George Sewall Boutwell

Why I am a Republican

A History of the Republican Party, a Defense of its Policy and the Reasons which

Justify its Continuance in Power

George Sewall Boutwell

Why I am a Republican
A History of the Republican Party, a Defense of its Policy and the Reasons which Justify its Continuance in Power

ISBN/EAN: 9783337416997

Printed in Europe, USA, Canada, Australia, Japan

Cover: Foto ©Suzi / pixelio.de

More available books at **www.hansebooks.com**

I AM A REPUBLICAN.

A HISTORY OF THE REPUBLICAN PARTY, A DEFENSE OF ITS
POLICY, AND THE REASONS WHICH JUSTIFY
ITS CONTINUANCE IN POWER,

WITH

BIOGRAPHICAL SKETCHES OF THE REPUBLICAN CANDIDATES.

BY

GEORGE S. BOUTWELL.

HARTFORD, CONN.:
WM. J. BETTS & CO.
1884.

COPYRIGHTED BY
WM. J. BETTS & CO.
1884.

PRESS OF
THE CASE, LOCKWOOD & BRAINARD CO.,
HARTFORD, CONN.

CONTENTS.

CHAPTER I.

The Provisions of the Constitution of the United States in relation to slavery, and their force in the Politics of the country, ... 7

CHAPTER II.

The Missouri Compromise and its repeal. 11

CHAPTER III.

The organization of the Republican Party, the contest in Kansas, and the elections of 1856. 22

CHAPTER IV.

The Senatorial contest of 1858 in Illinois, and the election of Mr. Lincoln in 1860. 26

CHAPTER V.

The Inauguration of Mr. Lincoln and the political and military questions then forced upon the country. 32

CHAPTER VI.

The Proclamation of Emancipation and the amendments to the Constitution. 38

CHAPTER VII.

The election of 1864 with a view of the position of the Democratic and Republican parties. 52

CHAPTER VIII.

The Financial Policy of the Republican party and its results.   64

CHAPTER IX.

The Protective Policy of the Republican Party, and its effects upon the wages of laborers and upon the prices of commodities. 74

CHAPTER X.

The Policy of the Republican Party in regard to the Public Lands 83

CHAPTER XI.

The Policy of the Republican Party in favor of universal education. 88

CHAPTER XII.

The Increase of the country in Population and Wealth since 1860. 91

CHAPTER XIII.

The Questions at Issue in the pending contest. . . . 95

CHAPTER XIV.

The Influence of the United States in the affairs of the World, due to the administration of the government by the Republican Party. 107

PUBLIC SERVICES OF JAMES G. BLAINE. . . . 165

PUBLIC SERVICES OF JOHN A. LOGAN. . . . 185

ADDRESSES, PLATFORMS, ETC.

Abraham Lincoln's speech at Springfield, Ill., June 17, 1858.. 114

Abraham Lincoln's Inaugural Address, March 4, 1861. . . 122

Proclamation of Emancipation, Sept. 22, 1862. . . . 131

Proclamation of Emancipation, Jan. 1, 1863. 133

Abraham Lincoln's Oration at Gettysburg, Nov. 19, 1863. . 135

Abraham Lincoln's Second Inaugural Address, March 4, 1865. 136

Republican Platforms, 1856–1884. 138

Democratic Platform, 1864. 163

INDEX. 196

INTRODUCTION.

It has been my purpose, in the preparation of this volume, to present at one view a history of the Republican party, a defense of its policy and the reasons which justify its continuance in power. I have not dwelt upon its errors and mistakes; it has committed errors, it has made mistakes, but those errors and mistakes have not interfered with its general policy nor affected in any sensible degree the good fortune of the country.

It accepted power when the industries of the country were insignificant in volume, limited in variety, and paralyzed by the constant and vigorous warfare upon every measure designed to foster labor or to add to the security of capital employed in manufactures and trade. The country was enslaved to the idea that agriculture might prosper while manufactures were neglected.

It accepted power when the country was on the eve of a gigantic war and when all the conditions and circumstances were unfavorable to its successful prosecution.

It has administered the government during a fourth part of its constitutional existence.

In that period the resources of the country have been so developed, its industries so multiplied and magnified that the era is marked as one of unexampled prosperity. In that period a new generation of men has come upon the stage, who cannot, out of their own experience, institute either contrasts or comparisons between the near and the more remote past.

I have sought to address myself to that class in the hope that I may enable them to see, as in one view, the beneficial changes that have been wrought by the Republican party in constitutional law, in public policy, in the educational and industrial condition of the people, and above all in the sentiment of nationality, which is better security for the preservation of the Union than can be had in statutes and constitutions.

GEO. S. BOUTWELL.

GROTON, MASS.

CHAPTER I.

THE PROVISIONS OF THE CONSTITUTION IN RELATION TO SLAVERY AND THEIR FORCE IN THE POLITICS OF THE COUNTRY.

THERE were three provisions of the original Constitution of the United States, and all relating to Slavery, that were in conflict with the opinions and principles of the founders of the States of New England, New York, and Pennsylvania.

The framers of the Constitution recognized the existence of the conflict, but they made no provision for its adjustment. As the formation of a more perfect Union was then a political necessity, there was, indeed, no possibility of an adjustment of the conflict between the system of slavery and the principles of human equality. In the presence of that necessity the advocates of Slavery achieved a decisive victory. It is not now important to trace the steps by which the victory was won, nor to know the names of members of the Convention who made motions or gave votes. It was then a higher duty to create a nation than to stigmatize or to shun an evil. But the victory was temporary, and in less than three-fourths of a century those provisions of the Constitution, which were designed to protect the system of Slavery, became the efficient if not the sole cause of its destruction.

By the Constitution the foreign slave trade was tolerated for twenty years, and thus the slave population was greatly augmented, the system was extended to new territories, and the number of persons interested, pecuniarily, in Slavery was largely increased.

By another provision of the Constitution the slave population was divided into classes of fives, and each class was counted as three free persons in the representation of the several States in the House of Representatives and in the Electoral Colleges for the choice of President and Vice-President of the United States. Thus it came to pass that by the importation of savage negroes from Africa, the South added to its political power in the government of the country, and thus for seventy years was the increase in the number of ignorant and non-voting slaves set off against the votes of the educated active, self-reliant, and enterprising freemen of the North.

As if it were a purpose to keep these impolitic and unjust provisions of the Constitution before the eyes of the people of the] States, the duty of returning fugitives from service to their mas was imposed upon the National Government. In the perform of that duty Congress denied to the alleged fugitive the righ trial by jury, and confided to subordinate officers of the courts authority to decide irrevocably the fate of every person arraignt as a fugitive from slavery.

The amalgamation of the races was one of the fruits of slavery, and as the child followed the condition of the mother, the system came to include, finally, many persons who had only a strain of African blood in their veins. And thus the surrender of persons apparently white was developed as an incident of the system.

From 1790 to 1860 the population of the North increased immensely. Following the lines of latitude it took possession of the Mississippi Valley north of the Ohio and the Missouri.

The love of liberty and a hatred of slavery were taught in all the schools and preached in all the churches, but with equal, if not with greater zeal the doctrine of obedience to the Constitution was taught also. Thus was the public sentiment of the North so wrought that it would concede to slavery whatever was stipulated in the Constitution; but it was ready, as well, to deny every fresh demand.

Under a system of intelligent, free labor, the tendency is to produce as much as is possible, and to consume only what is necessary. Hence wealth. Under the system of slavery the tendency is to produce as little as possible, and to consume whatever can be procured. This of the slaves, and hence poverty. The owners lived in idleness and indulged in prodigal ways. At the end the North was rich, relatively, and the South was poor. Slavery had exhausted the land, and the slave-owners had been impoverished by the habits born of the system. The slave-owners needed new lands for personal subsistence, and they needed new States for political power.

If the North had been indifferent to the system of slavery in a moral view of the subject, it would have resisted its appropriation of new territory, and upon the ground that it would not permit the constitutional system of political inequality to be extended and strengthened.

If the Constitution had abolished instantly the foreign slave-trade, if the basis of representation had been limited to free persons, and if had been provided that the question whether an alleged fugitive ṇn service was bound legally to perform such service should be ịded by a jury, the system of slavery would have continued for ..rs, and perhaps for generations, in the States of the Gulf of ,ico and the Lower Mississippi Valley.

lavery would have been without political power, and therefore it ver could have organized a rebellion against the Government. In .state of domestic peace there would have been no justifying cause for national interference.

In that condition of affairs, slavery would have existed in the several States until by the individual action of such States its abolition had been decreed. The effect, then, of the constitutional concessions to and guarantees for slavery was to endow the slave States with unequal political power for two generations, and then to dethrone them and leave them prostrate and under the absolute control of the free States.

The advantages which slavery and the slave-holding class derived from the guarantees of the Constitution were all temporary, and they all have disappeared. The compromises of the Constitution and the compromises under the Constitution are alike valueless. The annexation of Texas, the Mexican war, the struggles in Kansas, have all inured to the advantage of freedom.

When the three provisions concerning slavery were embodied in the Constitution, a conflict was inevitable. Whenever, in a free government, a conflict arises upon a topic that engages the thought of the majority, the contestants will either appropriate existing parties to their service or they will create new ones. When slavery demanded new guarantees, neither of the then existing parties was prepared to resist the demand. Hence the Republican party was a necessity, and its organization has been the instrumentality by which the people have destroyed slavery, reformed the Constitution, and reconstructed the government upon the two cardinal principles of the equality of States and the equality of men.

The contest is not ended. It will continue until the sentiments and traditions bred of slavery have disappeared from the States and communities once cursed by that institution. Hence the necessity remains for the continued existence of the Republican party. That party is the only political organization that is authorized to speak for or to defend what has been accomplished. The measures of which it may boast and on which its claim to continuing public confidence rests, have all been resisted, and often they have been denounced by the Democratic party. Execution of those measures yet remains to be done.

The great struggle through which the nation has passed was accepted and continued by the Republican party for the purpose of abolishing those features of the Constitution which recognized injustice as a force in the government. So much has been accomplished, but injustice in the administration of the government still exists. The Democratic party as an organization profited by the injustice of slavery, and therefore it resisted the overthrow of slavery. It now profits by the intolerance and persecution that prevail in the old slave States. That intolerance and persecution it now defends.

By the agency of the Republican party, and as a constitutional right, the equality of all men before the law has been secured; but upon the Republican party rest the obligation and the duty of securing that right, as a practical and conceded right, to all the citizens of the United States.

CHAPTER II.

THE MISSOURI COMPROMISE AND ITS REPEAL.

IT would not be just to assume that the framers of the Constitution foresaw the evils which have flowed from the provisions relating to slavery. Indeed, it is probable that the delegates from the South and the North alike expected the gradual destruction of the system, and that at no distant day.

Cotton-raising in the United States was then an experimental and unproductive application of labor. The total export of cotton in the year 1800 was less than 90,000 bales, weighing 215 pounds each, and the domestic consumption in factories did not exceed 500 bales. At that time there were only three spinning-mills in America. In the year 1790 there was neither domestic demand nor foreign trade in cotton. In 1764 eight bags of American cotton were seized in Liverpool upon the allegation that it could not have been grown in America. When it was released the spinners neglected it, doubting whether it could be worked profitably.

Between the year 1788 and the year 1800 two inventions were made, which added immensely to the profits of the cotton culture and to the value of slave labor. Eli Whitney invented the cotton-gin, and Jacob Marshall invented the cotton-press. Whitney was from Westborough, and Marshall was from Lunenburg, both in the county of Worcester and State of Massachusetts. Previous to those inventions, the seeds of cotton had been separated from the lint by hand labor or by rude mechanical devices, and the cotton destined for market had been trodden in round sacks or bags. The invention of the cotton-gin, especially, stimulated the importation of slaves from Africa, added to their value in the tobacco and grain-growing sections, inaugurated the trade in slaves between the States of the Potomac and the States of the Gulf of Mexico, and finally added the lust of gain to the love for political power, as inducements for the extension and defense of the system of slavery. Then came into public view a class of moralists and theologians, who maintained the doctrine that the rude and savage negroes of Africa had been transferred to a school of civilization and progress, and that slavery was not only not forbidden in the Jewish and Christian Scriptures, but that it was recognized and tolerated in all. Thus was slavery imbedded in the Constitution, and protected by moral, theological, and financial defenses and defenders. Law, wealth, and theology had combined for its protection.

In 1794 Congress passed penal statutes against the exportation of slaves from the United States, and prohibiting the use of American vessels for the transportation of slaves from one foreign country to another. This legislation satisfied the moral sentiment of the North, and promoted the pecuniary interests of the South.

In 1807 Congress proceeded to enforce the Constitutional inhibition against the importation of slaves. By the statute of March 2, 1807, any person found guilty of being engaged in the foreign slave-trade was liable to imprisonment for not less than five nor more than ten years, and to a fine not exceeding ten thousand dollars. The penalty of forfeiture was imposed upon vessels and their equipment, when found engaged in the slave-trade.

In this statute, by the seventh section, a very important concession was made to slavery. It was provided that all negroes and mulattoes found on any vessel arrested in the slave-trade should be delivered to the authorities of the State into whose port the inculpated vessel was brought. Under this statute the State of Louisiana enacted a law that all negroes and mulattoes delivered to the Governor of that State by virtue of the statute of 1807 should be sold as slaves. The object of the seventh section of the statute of 1807 was the protection of the Slave States against the presence of free negroes. Its effect was to add to the slave population of the country. The statute of 1807 remained in force until 1819, when the captors of any vessel engaged in the slave-trade were required to deliver to the President of the United States all persons of color found on board such vessel. Provision was made for the return of such persons to the coast of Africa.

The Free States and the Slave States did not antagonize each other upon questions touching the suppression of the foreign slave-trade. Georgia and South Carolina had insisted upon the right to continue the importation of slaves from Africa as a check to the monopoly of slave labor in the northern Slave States. The continuance of the trade for twenty years was a compromise between the Free States and the northern Slave States on one side, and the States of the extreme South on the other. Under the influence of the same motives Virginia and her associates of the border were willing to prohibit the foreign trade at the earliest day. They were also, and for the same reason, ready to provide for the return to Africa of all negroes found on board of slave-trading vessels. If Louisiana and her associates would have made them slaves, and if New York and her associates would have made them free, it was true that Virginia and her associates were not prepared to accept either alternative.

The return to Africa of all captured negroes may have been just, but manifestly it was a politic proceeding for the border Slave States. From 1789 to 1820 there was no other action by the Government of the United States which affected, or could in its results affect, the institution of slavery. Of the thirteen colonies, seven had become Free States, and six were Slave States. Of the nine new States admitted into the Union previous to the year 1820, five were Slave States, and four were Free States. Thus an absolute equilibrium of political power had been established. Eleven States were Free States, and there were eleven States that maintained slavery. The establishment of this equilibrium, and the tendency to its overthrow, were the cause or the occasion of the bitter sectional struggle which, commencing in 1820, even yet disturbs the harmony of the Republic.

The pro-slavery provisions of the Constitution gave rise to that struggle, and in its progress the antagonizing parties became sectional. The Whig party disappeared, and the Democratic party abandoned its principles.

The anti-slavery sentiment was organized in the Republican party, and so organized, it was destined to accomplish two historical results —the destruction of slavery, and the preservation of the Union.

As the Whig party, as an organization, would neither oppose nor defend slavery, it could not command efficient support either North or South. The Democratic party passed through the successive stages of Constitutional protection to slavery, non-interference by the National Government, the supremacy of the laws of nature over the question of slavery extension, and finally it subordinated its love for the Union, and yielded itself absolutely to the defense of the institution of slavery. With the formation of the Confederacy the Democratic party ceased to exist in the rebel States, and in the North, although it remained passive as an organization, it furnished a shelter to bodies of men who sympathized with the South.

When it was discovered by the leading men of the country that the equilibrium between the North and the South could not be preserved, the contest for supremacy began.

The equality of States and of representation in the Senate could not be changed, except by the admission of new States into the Union; but the increase of population in the contending sections could not be controlled by statutes, and at the close of every decennial period there was a new distribution of power in the House of Representatives and in the electoral colleges.

The re-distribution of political power was required by the Constitution, and thus by the Constitution was the equilibrium between the Free and Slave States destroyed. In 1790 the representative power of the Slave States to the Free States was as 87 to 100; in 1800 it was as 85 to 100; in 1810 it was as 92 to 100; in 1820 it was as 88 to 100.

The loss from 1810 to 1820 made it manifest that the equality of the South could not be maintained in the House of Representatives. It was then that the District of Maine applied for admission into the Union as a State. By the treaty of 1803 with France the territory of Louisiana was ceded to the United States. France had acquired the territory of Spain by a treaty made in 1763. It was claimed that the territory of Louisiana included all the country west of the Mississippi, except a small region near the Gulf of Mexico. Slavery existed in the territory. The application of Maine for admission into the Union was met by an application by the inhabitants of a portion of the territory of Missouri for admission as a Slave State. Missouri had been formed out of the original territory of Louisiana. After a long and bitter contest, the act for the admission of Maine was approved March 3, 1820, and on the sixth day of the same month an act was passed, authorizing the inhabitants of Missouri to form a constitution, and providing for the admission of the territory into the Union as a State. By the eighth section of that act slavery was prohibited in the territory acquired by the treaty of 1803, north of the parallel 36° 30'. Missouri was north of that parallel, but the new State was excepted from the inhibition. It was a hope, if not a confident belief on the part of the South, that Slave States could be formed from the territory south of that line, in set-off to the States that might be formed from the territory north of that line.

Arkansas was admitted into the Union in 1836, and in 1837 the equilibrium of States was re-established by the admission of Michigan. It then became apparent that the equality of States could not be maintained through the next decade. Of slave territory only Florida remained, while in the North there was the vast waste out of which the States of Iowa, Wisconsin, Minnesota, Oregon, Kansas, and Nebraska have been organized. The greatness of the future of these States was not foreseen, but their coming was anticipated and accepted on all sides as of the inevitable. The equilibrium of representation in the House had been destroyed, and the struggle was therefore intensified for the preservation of the equality of the Slave States in the Senate. As the slave-holding class ruled the South, it was possible always for that class to decide a presidential election, and hence the whig and democratic parties were rival bidders for southern support. The presidency was sold in the market. The South usually dictated the candidates of each party, and, unless the election of Harrison in 1840 was an exception, the South achieved a victory in every contest from 1828 to 1856 inclusive.

By the aid of organized bodies of men from the United States, and chiefly from the South, the State of Texas had declared its independence of Mexico, and organized a separate government. The governing force in Texas was composed largely of immigrants from the Slave States. Their policy was dictated by Southern statesmen, and directed to the annexation to the United States of the "Lone Star State," as Texas was then called. By the death of President Harrison, in April, 1841, John Tyler succeeded to the presidency. By birth, political training, and sectional feeling, he was allied to the slave-holding class, and his public policy was directed to the annexation of Texas as the leading and historical measure of his administration. In the canvass of 1844 Mr. Clay represented the Whig party, and Mr. Polk the Democratic party Both of those men were in the interest of slavery. Mr. Polk made no claim to anti-slavery opinions. He was an open advocate of the annexation of Texas. Mr. Clay may have had misgivings as to the system of slavery, but he was wanting in principle, or he lacked the courage to make a declaration of his real opinions, if they were hostile to the institution. The Whig party of the North was opposed to the annexation of Texas, but during the campaign Mr. Clay made a public surrender on the question, and by that surrender he lost the State of New York and the presidency.

The election of Mr. Polk was treated as an endorsement of the scheme, and the outgoing Congress, by a joint resolution approved March 1, 1845, provided for the annexation of Texas to the United States. The resolution contained a guarantee that States, not exceeding five in all, might be formed out of the territory, and admitted into the Union under the provisions of the federal constitution. The States formed out of the territory south of 36° 30' were to be admitted into the Union, either with or without slavery, as the people of each State asking admission might desire. In the States formed out of territory north of that line, slavery and involuntary servitude, except as a punishment of crime, were prohibited. As in the end there was no territory north of the line 36° 30', slavery gained one State in the outset, with the prospect of acquiring four other States, while the North gained nothing by the inhibition. Thus was an open way made for the organization of new Slave States, to be used in set-off against the coming States of the north-west.

The admission of Texas into the Union presented a fresh opportunity to the South, but it was an opportunity fraught with the gravest peril. When Texas declared its independence it named the Rio Grande as its southern boundary. On the other hand, Mexico made claim to the territory between the Rio Grande and the Nueces River. By annexation the United States accepted the controversy, and the war which then existed between Texas and Mexico. Mr. Polk was President. General Taylor was ordered to the left bank of the Rio Grande, near Matamoras. His army was first termed an army of observation, then an army of occupation, and finally it became an army of invasion. In the month of May, 1846, the war opened which ended in the capture of the City of Mexico by General Scott, and the treaty of Guadaloupe Hidalgo, signed the second day of February, 1848, by which a vast territory, including New Mexico and Upper California, was ceded to the United States. The Missouri compromise line had been extended across Texas by the joint resolution of March 1, 1845, but now the acquisition of a vast area, both north and south of that line, gave fresh consequence to the slavery issue. Of the new acquisition California alone contained a population sufficient for a State, and the larger part of its area, and much the larger part of its inhabitants, were north of the line 36° 30'. The Union was then composed of fifteen Slave States and fifteen Free States. The admission of California, whether as a Slave State or a Free State, would destroy the equilibrium. By the census of 1850 the representative power of the Slave States to the Free States was as 63 to 100.

The equilibrium in the House of Representatives and the Electoral Colleges had been destroyed, and beyond recovery. The cotton-gin had not only stimulated the growth of cotton, and increased the value of slaves, it had also stimulated the manufacture of cotton goods in the north and east, enhanced the wages of labor, added to the comforts of the laboring classes, and thereby encouraged immigration to the North.

In another form slavery itself contributed to the overthrow of the slave power. Wherever slavery existed manual labor was dishonored; and hence all the immigrants from Europe who had not the means and the ambition to become landholders chose their homes in the Free States. By the force of these combined agencies and influences the representative power of the South was broken down. By the annexation of Texas, the consequent war with Mexico, ending with the treaty of Guadaloupe Hidalgo, California was presented for admission into the Union as a free State, and at a time when the control of the House of Representatives was irretrievably lost to the South.

In this exigency Mr. Calhoun's dying speech was read in the Senate, March 4, 1850, by James M. Mason, of Virginia. He admitted the overthrow of the equilibrium between the Free and the Slave States, and he attributed it to the action of the general government. He closed with a demand for an amendment to the Constitution, by which equality of political power should be guaranteed to the South, and he coupled the demand with a threat of secession in case it should be refused. But Mr. Calhoun had then lost faith in the permanence of the institution. There is good reason to believe, but not the means to prove, that Mr. Calhoun, a few months before his death, said to a friend, "Slavery will go down, sir; it will go down in the twinkling of an eye, sir." His *Essay on Government* contained a statement of his plan for preserving, or rather for re-establishing the equilibrium between the Free States and the Slave States. He advocated an amendment of the Constitution, which should provide for two presidents, one from the South and one from the North. Their powers were to be equal, and consequently every executive act would require the concurrence of both presidents. The scheme was designed, manifestly, to effect a dissolution of the Union, and under circumstances which would enable each party to charge the responsibility upon the other.

The people of California framed a Constitution without the authority of Congress, and resistance to its admission into the Union was put upon that ground.

That position was a pretext. The exclusion of slavery was in fact the real reason. The bill for the admission of California was approved the 9th day of September, 1850. It was silent upon the subject of slavery, but two other bills were approved the same day—one for the organization of the Territory of New Mexico and the adjustment of the boundary between Texas and New Mexico, and the other for the organization of the Territory of Utah. Although the whole of the Territory of Utah was north of the line 36° 30', and although a part of New Mexico was also north of that line, both statutes contained a provision that the States that might be formed out of said Territories should be received into the Union with or without slavery, as their Constitutions might prescribe. These three measures, and the bill for the abolition of the slave-trade in the District of Columbia, and the bill for the surrender of fugitives from slavery, were carried under the lead of Mr. Clay. To Texas the sum of ten million dollars was paid for a surrender to New Mexico of the territory north of 36° 30', and thus were the Free States led to abandon whatever advantage was contemplated by the extension of the Missouri compromise line across Texas, by the joint resolution of March 1, 1845.

All the territory of Louisiana was slave territory at the time of its purchase from France in 1803. Hence the application of the Missouri compromise line was a gain to the free States, inasmuch as the region of country north of the line 36° 30' was relieved of slavery and consecrated to freedom.

All the territory acquired of Mexico by the treaty of Gandaloupe Hidalgo was free territory. Hence the provision in the statutes for the organization of New Mexico and Utah, by which the question of slavery was remitted to the inhabitants who might occupy those Territories when they should apply for admission into the Union, was a concession to slavery. Slavery was thereby made possible in a Territory theretofore free. Except for slavery, the question of the admission of California would have been considered by itself.

As the death of President Harrison in 1841 had made the annexation of Texas possible during the term for which he had been elected, so the death of President Taylor in July, 1850, made it possible for the slave-holders to secure the surrender of Utah and New Mexico to the chances of slavery. It was understood that General Taylor was opposed to the compromise measures of 1850. The most offensive of those measures was the Fugitive Slave Bill.

When these measures of compromise and conciliation had passed into statutes, and thus were made binding upon the country, their advocates and supporters North and South announced a peace—absolute and continuing peace—upon the subject of slavery. On that declaration the Democratic party achieved an easy victory in 1852.

One generation of men had been witnesses of and participants in the series of contests upon the subject of slavery, commencing in 1820 and ending in 1850.

In every instance the demand of the South had been accompanied by a threat that in case of failure the Union should be dissolved. By this threat, and by the assertion of its power to elect a President of either party, it subjected the political organizations of the country to its will, and reduced an entire generation of statesmen to a condition of moral and political servitude. In the presence of an attempt to nullify the laws of the Union, and, under the lead of General Jackson, a successful resistance was made in 1832 to the demand of the slave-holders. Their policy, however, was not changed. Indeed, the leaders in the treasonable scheme of nullification, including Mr. Calhoun, were soon restored to public confidence and advanced to new places of trust and power. In fine, as nullification was a means by which the slave-holders attempted to assert their power in the government of the country, and as the leaders in nullification were the leaders of the Democratic party of the South, and as the Democratic party of the country was dependent upon the Southern Democracy, the National Democratic party had no alternative but to recognize the leaders in nullification as leaders also in political affairs. Hence the defeat of nullification as a movement did not work the defeat and exile from politics of the leaders and apostles of that heresy. As long as slavery was a force in politics, and as long as the Democratic party was subject to that force, the leaders of the South were sure of place and power in the government of the country.

When the thirty-second Congress was about to end, a bill was introduced for the organization of the Territory of Nebraska. This bill was reported by Senator Richardson, a Democrat from Illinois, and it was supported by Senator Douglas from the same State. That bill recognized the exclusion of slavery, and, therefore, it was defeated under the lead of Senators from the South. Soon after the organization of the Thirty-third Congress in December, 1853, bills were introduced for the organization of the Territories of Kansas and Nebraska. Senator Dixon, a Whig from Kentucky, gave notice of an amendment abrogating the Missouri Compromise.

That suggestion was adopted by Senator Douglas of Illinois, and he thus became the responsible author of the scheme to repeal the compromise of 1820.

It was claimed that the concessions made in the bills for the organization of Utah and New Mexico were an abandonment of the principles of the compromise of 1820, inasmuch as the inhabitants of those Territories were endowed with power to establish or prohibit slavery. The claim had some foundation in the fact that all of Utah and part of New Mexico were north of the parallel 36° 30', but there was a careful concealment of the claim when the compromise measures of 1850 were before Congress and the country. It is a violent presumption that Mr. Webster and others whose opinions were in harmony with northern opinion, anticipated the claim thus based on the compromise measures of 1850, but it is no compliment to their intelligence to assume that they did not comprehend the nature and scope of the concession then made.

At the opening of the Thirty-third Congress President Pierce congratulated the country upon the settlement of the slavery controversy, and he volunteered the pledge that the repose then enjoyed should suffer no check if he had the power to avert it. The sincerity of his pledge cannot be questioned, but in proportion to its sincerity is the evidence of the power of slavery in compelling him to violate it, and to involve his administration and the country in the horrors of civil war on the plains of Kansas.

Mr. Douglas was the champion of the repeal of the Missouri Compromise. Many artful phrases were coined in the vain hope that the true intent and meaning of the act might be concealed from the public. The great facts could not be concealed. By the compromise of 1820 a vast region of country had been dedicated to freedom. By the repealing act of 1854 that country had been opened to slavery.

In the then excited condition of the public mind, the Territories were made the theatres of civil war.

The supporters of slavery and the devotees of freedom were invited to a contest of arms for the adjustment of a question which might and should have been settled by Congress. But if it had been so settled, the conflict would have been continued between the two forms of civilization, born, one of freedom, and the other of slavery. Without the spirit of prophecy, the declaration may be made safely that the civilization born of freedom would have triumphed in the end.

The repeal of the Missouri Compromise precipitated and made inevitable the contest of arms between the two forms of civilization, and in that contest the civilization of freedom was victorious.

It is no answer to say that the population of the North exceeded the population of the South. That excess was due to its superior civilization as certainly as was its supremacy in commerce, in manufactures, and in the inventive arts.

The words of repeal are these: "That the Constitution and all laws of the United States which are not locally inapplicable, shall have the same force and effect within the Territory of Kansas as elsewhere within the United States, except the eighth section of the Act preparatory to the admission of Missouri into the Union, approved March sixth, eighteen hundred and twenty, which, being inconsistent with the principles of non-intervention by Congress with slavery in the States and Territories, as recognized by the legislation of eighteen hundred and fifty, commonly called the Compromise Measures, is hereby declared inoperative and void; it being the true intent and meaning of this Act not to legislate slavery into any Territory or State, nor to exclude it therefrom, but to leave the people thereof perfectly free to form and regulate their domestic institutions in their own way, subject only to the Constitution of the United States."

It is no exaggeration to say that never elsewhere has a sentence of the English language been so freighted with consequences as was this. It invited the representatives of thirty million people to bloody strife on the borders of Missouri and the plains of Kansas; it annihilated the Whig party; it divided the Democratic party of the North; it organized, consolidated, and made invincible the Republican party of the Union, and finally it involved the country in a civil war, in which not less than two million American citizens took part, and not less than four hundred thousand gave their lives. All this was the fruit of the alliance between the slave-holders of the South and the Democratic party of the North.

CHAPTER III.

THE ORGANIZATION OF THE REPUBLICAN PARTY, THE CONTEST IN KANSAS, AND THE ELECTION OF 1856.

THE formation of a new political party, or the regeneration of an old one, is due always to events, and not to the schemes and purposes of men, except as events sometimes originate in such purposes and schemes.

It is a weak exhibition of genius and an utter waste of power, to attempt the creation of a new party by the force of mere will. On the other hand, when events demand a new party, or the re-organization of an old one, all resistance is borne down speedily.

The Republican party was the child of events. The pro-slavery provisions of the Constitution, the foreign slave-rade, the acquisition of Louisiana, the Missouri Compromise, the nullification scheme of South Carolina, the colonization and annexation of Texas, the Mexican War, the contest over the admission of California, the compromise measures of 1850, and finally the repeal of the Missouri compromise in 1854, were the events which rendered the formation of an anti-slavery party inevitable.

Its name was an incident only, and an unimportant incident; its principles and its purposes were the vital facts. No one can say why its organization was so long delayed; no one can say why its organization was not yet farther postponed.

During the colonial period and the years of confederation, the antagonism between slavery and freedom, or rather between the institutions of slavery and the institutions of freedom, had not taken form; but the inherent antagonism was organized in and developed under the Constitution, and for seventy years a struggle for the mastery went on. In every contest slavery had triumphed, and in every contest its victory was due to an alliance with one or both of the old political parties,—more frequently with the Democratic party.

This experience had destroyed confidence in the aged, this history had engendered suspicions in the young. Consequently, upon the repeal of the Missouri Compromise, the Democratic party of the North was divided, and the Whig party, as a national organization, ceased to exist.

As these bodies of Democrats and Whigs had rebelled against the political parties with which they had been identified, and for the same cause, they were driven necessarily into an alliance for self-defense as well as for the purpose of forming a barrier to the progress of slavery.

Neither men nor parties are the masters of events, and it is quite certain that the majority of the Republican party did not, at the time of its organization, anticipate its career and power in changing the institutions and controlling the fortunes of the country. There was, in the nature of the case, entire agreement upon the question of slavery extension, and a general concurrence in the opinion that persons arrested as fugitives from service should be surrendered only upon a verdict of a jury; but there was a divided sentiment as to the abolition of slavery in the District of Columbia, and a very general opposition to any interference with the institution in the States where it then existed.

It is to be admitted that the history of the Republican party is a singular commentary upon its first declaration of principles at Philadelphia, in 1856. There is in that declaration no reference to slavery in the States, to slavery in the District of Columbia, or to the rendition of fugitives from service. It demands the admission of Kansas as a Free State, and it denounces the proceedings in that territory, and especially the military and judicial usurpations, by which the people had been deprived of life, liberty, and property, without due process of law. Slavery and polygamy in the territories were condemned, and the projects for a railway to the Pacific Ocean, and the improvement of the rivers and harbors, were commended as within the scope of national authority. The platform was silent upon the questions of protection and free trade.

These declarations seem ridiculously weak and unaggressive, when measured and judged by the great movements and policies which the Republican party has originated, defended, and carried forward to final success. It met the enemy, however, at the point of attack. The South asserted its right to establish slavery in all the Union,— in the territory of Washington as well as in Kansas.

The Philadelphia platform declared that it was the legal right and the political and moral duty of the national government to prohibit slavery in all the territories of the Union,—South as well as North. Thus was the issue made between slavery and freedom. The Southern leaders well knew that when slavery was limited to existing territory it must begin to die. Limitation of the institution was not only loss of political power, it was abolition in a mild way, but in a way that led to the certain destruction of the system.

The devotion to slavery of one half of the Union for a period of seventy years, and the tolerance of the institution by the other half of the Union will, in a further like period of time, become the marvel of history. Other and not far distant generations of men, in the South as well as in the North, will be unable to comprehend the public sentiment of the age in which we are living. The institution of slavery has passed away; but the traditions, ideas, and habits of life bred by slavery yet linger among us. The Republican party, even, is not free from the influence of those ideas, traditions, and habits of life, and the Democratic party submits itself to their control as in the days of slavery. In large portions of the South the right of the negro to vote is denied practically by the suppression of the vote itself. The remedy of this wrong is within the scope of the original purpose of the Republican party, if its action in regard to slavery in the District of Columbia and in the States can be defended successfully.

It is not good ground for the charge of hypocrisy or insincerity, that a party does not at the outset unfold its purposes. The Revolutionary party did not announce its purpose to secure the independence of the colonies. Indeed, from 1765 to 1770, it asserted the contrary; but when, by long and painful experience, the leaders became convinced that equality of rights could not be secured under the union with Great Britain, they then resolved to destroy that union. Events were their masters.

In 1856 the exclusion of slavery from the territories was the leading issue between the contestants. The controversy over that issue led to secession, war, the abolition of slavery, the constitutional amendments, and the reconstruction of the government upon the basis of those amendments. As these events succeeded each other the Republican party had no choice of ways. It resisted secession, prosecuted the war, overthrew slavery, adopted the amendments to the constitution, and reconstructed the government upon the basis of the equality of men and the equality of States. The old government recognized the equality of States, and disregarded the equality of men. The new government asserts the doctrine that the equality of men is the only security for the equality of States. The Republican party asserts the equality of men as the only sure basis of the equality of States.

The Democratic party maintains the equality of States, and denies the equality of men. This is the issue, the constitutional issue born of slavery, and its sole survivor. And here again the Republican party has no choice of ways. If it were indifferent to every consideration not purely selfish, it would yet have no choice of ways. It has created a new system of finance, and it has identified itself in its history and in its policy with the doctrine of protection to domestic labor. Into those two policies are woven the interest of every capitalist, and the means of support of every workman in the North, and those policies can never be secure until the equality of men is recognized, and its benefits are enjoyed practically by the former slaves of the South.

In the old Slave States there are one million citizens of the United States whose votes should be received and counted in every State and national election, and it is probable that more than one-half of those men are deprived of their rights, either by force or fraud. This denial of the equality of men destroys the equality of States, and puts in jeopardy the financial and economical prosperity of the country. And thus again is the spirit of selfishness made subservient to the cause of justice.

Upon the repeal of the Missouri Compromise Kansas became the theatre of civil war. To that entertainment, indeed, the country was invited. The Democratic party was in power at Washington, and its influence was given to the scheme of making Kansas a Slave State. The South sent men and money. The North sent men and money. Contests of blood occurred, ruffian raids were tolerated, if not encouraged, towns were burned, hostile legislatures assembled, antagonizing constitutional conventions met, and vain appeals were made for the admission of the territory into the Union as a State. That event was postponed until January, 1861, but these proceedings of disorder and blood compacted and strengthened the Republican party for the struggles and responsibilities that it was soon to meet.

CHAPTER IV.

THE SENATORIAL CONTEST OF 1858 IN ILLINOIS, AND THE ELECTION OF MR. LINCOLN IN 1860.

THE Republican party of the State of Illinois held a convention at Springfield, June 17, 1858, and nominated Abraham Lincoln for the seat in the United States Senate then held by Stephen A. Douglas. The nomination of Mr. Lincoln was anticipated, and he had prepared a speech, which he then delivered. In that speech he set forth the doctrines of the Republican party, arraigned the administration of Mr. Buchanan, and denounced the repeal of the Missouri Compromise under the lead of Senator Douglas. That speech inaugurated a discussion which has no equal in the history of American politics. It introduced Mr. Lincoln to the country generally, and prepared the way for his nomination to the Presidency two years later.

In that speech, Mr. Lincoln made the declaration, then characterized as extravagant, but accepted, finally, as prophetic: "I believe this Government cannot endure permanently half slave and half free."

On this phrase Mr. Douglas based many arguments, in the vain attempt to prove that Mr. Lincoln was a disunionist. The context showed that Mr. Lincoln attempted only to establish the proposition that a tendency towards freedom, or a tendency towards slavery, must, in the nature of the case, be developed, and that the Union would in time become all slave or all free.

In that speech, and in the debate that followed, he characterized the repeal of the Missouri Compromise as a step towards making the Union all slave, and he contrasted the act with the ordinance of 1787 for the government of the Northwestern Territory, by which all the unoccupied lands within the jurisdiction of the old Confederacy were made forever free.

(26)

Mr. Lincoln claimed, and claimed justly, that at the formation of the Union the opinion was entertained generally that the institution of slavery was temporary. The ordinance of 1787 made it local. The magnitude of the surrender under the lead of Mr. Douglas may be best expressed in the statement that at the time of the adoption of the Constitution there was not one foot of territory outside the jurisdiction of the thirteen States that was not dedicated to freedom; and that after the passage of the act for the organization of Kansas, there was not one foot of territory within the jurisdiction of the United States that was not open to slavery.

Mr. Lincoln's first fame rests on that great debate. Judge Douglas was an experienced politician and a skillful debater. He had already taken a place amongst the able men of his time. In the month of June Mr. Lincoln was unknown outside of Illinois and Indiana. In September his character was understood and his ability was recognized in all the non-slave-holding States of the Union. His mastery over Douglas had been complete. His logic was unanswerable, his ridicule was fatal, and every position taken by him was defended successfully. At the end Douglas had but one recourse. He misstated Lincoln's positions, and then assailed them; but Lincoln was ever ready to expose the fallacies, and to hold up their author to the derision or condemnation of his hearers.

In the month of September Mr. Lincoln delivered a speech at Cincinnati, in reply to Mr. Douglas. In that speech he addressed himself to the citizens of Kentucky, and advocated the nomination of Mr. Douglas to the Presidency, upon the ground that he was more devoted to the South than were the Southern leaders themselves, and that he was wiser in methods for defending their rights. This was a form of attack which Douglas did not anticipate, and which he could neither resent nor answer.

In all that debate it was the constant effort of Mr. Douglas to present Mr. Lincoln as the opponent of the Constitution and the Union. That effort led Mr. Lincoln to place himself conspicuously upon Constitutional, Union ground. The sentiments that he thus expressed and taught were woven into all the platforms of the party in every section of the country. To those sentiments he adhered when he became President, and in every step of his great career he tested his acts by the fundamental law. He aided in the organization of the Republican party, and to him more than to any one else is the party indebted for its character, its measures, its success. He is the first personage of its history, and the second personage in the history of the Republic.

The nomination of Mr. Lincoln at Chicago in May, 1860, was not accomplished without a severe contest, nor without doubts and misgivings on the part of many members of the convention. Mr. Seward was the recognized leader of the party, and he was supported by the State of New York. The State of Ohio presented Mr. Chase, who in standing and influence was second only to Mr. Seward. The votes of Pennsylvania were given for General Cameron, and thus the three leading Republican States were divided.

After several ballots, the nomination of Mr. Lincoln was made. The result was received with enthusiasm in the Northwestern States, with feelings of disappointment in New York, but with hope and confidence elsewhere. By the month of September all disappointments had been allayed, and the party was not united merely, it was compacted as firmly as was ever any military organization. It was sustained by its principles and rendered enthusiastic by the certainty of success.

The declarations made at Chicago were aggressive, and in many particulars the platform of 1860 was a contrast to, rather than a growth from, that of 1856. It asserted that the normal condition of all the territory of the United States was that of freedom; it denounced the outrages in Kansas, and demanded its immediate admission into the Union with her Constitution as a free State; it branded the re-opening of the African slave-trade as a crime, and in expressing the abhorrence of the Republican party to all schemes of disunion, the Democratic party was arraigned for its silence in the presence of threats of secession made by its own members. The doctrine of encouragement to domestic industry was announced, the sale of the public lands was condemned, the coming measure of securing homesteads for the landless was approved, and a pledge of protection was given to all citizens, whether native or naturalized, and whether at home or abroad.

The party was again pledged to the construction of a railway to the Pacific Ocean, and to the improvement of the rivers and harbors of the country.

In the primary declaration, the platform asserted the necessity for the existence of the Republican party, coupled with the assurance of its permanency.

It was assumed in the platform that the Republican party was soon to enter upon the work of administering the Government. It pledged itself to economy, to the Union, to the rights of the States, and to unending hostility to every form of human servitude.

The aggregate popular vote exceeded four million six hundred and eighty thousand, and of the total one million eight hundred and sixty-six thousand votes were given for Mr. Lincoln, and of the three hundred and three electoral votes, he received one hundred and eighty. The Democratic party was divided. Mr. Breckinridge, the candidate of the South, received eight hundred and forty-seven thousand votes and seventy-two votes in the Electoral College, while Mr. Douglas received only twelve electoral votes, although his popular vote reached a million three hundred and seventy-five thousand. John Bell received thirty-nine electoral votes on a popular vote of less than six hundred thousand. The popular vote for Mr. Lincoln was nearly a half-million less than a majority; but his predecessor, Mr. Buchanan, was also a minority President.

Eleven States voted for Mr. Breckinridge, and of these, all, except Delaware and Maryland, became members of the Confederacy. The States of Virginia and Tennessee, that had voted for Mr. Bell, supplied the places in the Confederacy made vacant by the absence of Maryland and Delaware. The result showed that the Democratic party, as represented by Mr. Breckinridge, was in fact a secession party as well. The division of the Democratic party decided the election in favor of Mr. Lincoln.

Had that party supported Mr. Douglas in good faith, his election would have been secured, probably; but the South would have been left without excuse, if it had persisted in the scheme of secession. Therefore it came to pass that the Democratic party was disorganized by its own leaders, as a step preliminary to the election of Mr. Lincoln and the secession of the States of the South.

The election of Mr. Lincoln was made the pretext for disunion, but the leaders must have known that he would be powerless to do any act or thing contrary to their Constitutional rights while the members of Congress from the South retained their seats in the Senate and House of Representatives. They had, however, only a choice of ways. It was not possible to hold seats in the Congress of the United States and at the same time to organize a hostile government. If Jefferson Davis was to become the President of the Confederacy, it was necessary for him to surrender his seat in the Senate of the

United States. A like necessity attended the leading men by whom he was supported.

It was also the necessity of their situation that the new government should be organized during the administration of Mr. Buchanan. It is not necessary to assume any private understanding between the President and the leaders of secession. His message of December, 1860, contained declarations which justified Mr. Davis and his associates in assuming that Mr. Buchanan would not interfere with the organization of the new government. Of Mr. Lincoln, and of the administration that he might form, nothing could then be known.

Mr. Buchanan denied the right of secession as a Constitutional right, but he also denied to the Government of the United States all power under the Constitution to prevent secession by force. As a consequence the Union could exist only by the concurring and continuing consent of each and every State. Hence it was competent in fact, if not in law, for a majority of the voters in the smallest State, as Delaware, for example, to declare the Union at an end. Thus it came to pass that the Constitutional opinions of the President harmonized with the purposes of the secessionists. They took the responsibility of seceding from the Union, and the President took the responsibility of announcing that the general Government had no power under the Constitution to interfere with their undertaking.

Denying the right of the National Government to preserve its existence by force, the opinions of the President upon the abstract Constitutional question of the right of secession were of no practical value whatever.

Upon the admission of Mr. Buchanan, the Union ceased to exist on the 17th day of December, 1860, when the State of South Carolina adopted the ordinance of secession. It followed from Mr. Buchanan's position that the war, and all the incidents and consequences of the war, were unconstitutional.

The weakness of his position was shown by the impotence of the conclusions to which he was driven. Having surrendered all right of jurisdiction over the territory and people of South Carolina, he yet attempted to assert a right of property in the custom-houses and forts that had been constructed by the United States, although he could not visit those custom-houses and forts except as an act of war. Upon his theory of the Government, Mr. Buchanan was President from the 17th of December, 1860, to the 4th of March, 1861, of a part only of the country that had elected him to office.

Thus, by the aggressive acts of one wing of the Democratic party, and the non-action of the representatives of the whole party, the Union ceased to exist. One wing of the party said the Union had no right to exist. The other wing of the party said the Union had no Constitutional right to maintain its existence by force. Standing in the presence of the facts that existed the 22d day of February, 1861, and with a knowledge of the opinions entertained by Mr. Buchanan, the conclusion is outside of the realm of controversy that if he had had two years more of official life, the Confederacy would have been established firmly and recognized by the leading nations of the world.

The Union was dismembered and surrendered by the Democratic party.

The Union was re-established by the Republican party.

CHAPTER V.

THE INAUGURATION OF MR. LINCOLN, AND THE POLITICAL AND MILITARY QUESTIONS THEN FORCED UPON THE COUNTRY.

MR. BUCHANAN'S denial of the constitutional right of secession was an impotent abstraction in presence of his declaration that the national government had not a constitutional right to preserve its existence by force. The position of Mr. Buchanan was more favorable to the South than any other that he could have chosen. The only peril of the South was war on the part of the national government.

Under the administration of Mr. Buchanan there could be no war. His assertion of the right of property in the custom-houses, forts, and arsenals, implied the use of force for their recovery and possession, but jurisdiction over the remaining territory of a State was still to be exercised by the State. With that jurisdiction conceded, of what use to the national government would have been the possession of custom-houses, arsenals, and forts? In a short period of time they would have been surrendered to the State authorities.

The effect of his position was to unite the South by relieving the timid and conservative elements of all fear of war. He thus made it possible for the advocates of immediate secession to say that the only thing needed was the courage to act, as the act would be accepted as an accomplished fact.

If Mr. Buchanan had asserted the right of secession, his influence with the democratic party of the North would have been greatly diminished if not destroyed utterly; but his qualified position was sustained apparently by all of the democratic voters in the Free States who had not supported Mr. Douglas. Mr. Buchanan's policy consolidated the South and divided the North.

Mr. Lincoln asserted his own position in his inaugural address, and thus indirectly he controverted the position occupied by Mr. Buchanan. Mr. Buchanan denied the right of secession and admitted the fact; Mr. Lincoln denied the right and the fact as well.

A portion of the inaugural address is devoted to a critical analysis of the government, to which Mr. Lincoln added these significant sentences: "It follows from these views, that no State, upon its own mere motion, can lawfully get out of the Union; that resolves and ordinances to that effect are legally void, and that acts of violence, within any State or States, against the authority of the United States, are insurrectionary or revolutionary, according to circumstances. I, therefore, consider that in view of the constitution and the laws, the Union is unbroken, and, to the extent of my ability, I shall take care, as the constitution itself expressly enjoins upon me, that the laws of the Union be faithfully executed in all the States."

This declaration did not stop with the assertion of the right of property in custom-houses, forts, and arsenals; it announced a purpose to collect the revenues, to keep open the courts, to maintain the post-offices within the limits, and to carry the mails and transport troops and munitions of war over the territory of every State of the Union. It was an assertion of jurisdiction, with an assertion of all the powers incident to jurisdiction. Resistance on the part of any State to the exercise of that jurisdiction would be insurrection or revolution. Mr. Lincoln put the responsibility upon the disaffected States. He well knew, however, that they must either abandon the scheme of secession, or resist the jurisdiction of the United States. Indeed, South Carolina and other States had already asserted exclusive jurisdiction by seizing custom-houses and forts, and substituting State flags for the flag of the United States.

Under the lead of Mr. Buchanan it was impossible to re-establish the Union, as it had been impossible for him to preserve it. On the other hand, Mr. Lincoln did not admit that in a legal view the Union had been destroyed, and he announced his purpose to preserve it. He did not admit the right of secession, and he claimed that the so-called ordinances of secession were null and void.

Under a Democratic administration, and by the consent of its head, the Union was destroyed in fact if not in law. Under a Republican administration the Union was re-established in fact, as it existed in contemplation of law.

The months between the election in November and the inauguration in March were filled with rumors of schemes to assassinate Mr. Lincoln, and to seize the Capital. Whether these rumors had a foundation may not be known, but they so far influenced Mr. Lincoln's friends that he was induced to conceal his movements over the route from Harrisburg to Washington.

When Mr. Lincoln became President, all the forts, arsenals, and custom-houses in South Carolina, Georgia, Alabama, Mississippi, Louisiana and Florida, excepting only Forts Sumter, Pickens, Jefferson, and Taylor had been seized, and all their property, movable and immovable, had been converted to the use of the Confederate States. Mr. Lincoln's legal position was such that he would have been justified in a resort to force for their recovery. It was his purpose, however, to await the movements of the secession authorities, well knowing that they could not long remain inactive, and that an attack upon Union troops would arouse and consolidate the North.

The twelfth day of April, 1861, Gen. Beauregard opened fire upon Fort Sumter. This act transferred the contest from the theatre of discussion to the arbitrament of arms. It was followed by a proclamation from President Lincoln, calling for seventy-five thousand volunteers, whose first duty should be the recovery of the forts, places, and property which had been seized from the Union.

Thus the war was inaugurated, and under circumstances which placed the entire responsibility upon the actors in the Rebellion.

As slavery had been the cause of the war, the administration was brought face to face with questions growing out of the system. In the beginning the military authorities surrendered fugitives to their masters. Soon, however, that course of action was changed, upon the demand of the people and the concurring judgment of the administration.

As early as July, 1862, a law was passed which provided that the slaves of all persons engaged in the Rebellion, or giving aid and comfort thereto, who might escape and come within the Union lines, and all slaves captured from such persons or deserted by them, and all slaves of such persons found in any place occupied by rebel forces and afterwards occupied by the forces of the United States, should be forever free, and never again held as slaves.

This statute ended all controversy over the question of duty in regard to the rendition of fugitives from slavery, and its continuing operation would have ended the system in the eleven rebellious

States, even if the Proclamation of Emancipation and the Thirteenth Amendment to the Constitution had not been called into existence.

In the month of March, 1861, the Confederate authorities sent to Washington a commission, consisting of three persons, with instructions to negotiate a treaty of separation and peace. The commissioners assumed that they represented a government *de jure* as well as *de facto*, and that the question of the right of the Confederate government to exist was not to be considered. Mr. Seward declined to see them, and solely, as he said, upon public grounds.

In the months of January and February, the rebel authorities had seized forts and arsenals, the property of the United States, with all the movable effects, including one hundred thousand stand of arms. Having thus commenced a war, the Confederate authorities sought by diplomacy to negotiate a peace.

Mr. Lincoln occupied strong ground. He claimed to be the President of the whole Union, and he accepted the duty of executing the laws in every State. On this proposition there could be no negotiations, and certainly none which rested upon an admission that the Union had ceased to exist.

Thus again was made apparent the issue between Mr. Buchanan and Mr. Lincoln. Mr. Buchanan admitted the destruction of the Union, and denied the existence of any right in the national government to attempt its restoration by force. Mr. Lincoln treated the ordinances of secession as void *ab initio*, and claimed the right to enforce the laws of the United States in every State,—in those that had seceded as well as in those that were loyal to the Constitution. It is thus seen that he laid a foundation in law for every act of his administration, whether of legislation, of diplomacy, or of war. It is thus seen, also, that the Republican party, through its constituted agents, restored a Union and reorganized a government that had been assailed by one wing of the Democratic party, and abandoned by the other

The statute of 1850, for the rendition of fugitives from slavery, was one of the most barbarous acts of modern times, and its passage contributed more largely than any other measure, to the anti-slavery sentiment of the North. The statute of 1793 was a humane measure when compared with that of 1850. By the earlier statute the claimant was required to make his own seizures, and to prove his title to the fugitive before a judge of a circuit or district court of the United States, or before some magistrate of a county, city, or town corporate, wherein the arrest should be made; but by the law of 1850 the commissioners of the courts of the United States were authorized to act, marshals and deputy marshals were required to make the arrests, and in case of an affidavit by the claimant that he had reason to apprehend that an attempt would be made to rescue the fugitive, it became the duty of the officer making the arrest to employ assistants, and to return the fugitive to the State from whence he came, and at the expense of the United States. The alleged fugitive was not allowed to testify in his own behalf, but affidavits in behalf of the claimant were to be received, and the findings of a court in the State from which the person had escaped, as alleged, were conclusive. At the end the commissioner was entitled to a fee of ten dollars if the fugitive should be surrendered to the claimant, and five dollars only in case of his discharge. If a fugitive succeeded in making his escape from a marshal or deputy marshal the marshal was made liable to the claimant for the value of the service of the fugitive in the State or Territory from which he had escaped, and this whether the escape was with or without the assent of the marshal. In the execution of the process the officer was authorized to call upon the bystanders as a *posse comitatus*, and all the citizens of the United States were enjoined to aid the marshals and deputy marshals in the performance of their duty.

The fugitive slave bill of 1850 was passed by a majority of fifteen in the Senate, and thirty-five in the House. Each of the old parties contributed votes,—the Whig party less generously than the Democratic party.

When the Republican party came into power the amendment or repeal of the fugitive slave law was a subject of constant agitation in Congress and in the country; but it was not until the 28th day of June, 1864, that a repealing act was passed, and approved by President Lincoln. The repealing bill passed the House by the vote of ninety Republicans against a minority consisting of one Republican and sixty-one Democrats. The bill was supported in the Senate by the votes of twenty-seven Republicans against the votes of four Republicans and eight Democrats.

The delay in securing the passage of the bill repealing the fugitive slave law, was due in part to the protests of the border Slave States that had not joined the confederacy, in part to the necessity of providing means for the prosecution of the war, and in part to the opposition of the northern Democrats, who denounced every movement that threatened the institution of slavery.

The repeal of the measure was the work of the Republican party.

It is not easy to comprehend the public sentiment upon the rights of negroes during the years of the war. Speaking generally, the members of the Democratic party were opposed first to their freedom, and consequently they were opposed to every measure and movement designed to elevate or improve the race. It was not without opposition that negroes were allowed to ride in the street-cars of the city of Washington; that they were permitted to testify in courts of justice; that they were employed upon the fortifications, or enrolled in the army. The leading Democrats of the North insisted that slavery should be preserved with the Union, and that the restored Union should answer in every particular to the old Union. They insisted also that the States in rebellion were still States in the Union, and entitled to the same rights as the loyal States. This latter dogma was entertained by many Republicans.

Every attempt to secure equal rights for the negro was opposed vigorously, and it was not until the 3d of March, 1864, that the statutes of the country authorized the enrollment of colored persons as a part of the military force of the Republic.

Through these various stages, and by the action of the Republican party, the colored inhabitants of the country were advanced and secured in the enjoyment of some of the civil rights which appertain to citizenship.

CHAPTER VI.

THE PROCLAMATION OF EMANCIPATION AND THE AMENDMENTS TO THE CONSTITUTION.

THE organization called "The Confederate States of America" made the overthrow of the system of slavery possible as a military necessity; but the administration of Mr. Lincoln was confronted constantly with the opposition of the Democratic party of the North. The monitory Proclamation of Emancipation was issued the 22d day of September, 1862, and so general was the hostility to the proceeding that the Republican party escaped defeat by less than twenty-five majority in the House of Representatives. In the year 1862 elections were held in the loyal States only.

Nor was the opposition to emancipation confined to members of the Democratic party. Similar opinions were entertained by the Republicans and Union men of the border Slave States, with few exceptions, and the Proclamation was deprecated by the press, and by influential Republicans in the most advanced anti-slavery communities of the North.

The early declarations of the Republican party that it was not its purpose to interfere with slavery in the States were quoted, and thereon the charge of inconsistency was based. No allowance was made for the changes that had been wrought by eighteen months of flagrant war. No account was taken of the facts that the slaves in the rebellious States were employed upon the plantations raising supplies for the armies in the field, and providing sustenance and even protection for the families at home. The spirit of forbearance, and the sentiment of humanity exhibited during the war by the negro population of the South, when thousands of defenseless families were at their mercy, ought to command not just treatment merely, but the sincere and continuing gratitude of the white population of the eleven States. The slave-holders themselves have been compelled to testify to the presence of virtues in the negro race which were supposed, generally, to belong only to the most cultivated classes of society.

But neither the facts which are thus admitted, nor the admissions themselves, have wrought any change in the relations of the two races. The absence in the white race of the sentiment of gratitude and the sense of justice, is not due to the difference of race, but to the antecedent condition of slave and master. The slave was bound to render everything, while he was incapable of commanding anything. The master commanded everything, and he was bound to render nothing. Hence the humanity of the negro was accepted by the master as the performance of a duty, whose avoidance would have been a crime.

To the slave-holders the overthrow of slavery was the loss of property, the loss of political power, and the loss of social supremacy. To the northern Democrat the overthrow of slavery was the loss of a political ally for which no substitute could be found. When the country was divided into two parties, upon questions that did not touch slavery, the slave power was a contingent in politics, and ready to perform service for either party, but always upon terms most acceptable to itself. When, however, the Whig party was extinguished, and the Republican party was organized as an anti-slavery party, the slave power was forced into an alliance, or rather into a union with the Democratic party, and under circumstances which precluded all controversy as to terms. The slave power of the South was thus subordinated to the Democratic party of the North. Theretofore the slave power had ruled both political parties, but with the organization of the Republican party it became the servant of one of those parties.

This change of parties was fraught with two important consequences. The slave power accepted secession as a means of escaping from a condition of subordination to the Northern democracy, and the Northern democracy demanded "the restoration of the Union as it was," well knowing that slavery was a bond which would hold the South in perpetual alliance with the Democratic party of the North.

Upon the basis of these ideas the policy of the Democratic party was rational and logical. It claimed that the army should be used to aid the return of fugitive slaves to rebel masters; that fugitive slaves should not be employed in forts and arsenals; that negroes should not be accepted as soldiers; and that inasmuch as the thirty-seventh Congress had declared that the war was prosecuted solely for the restoration of the Union, the abolition of slavery, whether in the District of Columbia or in the States engaged in the Rebellion, was a breach of good faith. Its mottoes were, "The Union as it was;" "Once a State always a State."

There was a very considerable minority of the Republican party who in the early years of the war either accepted the positions taken by the Democratic party of the North, or hesitated to assert the contrary. Finally, however, the Republican party accepted the responsibility of refusing to return fugitive slaves to rebel masters, of employing fugitive slaves in the forts and arsenals, of enlisting negroes in the army, of abolishing slavery in the District of Columbia and in the States and parts of States engaged in the Rebellion. "The Union as it was" was not restored, and the cry, "Once a State always a State," was disregarded.

The primary object of war is the re-establishment of a condition of peace upon a basis more satisfactory to the conquering party. Measures, not inhuman, which tend to the restoration of peace, or measures which tend to render a condition of peace, when peace shall be restored, more stable or more agreeable to the parties, are measures which are justified by the antecedent reasons and by the results. Thus tested, the emancipation of the slaves in the States engaged in the Rebellion is justifiable, and justified as a measure of war.

The slaves were employed in the cultivation of the soil, by which the families of the soldiers were supported and the armies in the field were supplied with subsistence. They were also employed in the transportation of war material, and in the erection of fortifications, and the construction of roads and bridges. Emancipation was a pledge by the national government to every person held in slavery, that the relation of master and slave should never be re-established. As the old Union had failed, and as in that Union slavery had been the cause of the failure, there could be no reasonable hope of a permanent peace until slavery disappeared. The old Union was an impossibility. Would a system of representation based upon slaves have been again tolerated by the North? Or would fugitives from slavery have been returned to their masters? Thus was the Proclamation of Emancipation justified by the rules of war, and warranted by the then existing exigencies of the public service. In fine, it made possible the formation of a Union so acceptable that no one is now found to voice a dissent, while from 1789 to 1860 there was never a year when the capacity or the right of the Union to maintain its existence was not a subject of public debate.

The Democratic party demanded the re-establishment of a system of government which had failed under and by its leadership, and resisted the reorganization of the Union upon a basis which guaranteed alike the equality of men and the equality of States. On the issue thus raised the Democratic party was defeated, and its policy is now condemned by experience.

The restoration of the Union and its peaceful perpetuation to other times, depended upon two events, viz.: The prosecution of the war to a successful termination, and the abolition of slavery. The Democratic party, through its leaders, denied the rightfulness of the war, although many members of that party contributed a full share to its success. The Democratic party, as an organization, opposed the abolition of slavery, and not one of its representative men supported the Proclamation of Emancipation.

Thus it appears that if the fortunes of the country had been committed to the Democratic party the war would have been a failure, probably; or if the rebellious States had been subjugated by arms or conciliated by negotiations, the institution of slavery would have been preserved to foster divisions, encourage controversies, all to end finally in a renewal of the war. The Democratic party is thus shown to have been deficient in patriotism and in statesmanship.

Upon a proposition submitted to the House of Representatives, December 15, 1862, which declared that the Proclamation of the 22d of September, 1862, was warranted by the Constitution, and that the policy of emancipation was well adapted to hasten the restoration of peace, was well chosen as a war measure, and an exercise of power having proper regard for the rights of the States and the perpetuity of free government, only two members who were elected as Democrats gave affirmative votes, while seven members who were elected as Republicans, or Union men, as distinguished from Democrats and Republicans, voted in the negative.

During the first two years of the war there was a continuous struggle between the North and the South for supremacy in the border Slave States, Delaware, Maryland, Kentucky, and Missouri. They were disturbed by the emancipation of the slaves in the District of Columbia, and every act of the President was carefully examined by the inhabitants of those States. They protested against any step looking to emancipation, even if compensation were guaranteed. In March, 1862, the President recommended the adoption of a resolution in these words, viz.:

"*Resolved*, That the United States ought to co-operate with any State which may adopt gradual abolishment of slavery, giving to such State pecuniary aid, to be used by such State in its discretion, to compensate for the inconvenience, public and private, produced by such change of system."

This resolution was supported by four Democrats only in the House of Representatives, and two in the Senate. It was passed by a two-thirds vote in each House, but the proposition was not accepted. This was Mr. Lincoln's first effort at emancipation in the States that had not engaged in the rebellion, and his sagacity and far-seeing statesmanship were never exhibited more conspicuously.

The proposition thus made by the President and approved by Congress could not but weaken the position of the border States in the event of emancipation without compensation, as an incident or result of the war. If, on the other hand, the proposition should be accepted by the loyal Slave States, there would then be no obstacle to compulsory emancipation in the rebel States. Moreover, the proposition qualified, in some degree, the demand made for immediate and unconditional emancipation as a measure of war. It was a preliminary step in a path in which the President was well assured he must walk to the end,—unconditional, universal emancipation. There can be no doubt, however, that the President was sincere in his effort to secure the freedom of the slaves in the loyal States and in aid thereof to compensate the owners.

His proclamation of the 19th of May, 1862, in which the proclamation of Major-General David Hunter, declaring that the persons theretofore held as slaves in South Carolina, Georgia, and Florida were forever free, was revoked, contained a passage which showed that he then thought of emancipation as a military necessity. This was his language: "Whether it be competent for me as commander-in-chief of the army and navy to declare the slaves of any State or States free, and whether at any time, in any case, it shall have become a necessity indispensable to the maintenance of the government to exercise such supposed power, are questions which, under my responsibility, I reserve to myself, and which I cannot feel justified in leaving to the decision of commanders in the field."

In July the President sought an interview with the representative men from the border Slave States. In an address to them he urged his plan for emancipation, and expressed his regret that his efforts had not been supported. Again he indicated the peril to which the loyal slave-holders were exposed, by a reference to the effect upon his northern supporters by his repudiation of Gen. Hunter's proclamation. "In repudiating it I gave dissatisfaction, if not offense, to many whose support the country cannot afford to lose. And this is not the end of it. The pressure in this direction is still upon me, and is increasing."

This appeal to the border Slave States was followed by an earnest recommendation to Congress in December, 1862, to initiate amendments to the Constitution of the United States guaranteeing compensation to any State that should provide for the emancipation of its slaves at any time before the year one thousand and nine hundred. This recommendation was coupled with the statement that the adoption of the plan would not stay the prosecution of the war, nor interfere with the proceedings under the Proclamation of the 22d of September. The proposition was thus limited in the mind of the President to the Slave States that had not engaged in the Rebellion.

Mr. Lincoln was an anti-slavery man, but his conduct as a citizen, and his policy as President, were guided by the Constitution. It is probable that at the moment when the war became formidable, and the Confederate States were organized as a government, he anticipated that the time would come when the emancipation of the slaves would be justified as a means of subjugating the rebels and restoring the Union. As early as May, 1862, in a letter to a Union man in Louisiana he intimated a purpose to proclaim emancipation rather than lose the government. When Lee crossed the Potomac and invaded Maryland, the President made a resolve that whenever the rebels were driven into Virginia he would issue the proclamation. The battle of Antietam in September, 1862, and the retreat of Lee were the final events in a series which, in the opinion of Mr. Lincoln, required and justified the emancipation of the slaves as a means of ending the war and restoring the Union.

Events then future have vindicated the wisdom of the act.

In his second annual message Mr. Lincoln discussed and defended the emancipation policy. "Without slavery," said he, "the Rebellion could never have existed; without slavery it could not continue." This was his first public declaration of these important truths, but the truths must have been present in his mind for many months previous to the declaration. The difficulties of his situation were such that he was compelled to withhold all expression of opinions and purposes in regard to slavery until the moment arrived when it was wise to act. In each of the border Slave States there was a strong public sentiment in favor of the Confederacy. Every step taken by the government of the United States looking to emancipation was calculated to increase that sentiment. In Missouri, Kentucky, and West Virginia the war was flagrant, and the Union forces were often on the defensive. The public sentiment of those States was so equally divided that they were held to the Union by force. On the other hand, there were large bodies of men in the North who demanded the immediate abolition of slavery, without regard to the effects upon the border States.

It was the great good fortune of the country that Mr. Lincoln was superior to temporary influences. His comprehensive wisdom enabled him to so shape his policy as to meet the reasonable demands of those whose opinions corresponded with his own, without intensifying the hostility of his opponents. Eighteen months of war, and often at their own doors, had led the border States to sigh for peace, and at any price. The system of slavery had lost many of its attractions. Fugitives were not returned. The armies were ready to accept the services of negroes without inquiry as to ownership. The Proclamations of September, 1862, and January, 1863, were received with favor by Republicans in the old Free States, and in silent acquiescence by the Union men in the border Slave States. The measure was denounced by the Democrats, and the elections of 1862 were highly favorable to that party.

If the Proclamation had been issued twelve months, or even six months, earlier, the country would have rebelled against the measure. Under the circumstances the loss of confidence, even in the border States, was temporary. In a few weeks or months at most, the consequences of the shock had disappeared. The abolition of slavery in the rebel States was accepted as an accomplished fact, and the border States soon realized that the system was valueless to them.

Mr. Lincoln had sought to abolish slavery in the border States as a step towards its forcible overthrow in the Confederate States. Failing in this the process was reversed. Slavery was first abolished in the Confederate States. Its abolition there made it impossible to protect it in the border States. Thus was the way prepared for the Thirteenth Amendment to the Constitution, and the final extinction of the system in the United States.

The resolution proposing an amendment to the Constitution abolishing slavery, was agreed to by the Senate, April 8, 1864, by a vote of thirty-eight in the affirmative to six in the negative. Of the Democrats, two only, Senators Harding and Nesmith, voted in the affirmative.

When the resolution came up for consideration in the House of Representatives, Mr. Holman of Indiana moved its rejection. On this motion the yeas were fifty-five, and the nays were seventy-six. Upon the final question, June 15, 1864, the yeas were ninety-five, and the nays were sixty-six. So the resolution failed to pass, the constitutional majority of two-thirds not having been secured. Mr. Ashley of Ohio, who had voted with the minority in numbers for the purpose of moving a reconsideration, entered his motion at once, and all further action was then postponed. Of the Democratic party three members voted for the resolution, sixty-five voted against it, and twelve members neglected to answer to their names.

The elections of 1864 were favorable to the Republican party, and of the members returned to the House less than one-third were Democrats. The canvass had changed public opinion upon the subject of emancipation, and many Democrats accepted the conclusion that the abolition of the system of slavery was inevitable. The thirty-ninth Congress was pledged to the amendment to the Constitution. Further resistance was therefore vain.

Early in the second month of the second session of the thirty-eighth Congress, Mr. Ashley called up his motion to reconsider the vote by which the proposed amendment had been rejected. That motion prevailed, and upon the question of passing the resolution the yeas were one hundred and nineteen, and the nays were fifty-six,—all Democrats. Sixteen Democrats voted in the affirmative, and eight others declined to vote.

The elections of 1864 had secured the passage of the resolution by the thirty-ninth Congress, but its adoption by the thirty-eighth Congress was due to the affirmative action of sixteen Democrats, and the non-action of eight others. The amendment was submitted to the States the first day of February, 1865, and the eighteenth day of the following December the Secretary of State issued a proclamation declaring that it had been ratified by the legislatures of twenty-seven of the thirty-six States composing the Union.

Thus and then the system of slavery came to an end in the United States; and thus and then was an example given which is to be followed by all the nations of the earth.

This was indeed the most lustrous event in American history. Not the Declaration of Independence, nor the Constitution, even, can bear the test of a comparison with the measures of Emancipation and Abolition. The chains which were lifted or broken by the Declaration of Independence were not as burdensome and galling as those which were fastened upon the Free States by the compromises of the Constitution. Had the Union with Great Britain continued for half a century, an equality of power with the mother country would have been recognized and established, or the bonds of union would have been parted in peace. The evils of the colonial relation were temporary; the evils of slavery under the Constitution had assumed the character of permanent and growing wrongs.

First of all there was a denial of the equality of men as political forces in the government of the country. Not merely a denial of political rights to the negro race; the Constitution secured unequal political power to the voters in a Slave State, and that inequality was increased as the number of slaves was augmented. Slave-catching was made a national duty; and the glowing truths of the Declaration of Independence were repudiated or disregarded in the public policy of the country. Professing freedom, we were characterized justly as a nation of slave-holders.

The slave-holding class directed the policy of the slave-holding States, and the slave-holding States held the balance of power between the rival parties of the North. And thus were parties and politicians and statesmen, and the public policy of the country, subordinated to the slave-holders of the South. At the end, the value of the Declaration of Independence was not so much in its allegations against Great Britain as in the announcement by authority of fundamental truths which concern all men, and are applicable to all times and conditions of society. Those truths were the constant enemy of slavery, and they contributed essentially to its overthrow.

With this history, and upon this view of emancipation, the Republican party may claim the first place among parties, when measured and judged by the value of the achievement and the difficulties attending its accomplishment. At the end, twenty-four Democrats of the House of Representatives contributed directly or indirectly to the passage of the amendment, and in the States yet others may have aided in its ratification; but their aid came when success was assured. They gave no assistance to the movement in the days of its weakness. Indeed, the men who favored emancipation were denounced by leading Democrats as equally guilty with those who were engaged in secession.

Mr. Lincoln's great place in history is due to the circumstance that he had the courage, the solemn fortitude, to inaugurate a system of emancipation, and then to apply all the resources and powers of the office that he held to the aid of the undertaking. Our successes on the water and in the field were due largely to the skill and courage of the officers and men of the navy and army. The President and Cabinet, however wise in counsel, could only share with others the honor accorded to military successes.

The Proclamation of Emancipation was postponed, upon the judgment and in the wise discretion of the President, until the country was prepared to accept it and support it. West Virginia, Kentucky, and Missouri had been so ravaged and wasted by both armies that the inhabitants sighed for peace at any cost. Slaves had lost their value, and slavery its attractions. In September, 1861, those States would have rebelled against emancipation and joined the Confederacy; in September, 1862, it was accepted by some as a relief and a hope, and by others as a consummation of what, for a time, they had regarded as inevitable.

The Proclamation of Emancipation removed all fears of foreign interference, and at home it dissipated the illusion that the Union as it was could be restored. Unity of opinion in council, and unity of purpose in the field, took the place of divided opinions and conflicting actions.

To the Republican party, and to Mr. Lincoln as the head of that party, are due the honors that will be accorded to the authors and defenders of the measure, by every generation of American citizens, and by the general judgment of mankind in all the coming ages.

If we can now imagine the war ended, the Union restored, as it was the old Constitution preserved, slavery perpetuated and all its evils magnified, we can form a just conception of the consequences of the policy advocated by the Democratic party.

In contrast with those consequences the South may be summoned to testify as to the existing condition of affairs. Of the twenty years of freedom, the last ten have been distinguished by a degree of prosperity such as the South had never before experienced. Population and wealth have increased in a ratio heretofore unknown. For its present productive power there has been no example in its history. If we include the negro race, the average intelligence is higher than at any time previous to the war. Political evils and crimes have not disappeared, but they are temporary. Above all, the defenders of slavery are a meagre minority, and the spirit of disunion is suppressed absolutely. These beginnings indicate the future greatness of the old Slave States,—a greatness which slavery could neither create nor tolerate.

Mr. Lincoln was indebted to the Republican party for the opportunity to initiate these great reforms, touching not merely the rights and condition of the millions of slaves, but affecting also the union, peace, and prosperity of the States and people of the Republic. But the Republican party, the country, and mankind, are indebted to Mr. Lincoln for the courageous statesmanship that he exhibited in the most perilous crises of the nation's history.

President Lincoln excelled all his contemporaries, as he also excelled most of the eminent rulers of every time, in the humanity of his nature; in the constant assertion of reason over passion and feeling; in the art of dealing with men; in fortitude, never disturbed by adversity; in capacity for delay when action was fraught with peril; in the power of immediate and resolute decision when delays were dangerous; in comprehensive judgment which forecasts the final and best opinion of nations and of posterity; and in the union of enlarged patriotism, wise philanthropy, and the highest political justice by which he was enabled to save a nation and to emancipate a race.

The slaves emancipated were not thereby made citizens. By the overthrow of the Confederacy the States composing it were not restored to their places in the Union. Such was the public sentiment in the South that there was no ground for believing that the rights of citizens would be accorded to the freedmen except upon compulsion.

By the abolition of slavery the freedmen were counted as if they were citizens, in the apportionment of representatives among the States. Therefore the abolition of slavery gave to the white voters in the old Slave States greater weight in the government of the country than they had possessed in the days of slavery. Two methods of remedying the inequality were suggested: First, to extend citizenship and the right of suffrage to the freedmen, or, secondly, to base the representation in the House of Representatives upon the number of voters in each State. In 1865 and 1866 the prejudice against the negro race was so strong that the alternative proposition was adopted.

The Fourteenth Amendment to the Constitution was designed to remedy the inequality otherwise existing between the value of a vote in the old Free States and the old Slave States. This result was secured by the second section, which provided that when the right to vote for certain officers specified should be denied to any of the male citizens of any State, being twenty-one years of age and citizens of the United States, or in any way abridged, except for participation in rebellion or other crime, the basis of representation in such State should be reduced in the proportion which the number of such male citizens should bear to the whole number of male citizens in such State. In order to give full effect to this section, it is provided in section one that all persons born or naturalized in the United States, and subject to the jurisdiction thereof, are citizens of the United States and of the State wherein they reside. Equal rights and privileges are also guaranteed to all citizens.

By the third section certain disabilities were imposed upon classes of official persons who had been engaged in the Rebellion, subject, however, to the power of Congress, by a two-thirds vote, to remove such disabilities. This inhibition is now operative only upon a few persons.

By section four the validity of the public debt is recognized, including bounties and pensions to the soldiers. The assumption of debts incurred in aid of the Rebellion by the United States or by any State, is prohibited.

The Fifteenth Amendment to the Constitution has annulled the second section of the Fourteenth Amendment, which fixed the basis of representation; but the guarantee of citizenship and of equal rights to all, without regard to race, color, or nativity, will remain as long as a "government of the people, by the people, for the people," shall exist on this continent.

The Fourteenth Amendment was proposed to the legislatures of the several States the 16th day of June, 1866, and on the 21st day of July, 1868, Congress, by a concurrent resolution, declared that the amendment had been ratified "by three-fourths and more of the several States of the Union," it having, in fact, been ratified by twenty-nine States in all.

By the Fifteenth Amendment to the Constitution the right to vote is secured to citizens of the United States in so far that it cannot be denied or abridged on account of race, color, or previous condition of servitude.

The Proclamation of Emancipation and the three amendments to the Constitution are all the work of the Republican party. With the exceptions specified in regard to the Thirteenth Amendment, the Proclamation and the amendments were opposed by the Democratic party, and by Democrats generally.

The ratification of the Fifteenth Amendment was announced by the Secretary of State, March 30, 1870. The war was ended, slavery was abolished, citizenship, State and National, had been established, and the right to vote had been guaranteed to all without regard to race, color, or previous condition of servitude. The Constitution had been reformed and the nation regenerated in the short period of less than ten years.

The Republican party was drawn by its principles and driven by its necessities to the support of all these measures. The government was in its hands, it was pledged to the restoration of the Union, and to its restoration upon the basis of its perpetuity. Neither of these ends could be attained while slavery lasted. When slavery was abolished the Fourteenth Amendment became an imperative necessity, as the only means of securing an equality of political power in the hands of the men who had suppressed the Rebellion and re-established the Union. When the negro race, numbering more than a tenth of the population of the country, had been freed; when they had performed service in the army; when they had been endowed with citizenship, and all under the lead and upon the responsibility of the Republican party, that party was bound by its principles and forced by its necessities to extend the franchise to those whom it had made citizens.

By the force of circumstances, and in obedience to a logic equally inexorable, the Democratic party resisted all these changes. For thirty years and more it had supported slavery, and in return it had enjoyed the alliance and support of the slave-holding class. A generation of voters and of statesmen had been trained in the companionship and ideas furnished by such support and alliance. If not held to their former associates by the sentiment of gratitude, nor influenced by the hope of regaining lost power, they were constrained in their action by the fact that the Republican party commanded the confidence and support of the anti-slavery men of the country. The field was occupied. In truth, however, the Democratic party remained faithful to its ancient allies, not from a sentiment of gratitude for past favors, nor from the expectation of future advantages, but from an identity of ideas, to whose power it submitted itself with unreasoning and absolute deference.

CHAPTER VII.

THE ELECTION OF 1864, WITH A VIEW OF THE POSITIONS OF THE DEMOCRATIC AND REPUBLICAN PARTIES.

FROM the autumn of 1860 to the month of August, 1864, the Democratic party, as a national party, made no declarations of its opinions or purposes concerning the war, the re-establishment of peace, or the reconstruction of the government.

Conventions were held in the States, however, and declarations were there made. Generally those declarations contained a denial of the rightfulness of the war; or if, as in some cases, the duty or the necessity of prosecuting the war was recognized, the recognition was coupled with the claim that it should be conducted solely for the restoration of the Union. The declarations of the Democratic party assumed as an historical fact that the Union was a union between Free States and Slave States rather than a union between States without regard to their domestic institutions. Consequently, in the view of the members of that party, the restoration of the Union meant the restoration of the union of Slave States and Free States. Thus to them slavery and the Union were co-existent political facts and alike enduring. This position was consistent with the traditions of the party and it was well calculated to advance it to power in the future, if, indeed, the position was not taken for that special purpose. In the elections of 1836, 1844, 1852, and 1856 the success of the Democratic party had been due to its alliance with the slaveholding class of the South, and the leaders must have been filled with serious apprehensions that the overthrow of slavery would be followed by their defeat in the country. Those apprehensions have become history, and except for a policy of force and fraud in the South the Democratic party could not have commanded a majority in ten States in the election of 1876 or in that of 1880. Thus is it seen that the traditions and hopes of the Democratic party alike led it to engage in the defense of the institution of slavery in the days of its peril and as its end approached.

Following the defeat of 1860 and the overthrow of the leaders of the Democratic party who were not engaged in the Rebellion, Gen. McClellan was not only advanced to the command of the army by a Republican administration, but he was accepted also as the head of the Democratic party.

The latter relation was established firmly by his letter to President Lincoln, dated at Harrison's Landing, Virginia, July 7, 1862.

Three propositions were enunciated distinctly in that letter, all of which were declined or set aside by President Lincoln.

(1.) The President was advised to assume the absolute control of public affairs. These are the words of advice: "The time has come when the government must determine upon a civil and military policy, covering the whole ground of our national trouble. *The responsibility of determining, declaring and supporting such civil and military policy, and of directing the whole course of national affairs in regard to the Rebellion, must now be assumed and exercised by you, or our cause will be lost.* The constitution gives you power even for the present terrible emergency."

(2.) The President was advised, or notified rather, that "neither confiscation of property, political execution of persons, territorial organization of States, or forcible abolition of slavery, should be contemplated for a moment."

And (3.) Gen. McClellan made a tender of his services in these words: "In carrying out any system of policy which you may form, you will require a commander-in-chief of the army, one who possesses your confidence, understands your views, and who is competent to execute your orders, by directing the military forces of the nation to the accomplishment of the objects by you proposed. I do not ask that place for myself. I am willing to serve you in such position as you may assign me, and I will do so as faithfully as ever subordinate served superior."

These three propositions are indefensible, and the first and third are open to explanation only upon the theory that McClellan had lost faith in the ability of the government to suppress the Rebellion by constitutional agencies. Considered logically his scheme was this:

Mr. Lincoln was to assume the dictatorship. A dictatorship could be maintained only by the power of the army.

McClellan was at the head of the army of the East, and that army was devoted to his person and his leadership.

At the moment of the tender of his services he well knew that if Mr. Lincoln accepted his advice as to the dictatorship he must also accept his services as the head of the army. As the army was then constituted it would have been impossible for Mr. Lincoln to assume absolute power and at the same time supersede McClellan as commander-in-chief.

In fine, the commander-in-chief of the army would have been the real dictator. If any natural interpretation is given to the language used by McClellan his letter was in itself an admission that the government had ceased to exist, and that a military usurpation was the only possible means by which it could be restored.

Happily for the country Mr. Lincoln was undismayed by the disasters of the Peninsula. He did not attempt to direct the whole course of national affairs; he did not accept McClellan's tender of support and promise of fidelity and subordination; and he continued to hold in his own hand the power to destroy slavery as a means of suppressing the Rebellion.

If to any this criticism of McClellan's letter shall appear unjust, the way is open for them to tender an explanation of his language that is consistent either with wisdom in judgment, or patriotism in duty.

When Mr. Lincoln issued the monitory proclamation of the 22d of September, 1862, McClellan was at the head of the army. The particular thing against which he had advised in his letter of the 7th of July had now been done, or so inaugurated that its accomplishment was an accepted fact in the South and in the North.

By a general order, dated the 7th of October, Gen. McClellan announced the proclamation to the army. He counseled obedience and moderation of temper in discussion, and he declared that "the remedy for political errors, if any are committed, is to be found only in the action of the people at the polls." Time, reflection, and, perhaps, more than all, the battle of Antietam, had enabled him to recover himself from the delusion or from the unpatriotic thought that he could create a dictator and dictate his policy.

As Gen. McClellan was nominated by the Democratic party for the office of President some responsibility for his opinions was assumed necessarily, by that party.

If he is held to a literal construction of the language used by him, then his advice to the President was unpatriotic, if not treasonable. If he is excusable upon the ground that he did not appreciate the scope and force of the language that he employed, then, manifestly, he was not fit for the position he occupied.

In November, 1863, the Supreme Court of the State of Pennsylvania pronounced the act of March 3, 1863, entitled "An Act for Enrolling and calling out the National Forces and for other purposes," unconstitutional.

Judge Woodward was the Democratic candidate for the office of Governor, and he was a member of the court and of the majority. He was not an obscure man. Independently of this opinion, he was well and generally known as an avowed supporter of extreme State rights doctrines. The opinion which he and his associates gave, and which was for a time the law of Pennsylvania, if it had been accepted generally by the judicial tribunals of the country, would have ended the contest and established the Rebellion as an accomplished fact. In that dark period of the country's history the war could not have been prosecuted under the volunteer system, even when supported by large bounties.

Judge Woodward and his associates of the majority asserted and maintained the doctrine that the regular army of the United States could be recruited only by volunteers, and that in case of invasion or rebellion the only other military resource was in the militia of the several States.

This force, when called into the service of the United States, must be summoned and employed under the State organizations, and subject to the command of the officers appointed or elected by virtue of State laws.

Such was the opinion of the Supreme Court of the State of Pennsylvania,—an opinion which denied to the national government the right to command the services of its own citizens and to employ them in its own ways in defense of its own existence. The doctrine of State rights, which concedes to the Union the power to protect itself in its existence, its rights, and its honor, and by its own methods, and independently of the will of States, and which concedes to States the power to administer their domestic affairs in their own way, is a healthful and constitutional doctrine; and no other doctrine would have been advocated or even announced except for the early-formed purpose to defend the institution of slavery at any and every sacrifice, whether of honor, of constitutional obligations, or of national existence.

The opinion of the court was given in November, and while the case was pending and during the canvass for Governor, Gen. McClellan held a conference with Judge Woodward, and thereupon he announced himself a supporter of Judge Woodward's candidacy, in a letter dated October 12, 1863.

The circumstance that the Philadelphia Press had stated that Gen. McClellan favored the election of Gov. Curtin was the occasion for the letter.

Gen. McClellan said that it had been his earnest endeavor to avoid participation in party politics, but as he could no "longer maintain silence under such misrepresentations," he proceeded to say that he had had a conference with Judge Woodward, that they agreed in their views, and that in his opinion the election of Judge Woodward was called for by the interests of the nation.

If there were any reason to assume that Judge Woodward did not disclose his opinions fully in that interview, all doubt must disappear in presence of the statements made by Gen. McClellan. He says, "I understand Judge Woodward to be in favor of the prosecution of the war *with all the means at the command of the loyal States*, until the military power of the Rebellion is destroyed. I understood him to be of opinion that while the war is waged with all possible decision and energy, the policy directing it should be in consonance with the principles of humanity and civilization, working no injury to private rights and property not demanded by military necessity and recognized by military law among civilized nations.

"And, finally, I understood him to agree with me in the opinion that the sole great objects of this war are the restoration of the unity of the nation, the preservation of the constitution, and the supremacy of the laws of the country."

Three distinct propositions are deducible reasonably, from the language employed by Gen. McClellan.

(1.) The military force was that which should be furnished by the loyal States, that is, the State militia as distinguished from the army of the United States, whether composed of men who had enlisted voluntarily, or of men who had been enrolled and drafted into service by the exercise of supreme and exclusive authority on the part of the national government. Thus it appears that the agreement in opinion by Gen. McClellan and Judge Woodward was that the mode of coercion provided in the act of March 3, 1863, was unconstitutional.

Unfortunately for Judge Woodward and Gen. McClellan, others, and among them Judge Davis, of the Supreme Court of the United States, maintained the constitutionality of the Enrollment Act.

(2.) Gen. McClellan and Judge Woodward agreed in opinion that property in slaves was as sacred as other property and that the institution of slavery was to survive the war.

(3.) That the constitution as it was should be preserved.

All three propositions were unsound and all their purposes failed; but upon the basis so established by these two men Gen. McClellan became the designated leader of the Democratic party in 1864.

The Democratic Convention assembled at Chicago the 29th day of August, 1864, and nominated Gen. McClellan for the office of President and George H. Pendleton for that of Vice-President of the United States.

The convention was called to order by August Belmont, Chairman of the National Committee. Gov. Bigler, of Pennsylvania, was appointed temporary chairman, and Gov. Seymour, of New York, was chosen to preside over the deliberations of the convention.

Mr. Belmont judged the past, condemned the present, prophesied concerning the future; and in all he was in error.

Addressing the convention, he said, "In your hands rests, under the ruling of an all-wise Providence, the future of the republic. Four years of misrule by a sectional, fanatical, and corrupt party, have brought our country to the very verge of ruin. The past and present are sufficient warnings of the disastrous consequences which would befall us if Mr. Lincoln's reëlection should be made possible by *our want of patriotism and unity.* The inevitable results of such a calamity would be the utter disintegration of our whole political and social system, amidst bloodshed and anarchy, with the great problems of liberal progress and self-government jeopardized for generations to come."

All these prophecies were falsified by events, and one only of his suggestions has become an historical fact.

Mr. Lincoln's reëlection was in part due to a want of patriotism in the Democratic party. The country was not then on the "very verge of ruin," nor did the reëlection of Mr. Lincoln result in the disintegration of our whole political and social system, although it did result in the destruction of so much of the social system as rested upon the institution of slavery.

Gov. Bigler charged the Republican party with the responsibility of dissolving the Union, and he asserted that its restoration could be effected only by the overthrow of the administration. His statement of fact was erroneous, and his prophecy was not fulfilled.

Gov. Seymour's address was more elevated in tone, but the pivotal thoughts were the same. He condemned the administration and declared that it could not then save the Union if it would. He asserted that its proclamations, its vindictive legislation, its hate and passion, were obstacles which it could not overcome. Of the Democratic party he said: "There are no hindrances in our pathways to union and to peace. We demand no conditions for the restoration of our Union: we are shackled with no hates, no prejudices, no passions. We wish for fraternal relationship with the people of the South. We demand for them what we demand for ourselves—*the full recognition of the rights of States.*" It is manifest from the language employed that he treated the proclamation of emancipation as a nullity, and that he was prepared to receive the States of the South without inquiry and without terms. Slavery was to continue and all the obligations of the old constitution were to be recognized and enforced. He pleaded for an impossible policy.

The proclamation of emancipation and the war had so far undermined slavery that its overthrow was inevitable. Consequently, the restoration of the old Union was an impossibility. This Gov. Seymour did not comprehend. The proclamation had been in force more than two years, and the restoration of the Union was then possible only upon the basis of freedom. As Gov. Seymour and his associates could not comprehend existing facts, they were incapable, consequently, of devising a wise policy for the future.

Gov. Seymour's great error was the assumption that the Republican party was under the influence of passion, and that the Democratic party was free from passion. The Republican party was a party of principles. When it came to power it had only a choice of ways. When the war opened it was compelled either to abandon its principles or to prosecute the war for the preservation of the Union.

In the prosecution of the war the time came when it was compelled to abandon the cause of the Union and its doctrines of human liberty or to attack and overthrow the institution of slavery. The policy of the party was not dictated by passion but by necessity. The execution of that policy was tempered by every humanity possible in a condition of war. The former slaves were advised to preserve order and even to render obedience, and thousands of rations were distributed to the needy inhabitants of the South, white as well as black. The policy of the Republican party was not a policy of passion, but a policy of principle under the dictates of a rigorous necessity.

Disappointment is not in itself a passion, but it generates the sentiment of hate and the fatal passions of jealousy and envy.

The Democratic party was the subject of a disappointment such as never waited upon any other political party in the republic. Usually parties are defeated upon questions of administration and through a loss of public confidence for the time being. Such losses may be repaired, and sometimes they are repaired without delay; but in 1860 the Democratic party lost not only power and the public confidence, but it lost also a controlling element in politics on which it had relied for more than twenty-five years, and by whose influence it had acquired and retained power in the country. Passion is a dangerous master, and of all human affairs its rule is most perilous in the affairs of government. In all of its great undertakings the Republican party has succeeded, and its measures have inured to the advantage of the country. On the other hand, the prophecies of the Democratic party have been falsified by events, the measures that it has proposed have been condemned by the public judgment, and whenever it has acquired power in the government it has exhibited a melancholy inability for administration.

In August, 1864, the result of the war was not in doubt, and it was apparent that the end was near.

The battle of Gettysburg had been fought, Vicksburg had fallen, the Mississippi river was open from its head waters to the Gulf of Mexico. Maryland, Kentucky, West Virginia, and Missouri were in the quiet control of the Union forces, the sea coast was under an effective blockade, and a portion of every border State and portions of nearly every State resting on the Mississippi river, the Gulf of Mexico and the Atlantic ocean were in the possession of the armies of the United States. Foreign interference was no longer apprehended. The credit of the Confederate States was destroyed utterly. It was impossible to negotiate loans abroad, and the resources on which taxes had been levied had disappeared. The new recruits for the Confederate armies did not repair the waste caused by sickness, death, and desertion.

In 1861 and 1862 the Union armies had suffered many defeats. In

1863 and 1864 they had gained many victories and they had endured but few disasters.

The army aggregated nearly a million of men, most of whom were veterans, disciplined by hardships, encouraged by a succession of victories, and confident in their own persons and in the courage and skill of their leaders. Indeed, there never was a day after Gen. Grant assumed the command of the Army of the Potomac when the army, the administration, or the world at large, excluding the Democratic party of the North, had any doubt of the result.

It is a marvel of history, and a marvel which history itself cannot explain, that the delegates of the Democratic party should have failed to realize the facts, or, realizing the facts, should have failed to comprehend their value.

By the first resolution it was declared by the members of the Chicago convention that the Democratic party would "adhere with unswerving fidelity to the Union under the Constitution." In this they meant the old Union and the Constitution as it was, with all its obligations in regard to slavery. Adherence to the old Union meant the restoration of the States that had engaged in the Rebellion, and all without terms, conditions, or voluntary pledges. By its pledge of adherence to the old Union under the Constitution the Democratic party repudiated the Proclamation of Emancipation as an exercise of power not warranted by the Constitution, nor justified by the exigencies of war.

The Chicago platform of 1864 was the logical sequence of the position taken by Mr. Buchanan in 1860. If the national government had not a right to use force to prevent the secession of States, then the exercise of the war power by the President and Congress was unconstitutional. Therefore, every act of force designed to suppress the Rebellion and restore the Union was invalid. The proclamation of emancipation was such an act. Consequently, it was a void act.

Upon this interpretation of the leading resolution of the Chicago platform the second resolution becomes intelligible. It was in these words: "Resolved, That this convention does especially declare as the sense of the American people, that after four years of failure to restore the Union by the experiment of war, during which, under the pretense of a military necessity, or war power higher than the Constitution, the Constitution itself has been disregarded in every part, and public liberty and private right alike trodden down and the material prosperity of the country essentially impaired—justice, humanity, liberty, and the public welfare demand that immediate efforts be made for a cessation of hostilities, with a view of an ultimate convention of the States, or other peaceable means to the end that at the earliest practicable moment peace may be restored on the basis of the Federal Union of the States."

The failure of which the convention spoke was not the failure of the war in a military sense; nor was it a failure upon the ground that its prosecution had not tended to the reëstablishment of the government and the exercise of jurisdiction over all of the original territory of the United States; but it was a failure in the sense that its prosecution and its successes, in the ratio of its successes, had rendered the restoration of the Union as it was and under the old Constitution less and less probable.

The demand for a cessation of hostilities was the logical sequence of the declaration made by Mr. Buchanan in his message of December, 1860: "The fact is, that our Union rests upon public opinion, and can never be cemented by the blood of its citizens shed in civil war. If it can not live in the affections of the people it must one day perish. *Congress possesses many means of preserving it by conciliation; but the sword was not placed in its hand to preserve it by force.*"

The Convention did not demand an armistice, which implies that the war may be resumed, but a *cessation of hostilities*, which implies a final and complete abandonment of force as a means of attaining the desired result.

This view of the meaning attached to that language by the Convention itself is confirmed by the object to be attained, as it is set forth, in these words: "*With a view to an ultimate convention of the States, or other peaceable means, to the end that at the earliest practicable moment peace may be restored on the basis of the Federal Union of the States.*"

The propositions involved in the resolutions of the Chicago Convention were these:

(1.) The war to end by the voluntary withdrawal of the armies and navies of the United States from the theatre of operations, and never again to be resumed.

(2.) The Union to be restored by a Convention of States or by other peaceable means, and in case of failure to be abandoned, and upon the ground that the nation had no constitutional right to preserve its existence by force.

(3.) That inasmuch as the nation had no right to use force to prevent the secession of States from the Union, the war, with all its consequences and incidents, was unconstitutional, including the Proclamation of Emancipation.

If the Convention had spoken for the American people, as it presumed and assumed to speak, the soldiers of the Republic might have received sympathy, but not gratitude nor pensions; the freedmen, wherever found, would have been returned to their former masters; the Proclamation of Emancipation would have been treated as void; and the debt of the North would have been repudiated, or it would have been massed with the debt of the South and with it made a charge upon the labor and capital of the country. Indeed, if the war on the part of the North was unjustifiable, then there could be no good reason for making its debt a charge upon the country and requiring the States of the South to contribute to its payment. For the same reasons we of the North would have been bound to pay the debt of the South.

Upon these issues, not fully expressed, and not always understood, the Democratic party appealed to the country.

In a total vote of more than four million Mr. Lincoln's majority exceeded four hundred thousand. Of the electoral votes Gen. McClellan received twenty-one—seven in New Jersey, three in Delaware, and eleven in Kentucky.

Mr. Lincoln received two hundred and twelve electoral votes, given by twenty-two States.

And so ended the most important political contest, not of this Republic only, but of modern times.

In November, 1864, the South was exhausted utterly. The people had lost confidence in the leaders, the armies were wasting away, the treasury was empty, and masters and slaves were alike assured that the end was near. The hope that the Democratic party might succeed was the only hope remaining.

Not more fortunate for the North than for the South was the failure of that hope.

With success would have come an effort to reëstablish the institution of slavery. Fugitives would have been gathered by the military arm from every quarter of the Union, and slave-catching would have become a national vocation. When the public patience had been exhausted and the public conscience had been again aroused, resistance would have been made, border wars would have been provoked, and the contest for supremacy would have been renewed.

When Congress passed the act of July 17, 1862, entitled "An Act to suppress Insurrection, to punish Treason and Rebellion, to seize and confiscate the Property of Rebels, and for other purposes," the restoration of the Union upon a pro-slavery basis became an impossibility.

The Confederates were struggling to found a Republic upon Slavery; the Democrats of the North were struggling to reconstruct the Republic upon Slavery. The Republican party, wiser than all, reconstructed the government upon the basis of universal freedom, of the equality of men in the States, and of the equality of States in the Union.

CHAPTER VIII.

THE FINANCIAL POLICY OF THE REPUBLICAN PARTY AND ITS RESULTS.

WHEN the Republican party came to power in March, 1861, the treasury of the United States was empty, its credit was impaired, the navy was scattered over the waters remote from our own coasts, and the army was only sufficient for the protection of the frontier against the Indian tribes.

As "money is the sinews of war," it was only possible to create an army and to reconstruct the navy by first establishing the public credit.

In 1860 there had been a long period of peace with foreign nations. For eight years the government had been in the control of the Democratic party. At the close of the Mexican war the debt was a trifle more than sixty-three million dollars, and the annual interest charge was less than three million and six hundred thousand. The Indian wars, the war in Utah, and the troubles in Kansas had so absorbed the revenues that the public debt the 30th of June, 1860, was about two million dollars more than it had been the 30th of June, 1849. This circumstance was of small moment in itself, but it indicates a lack of administrative faculty when considered in presence of the fact that the population of the country had risen from twenty-three million in 1850 to thirty-one million in 1860.

The public debt was equal only to two dollars for each inhabitant, with an annual interest charge of twelve cents. In 1791 the public debt exceeded seventy five million dollars. This amount, distributed upon a population of less than four million, was equal to about twenty dollars for each inhabitant. That sum, so vast in comparison with the debt of 1860, had been paid in the year 1835, together with the cost of the war of 1812, which amounted to the sum of seventy-five million dollars in addition to the debt then remaining unpaid.

From the day when the State debts were assumed under the administration of Hamilton and Washington, the nation had exhibited a wise and resolute good faith in everything relating to the public credit; yet, in September, 1860, that credit was so impaired that the Secretary of the Treasury was only able to borrow seven million dollars under an authority to make a loan of twenty-one million and upon a call for bids to the amount of ten million dollars.

The impairment of the public credit is attributed, usually, to the apprehensions then existing in the public mind as to the result of the pending elections and the consequent fate of the country. This may have been so, but whether so or otherwise, the cause of the impairment of the public credit is to be found in the position of the Democratic party in reference to the threats and doctrines of the secession members of that party, or in its avowed or well-known opinions concerning the right of secession, or in the apparent indifference of its representative men, and especially of the President and his Cabinet, to maintain the Union by force, whenever it should be necessary to use force for that purpose.

The act of the 22d of June, 1860, which authorized a loan of twenty-one million dollars, was designed to provide the means of redeeming a like amount of Treasury notes then outstanding and soon to be due and payable. The failure of this loan compelled the Secretary of the Treasury to ask for authority to issue new Treasury notes to the amount of eleven million dollars with which to redeem the old notes then outstanding. As security for the payment of these notes he recommended a pledge of the public lands. This pledge Congress refused to give, but the bill authorizing an issue of Treasury notes to the amount of ten million dollars was approved the 17th of December, 1860. The notes were to be issued or sold at par, but at such rates of interest as might be agreed upon by the bidders and the Secretary. Under this license bids were received and the notes were sold at par and varying rates of interest, averaging between eleven and twelve per cent.

There was a balance in the Treasury the first day of January, 1861, of two million, two hundred and thirty-three thousand, two hundred and twenty dollars; a sum inadequate for the safe management of a first-class bank.

The deficiency for the fiscal year, estimated on a peace basis, amounted to twenty-four million dollars. By an act approved the 8th of February, 1861, Congress authorized a loan of twenty-five million dollars. The bonds were to bear interest at a rate not exceeding six per cent., payable semi-annually. The principal was payable after ten and within twenty years.

The Secretary of the Treasury advised Congress to tender to the purchasers of bonds a pledge of the claim against the several States for the surplus revenue deposited with them a quarter of a century before. This advice Congress did not follow. Only eighteen million of the bonds were taken and these were sold at an average price of 89.03 per cent. of their par value.

Such was the condition of the national treasury and such the credit of the government when the Republican party came to power in March, 1861.

If at that moment the Republican party was in any degree responsible, that responsibility proceeded from one or all of three facts: Its election of a president through the divisions in the Democratic party; or in its refusal to submit to the claim that a State could secede from the Union; or, waiving the question of the right of a State to secede, upon its refusal to sanction the doctrine of Mr. Buchanan that the general government had no power, under the Constitution, to prevent by force the secession of a State.

On the 4th day of March, 1861, Mr. Buchanan, as the representative of the Democratic party, transferred to Abraham Lincoln a dissevered Union, a government in form only, whose treasury was empty, whose credit was broken, whose navy was dispersed, whose army was weak in numbers and led in part by untrustworthy officers, with an impending war whose magnitude at the end was to be estimated by the loss of hundreds of thousands of lives and the expenditure of thousands of millions of treasure.

This statement indicates the nature of the undertaking to which the Republican party was called, but it does not disclose fully its magnitude. At the extra session of Congress, which began the 4th day of July, 1861, the President asked for authority to borrow four hundred million dollars. The Secretary of the Treasury estimated the expenses of the current fiscal year at three hundred and eighteen million dollars.

At the end of the year it appeared that the expenses, exclusive of payments on account of the public debt, had been swollen to the enormous sum of four hundred and seventy million dollars.

At the extra session of Congress acts were passed authorizing the issue of bonds and Treasury notes to an amount in the aggregate of more than three hundred million dollars, and at a rate of interest not exceeding 7.3 per cent. per annum. Such was the effect upon the public mind of a vigorous administration of affairs, and such the confidence inspired by the purpose of the government to suppress the Rebellion and sustain the Union, that the loan was obtained and the means of prosecuting the war were secured.

The rate of interest was two-thirds only of what had been paid in Mr. Buchanan's administration and the loan was ten-fold greater. In a period of war, in an exigency, it is not possible for a nation to dictate the rate of interest that it will pay upon loans. The ability to dictate terms depends upon two concurring conditions: First, a well-established credit; and secondly, having tendered a loan to the public, the ability to wait until capitalists are prepared to accept the terms. In 1861 and in 1862 the credit of the government was not established, and its necessities were such that no delays were possible. When due weight is given to the circumstances then existing, it is not easy, even in this period of great fortunes and gigantic financial operations, to realize the fact that loans were made at the rate of a million dollars a day and upon moderate terms.

The financial policy of the Republican party was dictated in the outset by the exigencies of war, but it was afterwards adapted to the circumstances and conditions of peace.

The measures of that policy are divided, naturally, therefore, into two classes. As the credit of a government can neither be established nor preserved unless revenues are provided by systematic processes, it is wise in time of peace to meet every current expenditure, to which should be added payments upon the principal of any debt that may exist; and in time of war to so enlarge the revenues as to give assurance that the credit of the nation will be preserved until the return of peace.

The secession of States and the resignation of Senators and Representatives left the two houses at the end of the thirty-sixth Congress in the control of the Republican party. By an act approved the 2d of March, 1861, the customs duties were increased upon many articles of merchandise. This act was followed by the statute of the 5th of August, 1861, the statute of the 14th of July, 1862, and the statute of the 30th of June, 1864. It was the design, as it was the effect of these measures, not only to provide revenues upon the basis of a war policy, but also to give protection to the capital and labor of the country.

The gross receipts from customs for the year ending the 30th of June, 1861, were a trifle less than forty million dollars; but for the year ending June 30th, 1864, they had risen to more than one hundred and two million. In the meantime labor and capital were profitably employed in all sections of the Union then free from the presence of hostile armies.

Another important measure designed to support the public credit was the act to authorize the issue of United States notes and for the funding of the public debt of the United States, approved the 25th of February, 1862. The Secretary of the Treasury was authorized to issue United States notes to the amount of one hundred and fifty million dollars, without interest. Those notes were receivable in payment of all taxes, excises, debts, and demands of every kind due to the United States, except duties on imports, and they were also endowed with the legal tender quality in payment of all debts, public and private, within the United States. The Secretary of the Treasury was required to receive such notes the same as coin and at their par value in payment of all bonds that might be thereafter sold or negotiated by him.

By the same statute, the Secretary of the Treasury was authorized to issue bonds bearing interest at the rate of six per centum per annum, payable semi-annually, to an amount not exceeding five hundred million dollars.

He was also authorized to receive deposits of money payable at any time after thirty days upon ten days' notice, and to allow interest for the use of the same at the rate of five per centum per annum. As the interest upon the bonds, so authorized, was payable in coin, it was provided that all duties should be paid in coin or in certain demand notes which had been issued to the amount of fifty million dollars under an at approved July 17th, 1861. The coin so received was pledged specifically, first to the payment of the interest on the bonds and notes of the United States, and secondly to the purchase or payment of one per centum of the entire debt of the United States, to be withdrawn each fiscal year after the first day of July, 1862. The bonds so purchased were to be set apart as a sinking fund, and the interest accruing thereon was to be paid to the credit of the sinking fund and made part of the capital thereof. The residue was to be paid into the Treasury of the United States. This act, in connection with the statutes which provided for the increase of the customs duties and the act passed in the month of July following, levying a direct tax upon the States for twenty million dollars and providing a system of internal revenue, established the public credit so firmly that the government of the United States was able to create a debt of nearly three thousand million dollars and to prosecute the war without any delay due to the absence of the necessary means.

The statute establishing the internal revenue system was approved July 1, 1862, and it was put into operation in the months of September and October of the same year. The revenues from that source for the fiscal year ending June 30, 1863, amounted to thirty-seven million dollars, and for the year 1865 to two hundred and nine million. The total revenue created under that system, from its inauguration to the close of the last fiscal year, was three thousand and ninety-eight million dollars, a sum greater than the public debt of the United States at any one time. This was the largest branch of a government ever organized in historical times. As early as the first of January, 1862, its business was greater than that of the entire Treasury Department at any time previous to March 4, 1861.

Of all the measures of the war designed to establish the public credit, and to provide means for its prosecution, there was not one more important than the act establishing a national bank currency, approved the 25th of February, 1863. Previously to that time the paper currency of the country had been furnished by State banks, and under systems widely different, and generally without sufficient security for the redemption of the notes put in circulation. The national bank act required the corporators to deposit United States bonds in excess of the amount of circulation to be issued. The government assumed the redemption of the notes issued by the national banks and reserved the right to be reimbursed by the sale of the bonds. Several important advantages were secured by the national banking system. First, the redemption of the currency was secured absolutely, and secondly, its value was the same in all parts of the country.

In addition to these advantages the banks were required to purchase bonds of the United States and to deposit the same with the Treasurer for the security of their circulation. Thus a market for the bonds was created to the amount of three hundred million dollars.

Finally, the banks were enlisted actively on the side of the government as agents for the sale of bonds to corporations and private parties.

Of the leading financial measures of the war one only of them has been assailed, either in the courts or before the country. The authority given to the Secretary of the Treasury, by the statute of the 25th of February, 1862, to issue United States notes and to make them a legal tender in the payment of all debts then existing, as well as of those which might thereafter be contracted, has been debated, contested, and adjudicated finally by the Supreme Court.

That adjudication sustains the authority of Congress and vindicates the policy of the statute; but it is an error to suppose that any countenance is given either by the statute or by the decision of the court to the notion that United States notes should be issued except upon a pledge of redemption in coin.

The discretion, however, is vested in Congress, and upon the opinion given by Chief-Justice Marshall in the case of McCulloch v. The State of Maryland, the courts cannot interfere with its exercise.

Upon one branch of the subject there has been no difference of opinion. The constitutional grant to Congress of the power to borrow money is a grant so comprehensive in its terms that it of necessity includes the power to issue notes of any denomination, either with or without interest, and payable on demand or at any future time. With this concession, and in the presence of the opinion of the court in the case of McCulloch v. The State of Maryland, it follows that Congress may endow the notes which it authorizes with the legal tender quality, or it may refuse to so endow them. The power to borrow money and the power to levy taxes are supreme powers, and by processes of reasoning or by the exercise of the imagination many dangers may be demonstrated or suggested. But they are powers essential to national existence. They are powers that must be somewhere vested, and wherever vested there the discretion must be lodged also. Under our system the power is in Congress and the security against the abuse of the power is in the speedy responsibility of the representative to the constituency, through frequent elections.

In 1862 Congress had no alternative. The United States notes constituted the only means by which the army was to be paid, supplied, and kept in the field. If the legal tender quality had been withheld from those notes, during what period of time could the government have obtained supplies in exchange for a currency which the creditors of those who furnished the supplies might receive or decline at their pleasure?

Under our system, that figure of authority which we call *government* resides in citizenship, and each citizen is therefore an integral part of the government. Every sacrifice made, every duty imposed, every burden laid, when the proceedings are by due authority, is, in a constitutional sense, with the consent of all citizens. Every contract, which by its terms is not excepted out of the rule, is to be performed in the currency of the country at the time when the contract is liquidated. The power to decide the quantity and quality of that currency is an essential incident of sovereignty.

If, in 1862, there had been a persistent refusal to issue legal tender notes, there would have remained no means by which the Rebellion could have been suppressed. A like exigency may arise in the future, either from domestic disturbance or foreign war. In defiance of all criticism, but under the Constitution, a precedent has been made which assumes for the government the largest powers for its own preservation.

During the administration of President Johnson, the attention of Congress was directed chiefly to the measures of reconstruction and to the questions in controversy between the legislative and executive departments of the government.

Immediately after the inauguration of General Grant, an important act was passed, entitled "An Act to Strengthen the Public Credit." The bill was approved March 18, 1869, and it was the first legislative act of the Forty-first Congress. It is stated in the statute that the object was to remove any doubt as to the purpose of the government to discharge all just claims of public creditors and to settle the conflicting views of the laws by which such obligations had been contracted; and thereupon it was declared that the faith of the United States was pledged to the payment in coin, or its equivalent, of all the obligations of the United States known as United States notes and all interest-bearing obligations of the United States, unless it was expressly provided in such obligations that they might be paid in lawful currency, or other money than gold and silver.

At that time the public debt of the United States amounted to about two thousand six hundred million dollars, and its credit was so much impaired that the six per cent. bonds of the United States were sold for gold at the rate of eighty-three cents on the dollar. In December of the same year the Secretary of the Treasury recommended the passage of a law authorizing a new loan in the amount of twelve hundred million dollars, to be offered in three classes of four hundred million each, and to be payable at different periods of time.

The bonds of the several classes were to bear interest at the rate of five, four and a half, and four per centum per annum. In accordance with this recommendation, an act was passed by Congress and approved July 14, 1870, entitled "An Act to authorize the Refunding of the National Debt." Of the interest-bearing debt all but about three hundred million dollars was subject to the rate of six per centum per annum. Agreeably to the provisions of the act of 1870 and the acts in amendment thereof, the public debt has been refunded so that it now bears interest at the rates of three, three and a half, four, and four and a half per centum per annum. In the month of August, 1865, the debt of the United States, exclusive of cash in the Treasury, amounted to two thousand seven hundred and fifty-six million dollars, and the interest charge exceeded one hundred and fifty million. On the 30th of June, 1883, the total debt, exclusive of cash in the Treasury, was one thousand five hundred and thirty-eight million dollars, and the interest charge was fifty-one and a half million.

In the interval between the close of the war and the passage of the act to strengthen the public credit, serious doubts were entertained on both sides of the Atlantic, as to the ability and the disposition of the country to provide means for the payment of the interest and principal of the public debt. Although the act of the 25th of February, 1862, provided that the sinking fund system should be put into operation after June 30th of that year, the statute remained inoperative until the inauguration of President Grant.

In the first year of his administration, the Secretary of the Treasury made purchases of bonds for the sinking fund. This step was an assurance that the public debt would be paid—and paid in about thirty years—even if no other provision was made for its liquidation. All doubts were removed and threats of repudiation were not afterwards heard. Customs duties and taxes were collected, the revenues exceeded the expenses, and during the first term of President Grant's administration more than three hundred and sixty million dollars were applied to the payment of the interest-bearing debt of the country.

Thus, under the administration of the government by the Republican party, the two great problems of the war have been solved successfully. The Union has been restored and the enormous debt created for its preservation has been paid so rapidly that the four per cent. bonds of the government have been sold at the rate of twenty-five per cent. in excess of their par value.

The history of the world furnishes no example for the financial successes of the government of the United States. For these successes the country is indebted to the skill, courage, and integrity of the Republican party.

CHAPTER IX.

THE PROTECTIVE POLICY OF THE REPUBLICAN PARTY, AND ITS EFFECTS UPON THE WAGES OF LABORERS AND THE PRICES OF COMMODITIES.

IT is not the duty of a government to give employment to its subjects or citizens, but it is a duty to create and secure opportunities for employment.

In every community the labor of many persons is required for the support, education, and comfort of its members. If all the citizens or subjects of a government are regarded as members of one community, it is reasonable that their labor should be directed to their own support in every branch of industry that is free from natural obstacles to its successful prosecution.

At the close of the Revolutionary War, England, France, and Holland were in possession of all the skill in manufactures and the productive arts that was common to the western world. Those nations possessed capital sufficient for every reasonable undertaking.

England had discouraged manufactures in the Colonies, and the States of the new Republic had neither capital nor skilled labor. Political independence is not by necessity the equivalent of national freedom. The latter exists only when the internal resources of a nation are such that it may defy blockades by sea and frontier fortifications on the land, and yet continue in the uninterrupted possession and enjoyment of the comforts and conveniences essential to domestic and social life.

The possibilities of an agricultural community are limited to the productions essential to human existence, and in such variety only as the soil and climate will encourage or tolerate. A surplus of these productions may, through commerce, be exchanged for the manufactures of other communities; but as a condition of peace cannot be assumed of any nation, and as commerce is the first and easiest victim of war, a constant and sufficient supply of the comforts and conveniences of life can be secured only by the application of domestic labor to manufactures and the arts.

Of all the provisions of the Constitution, no one has contributed more to the industrial freedom of the United States than the paragraph which authorizes Congress to "promote the progress of science and the useful arts, by securing, for limited times, to authors and inventors, the exclusive right to their respective writings and discoveries." Herein is found the extremest form of the doctrine of protection, yet there is no other provision of the Constitution that has contributed so largely to the material prosperity of the country and to the comfort of the people. Nearly every improvement in machinery, by which articles of consumption by the people generally have been reduced in cost and placed within the reach of all, is due to an invention that would not have been made had not the inventor been assured that he would enjoy the exclusive use and benefit of his invention for a period of time. Nearly every advance in manufactures, from the hand-loom and spinning-wheel, is due to the stimulus given to the inventive faculties of man by the protection accorded to inventors. That protection has sustained the great body of inventors in their struggles against poverty, prejudice, and the disinclination of mankind to accept new ways in place of the old. Of the mass of inventors whose inventions have contributed to the prosperity and comfort of mankind, a few only have received adequate returns, either in fame or money. The private emoluments bear no just relation to the public benefits.

If, to-day, the results of the system of protection to inventors could be destroyed, there is not a family upon the continent that would not be deprived of much the larger share of its comforts, conveniencies, and luxuries.

The invention of labor-saving machines was stimulated by the laws framed for the protection of their inventors; but the use of labor-saving machines could be secured only by protecting those who were employed to construct and operate them. Such protection, however, was not practical, nor would it have been useful, as between the citizens or inhabitants of our own country.

As the knowledge and use of labor-saving machines cannot be limited to the country in which the inventions are made, a duty upon the products of such machines is the only adequate means of protecting our domestic labor, by giving to its results an advantage in the markets of the United States. The benefits of such a system are indirect as well as direct. The laborer in the mine, shop, or mill is saved from the full competition of the laborer in another country, who, from the circumstances in which he is placed, is compelled to give his labor for small compensation.

Beyond this fact, it is also true that the supplies consumed by the laborer and his family are, in a large part, obtained from the vicinity. Those supplies, in the main, are furnished by the agricultural population. The farmers of England supply the laborers of Birmingham and Manchester; the farmers of the United States supply the laborers of Pittsburgh and Lowell. If the goods now made in Pittsburgh and Lowell were made in Manchester, Sheffield, and Birmingham, the demand for the products of agricultural labor would be diminished in the United States, and proportionately increased in England.

Nor is it an answer to the claim that the protective system benefits the laboring classes, to maintain that, as an increase of wages in the United States is followed by the migration of laborers from Europe, an equilibrium of prices is secured in the end, and the laboring populations of the countries whose commercial relations are intimate are brought, finally, to the same level. If this were true, the fact that it is better for the American farmer to have the exclusive control of a near market than to take a chance in a distant market, would also be true. If, therefore, the operatives in a mill at Pittsburgh were all of foreign birth, the articles for their subsistence would be furnished by American laborers in other departments of industry.

Washington and Jefferson were advocates of protection to domestic labor, and the advantages of the system were as well stated and argued by Hamilton as they can be now stated and argued after a century nearly of experience under a protective system at times, and a system of free trade at other times.

It is a singular historical fact, which admits of no explanation that can be justified to the reason of mankind, that the political party in the United States most hostile to Great Britain was also the party that was most hostile to a system of protection to domestic industry by which America, in the highest national sense, could be made independent of the mother country.

Hamilton was an advocate of the British Constitution, and there was a period in his career when he would have accepted it as a model for the United States; yet he and the party which he founded were in favor of so organizing the policy of the new nation that it would be free, absolutely, in all its industrial and financial affairs. On the other hand, the party which had no sympathy for the political institutions of Great Britain, originated and maintained a policy of free trade, under and against which our infant manufactures struggled for more than half a century. The tariff acts of 1816, 1828, and 1842, gave temporary encouragement to the manufacturing industries of the country, but as the policy was controverted by the Democratic party, it was not easy to command either confidence or capital for new undertakings.

In the year 1860, at the end of seventy years of national life, distinguished by a vacillating policy upon the subject of protection, our manufactures in the aggregate amounted to no more than eight hundred and fifty-five million dollars upon an invested capital of one thousand and ten million dollars.

Employment was thus given to 1,311,246 persons, to whom was paid, in the aggregate, the sum of $378,878,966 as annual wages. The laborers received an average of $288 each per annum.

In 1880, the capital invested in manufactures amounted to $2,790,272,606. The product had risen to the sum of $1,972,755,642. The wages paid to 2,732,595 operatives amounted to $947,953,795, or an average annual earning of $346. From the year 1860 to the year 1880, the wages of the operatives, including men, women, and children, had been advanced twenty per cent. In other words, the operatives who were employed in 1880 were in the receipt each year of the enormous sum of one hundred and sixty million dollars in excess of the amount that would have been paid to them upon the basis of the wages allowed in 1860.

The aggregate wages paid in 1880 were one hundred and fifty per cent. greater than in 1860, while the increase in the number of hands employed was only one hundred and eight per cent.

A statement made by the "Clark Thread Company," doing business at Paisley, Scotland, and Newark, New Jersey, proves beyond controversy the fact that the ability to manufacture in this country the thread furnished by that company is due, solely, to the protection given to it, unless, indeed, the wages of the operatives were reduced something more than fifty per cent.

The correspondence between that company and Joseph Nimmo, Jr., Esq., Chief of the Bureau of Statistics, contains information of great value. The "Clark Thread Company" have transferred a portion of their manufacturing business from Paisley to Newark. Two advantages accrue to the company: the goods are made near the market, and the duties are avoided. The advantages to this country by the transfer of the business are many. The buildings for the business and the houses for the operatives are the product of American labor, and the subsistence of the operatives gives employment to mechanics and artisans in other departments, and creates a market for agricultural products.

A comparison of the wages paid by this company in Paisley and in Newark shows that, except for the custom's duties, not one spool of thread would be made in Newark, unless the wages of the laborers were reduced about one-half.

CLARK THREAD COMPANY,
NEWARK, N. J., January 31, 1882.

DEAR SIR: Your favor of yesterday is received.

In reply to your question as to what number of hours the employés work in either place, would say that in Paisley the factories work ten hours daily, five days in the week, and Saturdays to 12 o'clock noon, making a half holiday for Saturdays. In Newark we work ten and one-half hours, five days in the week, and stop on Saturdays at half-past one, making for Newark 50 hours as against 55 for Paisley.

With regard to your question as to the effectiveness of labor here and in Paisley, would say that my experience is about equal in both places, and the employés in either place, with the same machinery, will produce about the same amount of work, and work as steadily in the one place as in the other. . . . Our business of making spool-cotton is only in process of development in this country, as there is still large quantities of six-cord imported, but is becoming less as we get our means of production extended.

Any further information I can give you, will be glad to do so; as I think it is best for you people to know the true inwardness of the business.

Yours, respectfully,   WILLIAM CLARK.

J. NIMMO, JR., Esq.

CLARK THREAD COMPANY,
NEWARK, N. J., March 31, 1882.

DEAR SIR: Yours of the 29th came duly to hand, and contents noted, and in reply would answer the statements contained therein, as under, which we trust will be what you require to close up your report.

1. In regard to the machinery used in our two factories, would say that it is used in the same manner, but in a little larger extent in Paisley than in Newark.

2. The organization of labor is similar.

3. The methods pursued in the employment of labor is similar.

4. The physical and intellectual ability of the operatives in both countries are about equal.

5. The following is a statement of the wages paid in both countries to the same class of workers, and the percentage of one over the other:

GIRLS.	Paisley.	Newark.	Newark over Paisley.
	Per week.	Per week.	Per cent.
Spoolers	$3 60	$8 00	122
Reelers	3 60	8 00	122
Cop winders	3 60	8 00	122
Twisters	2 35	5 50	135
Slippers	1 65	3 00	81
Bobbin cleaners	1 50	2 50	66
MEN.			
Carpenters	7 25	17 00	135
Machinists	7 25	18 00	148
Dyers	7 00	15 00	114
Bleachers	6 50	13 50	108
Firemen	6 00	12 50	108

Hoping above will be satisfactory, we remain, yours truly,

CLARK THREAD COMPANY,
Per CONTRELL.

JOSEPH NIMMO, JR., ESQ.

CLARK THREAD COMPANY,
NEWARK, N. J., April 3, 1882.

DEAR SIR: We did make an error in our estimate of March 31, having omitted to take the difference in time of working hours between the two countries, but having looked it over and made that correction, we find the following result, which we think correct: Girls' average, Newark over Paisley, 99 per cent.; men's average, Newark over Paisley, 104 per cent., or 101¾ per cent. total average.

This is as near as we can get at it, and think you can safely take it as conclusive.

Yours truly, CLARK THREAD COMPANY,
Per CONTRELL.

JOSEPH NIMMO, JR., Esq.,
Chief of Bureau.

It is thus apparent (1) that the laboring population of the United States, engaged in manufactures, is much better paid than is the laboring population of Great Britain; (2) that the ability to manufacture many kinds of goods and to pay the present rates of wages is due to the protective system; and (3) that the operatives employed in the manufactories of the United States are in the receipt of better wages and in the enjoyment of more of the comforts of life than they could command in 1860.

Nor is it true that the cost of maintaining a family in 1880 was greater than in 1860, assuming always the same facts as to the scope of the purchases made.

The statement of the prices of leading articles of general use, prepared by the Chief of the Bureau of Statistics, but based upon a report made by the Director of the Mint, with the aid of other authorities noted, establishes the proposition in a general sense.

In a period of twenty years the habits of a people undergo great changes, and in many instances the laborer's savings are not greater at the end of the period than at the beginning; but, in the meantime, he and his family have enjoyed a larger share of the comforts and conveniences of domestic life.

If the deposits in the savings banks are a test of the relative condition of the laboring classes as to the possession of capital, their aggregate accumulations were immensely greater in 1880 than in 1860.

Statement of Prices of leading articles in the New York market in 1860 *and* 1880.

(Report of the Director of the Mint, 1881.)

	1860.	1880.
Flour, superfine, bbl.,	$5.190	$4.135
Pork, mess, "	a 18.090	a 13.230
Beef, mess, "	5.170	11.119
Hams, lb.,	.096	.084
Lard, "	a .117	a .079
Sugar, Cuba, "	.085	.070
" Loaf, "	.098	.086
Tallow, "	.100	.063
Molasses, New Orleans, gallon,	.465	.370
Leather, lb.,	.215	.212
Standard Sheeting, 36 in. wide (unbleached),	c .071	b .077
" Shirting, 28 in. wide (unbleached),	c .070	b .053
	$29.767	$29.658

a. From Report of N. Y. Produce Exchange of New York, 1880.
b. Data furnished by Edward Atkinson of Boston.
c. From N. Y. Shipping List for 1860.

This table indicates that the cost of living was not greater in 1880 than in 1860, and the census tables prove that the wages of the operatives in the mills were increased in that period by an addition of twenty per cent., showing an annual gain to that class of laborers of one hundred and sixty million dollars. That vast sum they have either held as capital or they have expended it in additions to personal and family comforts.

But the advantages of protection do not end thus. A system which adds twenty per cent. to the wages of one class of operatives affects equally the wages of every class of laborers within the influence of the system.

In 1880, the number of inhabitants in the United States of the age of ten years and upwards was nearly thirty-seven million, and of these more than thirteen million were employed in agriculture, trade, transportation, mechanics, manufactures, and mining. Of the thirteen million, two million and seven hundred thousand, or one-fifth of the whole, were employed in manufactures. Upon the basis of a direct gain to them by virtue of the system of protection of one hundred and sixty million dollars annually, and upon the theory that the laborers in other branches of industry enjoy equal benefits, the total gain to the laboring population is swollen to the enormous sum of eight hundred million dollars.

If liberal allowances be made for errors, or even for exaggerations, there will remain a substantial quantity of truth justifying the statement that any change of policy which affects unfavorably the manufacturing industries of the country, and especially any change which transfers the business in any sensible degree to England or to the Continent of Europe, is a policy fraught with peril to every laborer and to every capitalist in the land.

The transfer of half a million of laborers from the mills to mining and agriculture would prostrate the entire system of labor for the whole country.

When the demand for labor is checked the demand for the products of labor diminishes also.

A single illustration will give voice to the magnitude of the evils that are incident to a loss of the means to purchase the products of industry in accustomed quantities.

Of the entire population of the country, not less than thirty million are dependent directly upon the proceeds of labor for the means of subsistence.

If these means are reduced annually to the extent of ten dollars only for each person, the aggregate decrease in the demand for the products of labor is three hundred million dollars.

Under the protective system, one interest, and one only, has languished, — the foreign carrying trade upon the ocean.

Business upon the ocean is attended with more perils than wait upon business on the land, and the returns are more uncertain.

During the war period the added dangers not only prevented the increase of our commerce, but they caused the destruction of that which existed. Upon the return of peace, the opportunities for employment in agriculture, in manufactures, in the construction of railways, and in operating them, were so many and attractive that the ocean was neglected.

The overthrow of our manufacturing system would be attended with the loss of these opportunities, and thousands of laborers would be driven to the sea for employment and subsistence.

As long as this nation is, in its domestic industries, the most prosperous of the nations having intimate commercial relations with each other, so long will our doings upon the ocean be very insignificant when compared with our business upon the land.

It is understood that the Republican party is so pledged to the system of protection that no changes can be made under its lead or with its consent that shall tend to transfer the business of manufacturing to other countries, or in any sensible degree impair the demand for labor in the United States, or lessen its rewards.

It is understood, also, that the Republican party favors protection to agricultural products and raw materials, coupled with a system of drawbacks on the exportation of goods composed in whole or in part of materials on which duties have been paid.

CHAPTER X.

THE POLICY OF THE REPUBLICAN PARTY IN REGARD TO THE PUBLIC LANDS.

FOLLOWING the close of the Revolutionary War, and previous to the adoption of the Constitution, the States that claimed title by virtue of the colonial charters to the lands lying west of the thirteen original colonies, and east of the Mississippi River, ceded their rights to the United States. These lands so added were the subject of a Constitutional provision in these words: "The Congress shall have power to dispose of and make all needful rules and regulations respecting the territory, or other property belonging to the United States."

For the first half century after the organization of the government, these lands were a source of revenue to which prominence was given in all the estimates of the Treasury Department, and in the financial debates in Congress.

Grants were made to new States for educational purposes, and for public improvements. Bounties of lands were given to soldiers and sailors, and finally large concessions were made by alternate sections to companies authorized to construct railways over the public domain. When grants were made to railways the price of the reserved lands was increased one hundred per cent.

By a statute passed in 1841, all the public lands not specially reserved were made subject to preëmption by actual settlers at one dollar and twenty-five cents per acre.

Rights were limited to one hundred and sixty acres. Previous to the passage of that act settlers who were upon the public lands had a right of preëmption extended to them for a like quantity of land, and at the same price, when the claimant was in actual possession.

The policy of the government for the first fifty or sixty years was marked by five distinct features: (1.) Sales of lands for revenue; (2.) grants to States for educational and other public purposes; (3.)

bounties to soldiers; (4.) grants to railways; (5.) preëmption rights to actual settlers.

When the Republican Convention met at Chicago in May, 1860, the House of Representatives had passed a homestead bill that was then pending in the Senate. The convention endorsed the House bill and demanded its passage. The Senate laid aside the House bill, and passed a bill reported from its own committee. Upon conference the two houses were brought to an agreement, and the bill was submitted to the president, who returned it to the Senate with a message containing his objections.

Upon the question: "Shall the bill pass, the objection of the president to the contrary notwithstanding," the yeas were twenty-seven and the nays were eighteen. Mr. Johnson of Tennessee voted in the negative for the purpose of moving a reconsideration. Upon the passage of the bill originally the yeas were forty-four and the nays eight. The seventeen negative votes on the question raised by the veto message were given by Democrats, and of these eight had voted for the bill upon the question of its passage.

The veto message of President Buchanan made a distinct issue, and thenceforth the scheme assumed a political character. A nominal price of twenty-five cents had been fixed in the bill. That sum was designed to meet the cost of making the surveys and maintaining the land offices. The bill also granted to States certain lands that were within the jurisdictions of the respective States.

The president treated the grants to States and to settlers as gifts. In this view he was supported by the text of the bill, but he committed a grave error when he denied to Congress the power to dispose of the land for any purpose except revenue. A contrary practice had prevailed for more than half a century, and that practice was an authoritative commentary upon the meaning of the words, "The Congress shall have power to dispose of and make all needful rules and regulations respecting the territory and other property belonging to the United States."

If Congress could endow a system of schools in a State by a free gift of the public lands, with stronger reason could it grant a homestead out of those lands to the head of a family whose children were to be educated in the schools.

The constitutional grant to Congress of power to dispose of the public lands was a broad power. It would have been equally easy, and more natural, to have limited the power to the sale of the lands, if such had been the purpose of the convention. That this was not done justifies the inference that it was the intention to allow Congress to dispose of the lands in that way which seemed most conducive to the public interest.

Previous to the passage of the act, approved the 20th of May, 1862, granting a homestead upon the public lands to certain persons named in the act, the title from the United States could be acquired only by virtue of the preëmption laws which authorized the head of a family, or widow, or a single person, over twenty-one years of age, and a citizen of the United States, to make a location of one hundred and sixty acres at a cost of one dollar and twenty-five cents per acre, or by the location of bounty land warrants which had been issued to officers and soldiers who had performed service in some one of the wars in which the country had been engaged. Aliens who had filed an intention to become citizens of the United States, were also entitled to the benefits of the preëmption laws. Since the act of May, 1862, was passed, no authority has been given for the issue of bounty land warrants, but, by the statute of the 8th of June, 1872, every sailor, soldier, and officer who had served ninety days during the late Rebellion was authorized to enter upon any of the reserved sections of the public lands along the line of any railroad, and locate a quarter section of one hundred and sixty acres, and receive a patent therefor. The alternate section of lands along the the lines of railroads for which grants had been made, were reserved by the government, and valued at two dollars and a half an acre. Other public lands could be taken under the preëmption laws at a dollar and a quarter per acre. Every sailor, soldier, and officer who was thus authorized to make entry upon the reserved lands was allowed six months after the location to make entry and commence his improvements.

By the act of 1862, every person who was the head of a family, or who had arrived at the age of twenty-one years, and who was a citizen of the United States, or, who, being an alien, had declared his intention to become such, was authorized to make entry of one quarter of a section of land as a homestead, of any of the lands subject to preëmption at a dollar and a quarter per acre, or eighty acres of the reserved lands, and subject to preëmption at two dollars and a half an acre. The title, however, could be acquired only by five years' continuous residence unless the settler should plant trees upon the same in the proportion of one acre of forest to every sixteen acres of land. In such case the title could be acquired at the end of three years. All mineral lands are excluded from the operation of the preëmption and homestead laws, but, by the statute of the 10th of May, 1872, they were declared to be free and open to exploration and purchase whether the same had, or had not, been surveyed. By the same statute the limits of each location were prescribed.

Claimants are required to expend at least five hundred dollars in labor upon each claim. After public notice of the existence of a claim, and the expiration of sixty days therefrom, if no contestant appears, the claimant is entitled to a patent upon the payment of five dollars an acre to the proper officer. For the homestead system the Republican party is responsible.

In every country, and under every system of government, the ownership of land by the larger portion of the people has been a cause for congratulation, and the fact has been treated as evidence of stability in the government. The wisdom of the homestead act can be demonstrated by whatever resonable test is applied. And first of all as to revenues. When President Buchanan vetoed the homestead bill in 1860, the Secretary of the Interior estimated that the revenue from the sale of lands would be four million dollars for the next fiscal year.

Can there be a doubt that the increase of population, due to the homestead act, has added to the customs and internal revenue receipts a sum very much in excess of four million dollars annually?

The homestead system has stimulated migration from the older and most densely populated States to the frontier States and the territories, diminishing consequently the number of persons who depend for subsistence upon the sale of their labor, and increasing the number who depend for subsistence upon the sale of the products of their labor. The sale of labor is a necessary incident in the prosecution of business, but it is less conspicuous in agriculture than in manufactures, commerce, and the mechanic arts.

Population tends to the commercial cities and manufacturing towns. Any surplus of population, or of labor, in cities and large towns, generates, speedily, social and political evils of the gravest sort. The homestead system has counteracted this tendency, and multitudes of men who otherwise could not have escaped from the condition of dependent laborers, are now independent landholders and influential citizens of great and growing States.

The productive powers of mankind are now so vast, the competition so active, the relations and interests of nations are so intimate and interwoven with each other, that it is no longer possible, even in the United States, to exclude the paternal quality of government from the administration of our affairs.

The chief problem of all is to so encourage and diversify industries as to secure constant and profitable employment upon the land for the largest possible proportion of our inhabitants.

CHAPTER XI.

THE POLICY OF THE REPUBLICAN PARTY IN FAVOR OF UNIVERSAL EDUCATION.

WHEN the Republican party was formed its power was in those States that had been distinguished for their interest in systems of public instruction.

Indeed, it may be assumed that the general intelligence of the people in the old Free States, is due to the system of free schools, and that except for that general intelligence the Republican party could not have been organized into a controlling majority. As in the beginning the party was composed of men who did not agree in measures of public policy outside of the slavery question, the organization of the party could only be preserved and its growth increased by concessions upon subordinate topics.

Such concessions are made only by men whose intelligence is so great that they can discriminate between measures and policies that are vital and those which are expedient.

The Free State party in Kansas was composed of men who represented fairly the States that supported Gen. Fremont in 1856.

Torn and wasted as Kansas had been by the invasions of slaveholders and Federal troops in the vain attempt to make it "slave" territory, that border community of hardy Republicans incorporated into its first organic law a free, public, *graded* system of schools, embracing "common, normal, preparatory, collegiate, and university departments." It established a public school-fund which now amounts to about $2,500,000.

The confidence of Congress in the final triumph of the government was manifested in the passage of the bill "donating public lands to the several States and Territories which may provide colleges for the benefit of Agriculture and the Mechanic Arts," approved July 2, 1862.

The darkest period of the war was the summer of 1862. The credit of the government was impaired, and a complete system of taxation had not been devised; yet such was the confidence of the Republican party in the ultimate triumph of the North, and such its interest in general education, and especially in agricultural education, that an appropriation was made which has absorbed more than nine million acres of public land.

In the year 1859, Congress passed a similar bill, which was vetoed by Mr. Buchanan. His objections were based in part upon the Constitution. He claimed that Congress had no power to make a grant of the public lands as a gift, and yet he admitted that the concessions to the new States of one or two sections in each township in aid of public schools was within the constitutional power of Congress, inasmuch as a wise landholder, who had large bodies of land for sale, would make a similar donation.

This concession was fatal to his argument. If the authority given to Congress "to dispose of the territory" of the United States could be so construed as to justify a free grant for education, then the theory that Congress had only power to sell the lands was a false theory. If Congress might in its judgment grant a section of land in each township for the use of schools, and the act be justified upon the ground that the concession was beneficial indirectly to the grantor, might not Congress make a similar grant for any other purpose that in its judgment would inure to the benefit of the United States?

A charter was granted for the city of Washington in 1802, but no provision was made nor powers given for establishing public schools, nor did Congress grant any aid to the struggling city for educational purposes. When the charter was amended in 1820, the corporation was authorized "to provide for the establishment and superintendence of public schools," but no endowment or other help was given. In 1848, Congress again amended the charter, allowing the corporation to collect a tax of one dollar per annum from free, white, male, adult citizens for the support of common schools.

Mr. Jefferson, President of the United States, was a member of the school board for three years (1805–1808), and although much private and some public spirit was manifested occasionally in behalf of public education, all municipal action related to schools for *whites* only. When the war began in 1861, there were eleven flourishing schools in the District of Columbia, for the education of colored children, but they were private enterprises. It was under the Republican party, that the acts of Congress, approved May 20th, May 21st, and July 11, 1862, were passed, whereby public instruction for youth of both races was provided. Under the rule of the Republican party new and spacious school buildings have been provided, capable teachers are employed, and such appropriations are made as warrant the prediction that the city is to take rank with the most advanced cities of the country in whatever relates to public education.

The emancipation of the colored people in the South was followed in 1865, by the Act of Congress establishing the Freedmen's Bureau, designed to supply an agency which should discharge the moral obligations incurred by the National Government to the refugees and freedmen of the disorganized Southern States, till such time as returning peace and civil order should permit the formation of new governments and institutions, state and local, adjusted to the conditions of the new era. Hundreds and thousands of schools were opened or assisted by the Freedmen's Bureau; and during the seven years of its existence it expended about $5,000,000 for educational purposes. At the close of the war the States that had been engaged in the Rebellion were reorganized under the direction and subject to the control of the Republican party.

In the new constitution of each State, provision was made for a system of public instruction.

In March, 1867, a law was enacted which authorized the establishment of a Department of Education at Washington for the purpose of collecting such statistics and facts as would show the condition and progress of education in the several States and Territories, and also for the purpose of diffusing information respecting the organization and management of schools, school systems, and methods of teaching.

The Department of Education has been in operation for a period of sixteen years. The work it has done has removed all doubts as to the wisdom of the undertaking.

It would not be just to claim for the Republican party exclusive merit for the educational systems of the country; but its policy in the South during the period of reconstruction has given to the old Slave States a system of public schools, and imposed upon them a constitutional obligation to maintain them.

CHAPTER XII.

THE INCREASE OF THE COUNTRY IN POPULATION AND WEALTH SINCE 1860, AND THE POLICY OF THE REPUBLICAN PARTY IN RELATION TO THE RIGHTS OF CITIZENS AT HOME AND ABROAD.

BY the census report for 1860, the property of the country was estimated at more than sixteen thousand million dollars. The valuation, as made in 1880, shows a total of less than seventeen thousand million dollars.

Manifestly, the estimates made in 1860 were erroneous to the extent of thousands of millions. Their erroneous character is admitted by the superintendent of the census. In his preliminary report, he says; "The marshals of the United States were directed to obtain from the records of the States and Territories, respectively, an account of the value of real and personal estate as assessed for taxation. *Instructions were given these officers to add the proper amount to the assessment, so that the return should represent as well the true or intrinsic value as the inadequate sum generally attached to property for taxable purposes.*"

Under these instructions there could have been no uniformity of action by the marshals and their numerous deputies, and, consequently, the results were of no importance whatsoever. The value of statistics depends usually upon their accuracy and completeness. Statistics in regard to property cannot be accurate, however, in the sense that statistics of mortality may be accurate; but if they are gathered upon a basis that is systematic, and of record, the results of one period are valuable for comparison with the results of other periods. As the imagination or the opinions of the marshals and deputy marshals were the guides in the valuation of property in 1860, the results reached were then of no importance nor can they now be quoted for the purposes of comparison.

Slave property was then included and it has now disappeared.

The population of the country, in 1860, was hardly more than three-fifths of what it was in 1880.

Common observation demonstrates the fact that the average condition of the people, as to property, was less favorable in 1860 than it now is. If the estimated value of slaves be excluded from this calculation the statement is as true of the old Slave States as of the Free States. The productive power of the Slave States was never, previous to the year 1860, equal to what it is at present.

In 1860, the property of Massachusetts was estimated, for the purposes of taxation, at eight hundred and ninety-seven million dollars; in 1880, it was estimated for the same purpose at one thousand five hundred and eighty-four million dollars.

The gain in Massachusetts was about seventy-six per cent. for the entire period of twenty years.

If the same ratio of gain be accepted for the whole country the true valuation, in 1860, could not have exceeded nine thousand and five hundred million dollars.

It thus appears that the gains of the country in wealth during the first twenty years of Republican administration were equal to more than three-fourths of the total accumulations in the previous period of nearly two and a half centuries.

An administration whose policy is so wise that such results are possible is entitled justly to public support. This would be true if that policy were wholly negative. The faculty in government which allows the people to so use their capacities and capital as to secure the largest results may well be dignified as a political virtue. To do this when an expensive war was waged and heavy taxes were levied was the fortune of the Republican party.

Its management of the finances, its system of protection to labor, by which agriculture, the mechanic arts, and manufactures were stimulated, and the field of their operations extended, and the homestead act which induced multitudes of intelligent Europeans to transfer their allegiance to the United States, were among the chief material agencies by which the general prosperity was promoted and the wealth of the nation augmented.

Until recently the public law of Europe did not recognize the right of the individual to choose the government to which he would render allegiance; and it was only upon the passage of the law of the 27th of July, 1868, that the doctrine of expatriation was accepted as the fixed policy of the United States. Previous to that event jurists, statesmen, and diplomatists, had entertained differing opinions and the authorities were in conflict with each other.

Manifestly, there could be no legal nor logical basis for national interference in behalf of a naturalized citizen of the United States, who, in his native country, might be required to perform military service, unless the right of expatriation were first asserted as well as recognized.

The right was asserted in the statute of 1868, and the consequent duty of the United States Government was also set forth in these words: "Whereas the right of expatriation is a natural and inherent right of all people, indispensable to the enjoyment of the rights of life, liberty, and the pursuit of happiness; and, whereas, in the recognition of this principle, this Government has freely received emigrants from all nations, and invested them with the rights of citizenship; and whereas it is claimed that such American citizens, with their descendants, are subjects of foreign States, owing allegiance to the governments thereof; and, whereas, it is necessary to the maintenance of public peace that this claim of foreign allegiance should be promptly and finally disavowed; therefore, any declaration, instruction, opinion, order, or decision of any officer of the United States which denies, restricts, impairs, or questions the right of expatriation, is declared inconsistent with the fundamental principles of the Republic."

"All naturalized citizens of the United States, while in foreign countries, are entitled to and shall receive from this government the same protection of persons and property which is accorded to native-born citizens."

There is no evidence that, previous to the year 1868, either Great Britain or any of the principal continental nations of Europe, with the exception of France, recognized the right of expatriation as a personal right. Two theories and two rules of action existed. Great Britain and Austria maintained the doctrine that subjects could not assume any of the obligations of citizenship in another government without the consent of the mother country, first obtained. On this theory expatriation could not be asserted as a right, but it might be obtained as a grant. In other States it was admitted that the subject could assume the duties of citizenship in a foreign government, but that upon his return to his native land all his obligations as a subject would be revived. In this theory there can be found no quality of the doctrine of expatriation as a right.

Upon the issues thus raised, Great Britain claimed the right to seize and search American vessels, and to take therefrom British-born seamen, and that without reference to the fact that in some instances they had become citizens of the United States. This claim led to the war of 1812, and there was no waiver of the claim in the treaty of peace.

Upon the issues thus raised Prussia claimed the right to exact military service of naturalized citizens of the United States, who, having been born in Prussia, might be sojourning temporarily in that country.

These claims were supported in a measure by a reference to congressional, diplomatic, and judicial proceedings in the United States.

The increase in the United States of foreign-born citizens, who, with their immediate descendants, were claimed as subjects by other governments, led to the passage of the law of 1868, and to the formation of treaties with the principal nations of Europe, excepting France only, in which the doctrine of expatriation is recognized as a personal right. Beginning in 1868, twelve such treaties have been made. The chief contracting parties are Great Britain, Austria, Belgium, Denmark, Norway, Sweden, and the North German Empire, represented by the King of Prussia.

Thus has the public law of Europe been changed by the agency of the United States. The ability to dictate that change was due in a large degree to the supremacy of the United States as a military power, and its recognition as such by the nations of Europe. Thus has been secured to each of the thousands of naturalized citizens the right to return to his native land free from any apprehension that military or other service will be required of him.

CHAPTER XIII.

THE QUESTIONS AT ISSUE IN THE PENDING CONTEST.

THE history of a political party furnishes better means for testing its quality and estimating its claims to public confidence than can be deduced from the professions of its leaders or the platforms of its conventions.

The government of the country was in the hands of the Democratic party during four Presidential terms of the six terms next preceding the inauguration of Mr. Lincoln.

Upon the death of General Harrison and the succession of Mr. Tyler in April, 1841, the administration was controlled in a large degree by the leaders of the Democratic party.

In the long period, therefore, of twenty-four years, from 1837 to 1861, there were only temporary interruptions to the domination of the Democratic party, as represented by the Southern leaders, in the government of the country.

The annexation of Texas, the consequent war with Mexico and the vast acquisitions of territory, which followed, have inured to the benefit of the country, but the scheme of annexation was designed and executed for the advancement of the system of slavery. It is not to the credit of the Democratic party that a scheme designed to foster that system has been controlled for the advantage of freedom and the extension of free institutions.

Of the legislation of those twenty-four years one measure only of importance remains upon the statute books of the country. The independent treasury system exists. In all other respects its financial experiments have failed, and its financial theories have been abandoned.

Its ancient doctrine of State rights, by which the national government was subordinated to the will of individual States, has become odious to the people. In obedience to this doctrine of State rights the party continued in a persistent defence of the institution of slavery. At the end, the Southern half of the party engaged in rebellion; a portion of the Democratic party of the North either encouraged or tolerated the treasonable conduct of their brethren of the South; while a minority, not exceeding one-fourth of the entire organization, united their fortunes with the Republican party, and contributed their full share to the prosecution of the war and the destruction of slavery.

If the Democratic party is to be judged by its record from 1837 to 1861, there is no ground for the belief that it would so administer the affairs of the government as to meet the demands of the present period. When it lost power in 1860, its tariff policy, and its financial ideas were alike distasteful to the people. Not to Republicans only; the failure of their policies was admitted by themselves.

From 1860, to the present time, the Democratic party has resisted every new measure, and more especially those relating to human rights, —but when those measures had been adopted by the country it has been constrained to give them a tardy approval. Each year has produced a new issue, and each year has found the party yielding assent to some measure which it had previously condemned.

It opposed Emancipation, and it opposed each of the three Amendments to the Constitution, nevertheless it has been compelled to accept and endorse them all.

It opposed the homestead laws, the policy of making grants of lands to the agricultural colleges, and the system of improving the rivers and harbors at the public expense. Now it dare not avow its opposition to those measures, or to the policies in which they have their origin.

The National Bank System was introduced and adopted as a measure of Mr. Lincoln's administration, but it was opposed by the Democratic members of the Senate and House of Representatives, and with great unanimity.

The bill passed the Senate by a vote of thirty Senators in the affirmative and nine in the negative. The affirmative votes were given by Republicans. In the House of Representative the bill was agreed to by a vote of eighty Republicans in the affirmative over the vote of sixty-four Democrats and two Republicans in the negative. Of the two Republicans, one was from Maryland, and the other was from Missouri.

The opposition of the Democratic party was due to its State rights notions which then found expression in a fear of centralization. That fear was groundless, if any injurious results to the public welfare were apprehended.

There are two thousand and five hundred national banks, with an aggregate capital of five hundred million dollars. They are doing business in all the States and Territories of the Union. They are managed by citizens whose interests are identified with those States and Territories. The assumption by the general government of the power to provide a currency for the whole country was an act of centralization; but there is no centralization of capital or of management that might not have existed under the State system.

There is a class of duties that may be performed by States in case the National Government does not assert its better right. The banking system belongs to that class. Until the year 1863, the business of furnishing a circulation of paper was left to the States. The exigencies of the war compelled Congress to assume jurisdiction of the subject. It is a noticable fact that the Democratic party never admitted that the exigencies of the public service required a change of policy on its part.

Assuming always that the war was unnecessary, it followed that exigencies should not control the public policy. In the opinion of the Democratic party an easy way was before the country. The remedy was peace.

Within the limits prescribed by the Constitution, the question, whether a particular power should be exercised by the general government or left with the States, is a question for Congress. Congress is composed of representatives of the States and of the people. If our theory is not false in a fatal degree, those representatives will confer power upon the general government or withhold power as may seem most advantageous to the public interest. Anything in the nature of a usurpation is impossible. The parties are the same. The citizens of the States are citizens of the United States also. They have but one interest, and that is to lodge the exercise of the power where the advantage will be the greatest and the injury the least.

Within constitutional limits the people may concentrate the exercise of discretionary powers in the hands of the general government or they may confide their exercise to the States.

The power to furnish a bank currency is now lodged with the general government, and after an experience of twenty years the claim may be made safely, that the system has never been excelled, in this or in any other country. It embodies every advantage that was claimed for a national bank, when, in the administration of General Jackson, the Whig party sought to recharter the United States Bank, and it avoids every evil that the enemies of that institution alleged against it. The system is free, and the currency being equally valuable in every part of the Union, the old evil of domestic exchange has disappeared. While the State Bank System existed the question of exchange between cities distant from each other, as New York and New Orleans, was an element of trade more important than is now the rate of exchange between New York and London.

The preservation and perpetuation of the system is a subject of large public concern. As the bonds of the United States are the basis of the circulation, and as these bonds are now subject to purchase and payment at a rate which will lead to the withdrawal of those now held as security for the redemption of bank notes, a friendly hand is needed to so adjust the revenues of the country to its expenditures as to continue the system for an indefinite period.

As the Democratic party opposed the system at the outset, and as it has never exhibited any friendship for it, there can be no violence in assuming that it would willingly see it die.

The capital invested in national banks exceeds five hundred million dollars, their loans aggregate a thousand and three hundred million dollars, and their other assets are not less than one thousand million dollars more. The overthrow of this system, even if it were possible to substitute a better one, or its gradual disappearance, would be attended with financial evils that would reach and embarrass every branch of business. The loans are generally to men of business whose capital does not equal their opportunities for the employment of capital. A financial change which should require the business men of the country to pay these loans, would cripple them while other sources of capital were sought and secured. In the meantime, production would diminish, laborers would lose employment, sales would fall off, all to be followed by still greater reduction in manufactures, trade, and consumption.

There is in the country a body of men who advocate the issue of United States notes without an accompanying pledge or promise of payment in coin. This class of financiers, believers, as they are, in the capacity of the government to extemporize wealth, or the representative of wealth, are either members of the Democratic party or in close alliance with it. When the country is prosperous they either diminish in number, or they lose audience among the people. Their voice is not much heard in the land when capital and labor are employed and are in the enjoyment of adequate returns.

In periods of depression they offer an unlimited issue of irredeemable United States notes as the sure and only remedy. This heresy had many disciples in the year 1873, and afterwards, until the return of prosperity. So powerful was their influence in the Democratic party that old and trusted leaders of that organization yielded, temporarily, to its control.

The remedy for financial and business disorders which these theorists propose is most frequently the cause of those disorders.

Periods of depression in business will occur. They are inevitable. There is no system of finance, no skill of administration in government that can protect a commercial country against their recurrence. Bad harvests, war, peace, pestilence, may, one or all, either cause financial disasters or contribute to their severity.

A sure cause of such disasters exists always in a paper currency that is constantly increasing in volume as compared with the increase of wealth. A currency based upon and redeemable in coin has its limits; but there are no assignable limits to the issue of irredeemable paper money. Additions to the volume of currency advance prices, promote speculation, lead men into dangerous or visionary undertakings, increase personal and family expenditures, all to end, finally, in failures, loss of confidence, a sudden depression of prices, suspension of manufacturing industry, loss of employment by the laborers, and losses of fortunes by capitalists. A stable currency is the best security against such evil consequences. Most certainly the remedy is not to be found in a policy which would produce the disasters. The Republican party is pledged to the system of redemption of all paper money in coin. Of the Democratic party nothing can be assured in regard to the currency.

The policy of the Democratic party in regard to the tariff system is either uncertain or dangerous, and if uncertain it is probably dangerous also.

The history of the Democratic party from 1837 to 1860, would lead to the conclusion that it would favor free trade as a principle of public policy, and a tariff for revenue only as a wise application of the principle in a government that must rely upon customs duties as the chief means of support.

The history of the party and its traditions found expression in the platform of 1880. During the first session of the 48th Congress, Mr. Randall has taken ground as an advocate of the protective policy.

His defection has been sufficient, in alliance with the members of the Republican party, to prevent the passage of a bill framed upon the theory that the government should advance as rapidly as possible towards a free-trade system. The effect of the Morrison bill upon the existing industries of the country and its influence in promoting or retarding the introduction and development of new industries, are topics which demand attention; but the policy of the measure is of more consequence than its immediate effects. It is more important to understand the purposes of the authors of a tariff bill than it is to comprehend the effects of the measure itself. A bill framed by the friends of the protective system might prove injurious to some branches of industry, but the purpose being otherwise the country and the sufferers themselves would look for remedial legislation. On the other hand, when a bill is framed upon the theory that the price of American products should be controlled by the cost in other countries, the domestic manufacturers and the laborers may wisely assume that the business is to come to an end ultimately, or the wages of labor are to be reduced to the equivalent of the wages in that country where the laborer in each branch of industry is commanded at the lowest cost.

The proposition embodied in the policy which underlies every free-trade measure is that the American manufacturer and the American laborer are to be put into direct competition with the manufacturer and laborer in that country where the particular manufacture to which capital and labor are here directed, is produced at the least cost.

Under the protective system concessions may be made from time to time without injury to the industries to which the concessions relate. It is the theory of the protective system that protection should be granted to those industries only to which the country is so well adapted, in natural facilities and skill in machinery and in the use of machinery that we can rival the most favored or the most advanced nations within a reasonable period of time. This rule works the exclusion from the domain of the protective system of those industries to which the country is not adapted by nature and by circumstances.

When the country has attained to an equality with the nations farthest advanced, in the particulars of machinery and skilled labor, there will still remain a reason for the protection of the laborer in his wages and the manufacturer in his capital, in the matter of the rate of interest in the rival countries.

Equality of natural advantages being given, there remain four important elements to which competition in manufactures relate, viz.: (1.) Interest on capital. (2.) Wages of the operatives. (3.) Perfection of machinery. (4.) Skill of the operatives and mechanics who are employed in the business.

It has happened in some branches of industry that the skill of American operatives and mechanics was such as to defy competition; that our machinery was equal to that of other countries, and yet protection was needed as security against cheap labor and cheap capital. And even in cases where our skill is such as to defy competition a duty upon the importation of the article may be expedient. Assume that, in England, for example, there has been an overproduction of an article that is produced at the same cost as in the United States.

If the article can be sent to this country and sold without payment of duties the surplus would find its way to our shores.

As the price must be broken down in the United States or in England, it would be for the interest of the English manufacturers to save the home market and to crush the foreign market. The ruin of the foreign market, and the destruction of rival manufacturers would open the way for future sales at compensating prices. It is to be said also, that the imposition of a duty upon an article which is produced at home at its cost, in other countries adds nothing to the price of the article in the domestic market.

Practically there can be no such system as "a revenue system with incidental protection." If a system is devised for the purpose of obtaining revenue, the rate of duties must be such as to permit the importation of so much of each article as the country may need, and a rate of duty must be imposed, as heavy as can be levied, without encouraging the manufacture at home. The counter proposition is the true one. There may be a system of protection to domestic industry that shall incidentally yield a revenue.

A single example will illustrate both of these propositions. Assume that a ton of English pig iron can be laid down in New York, under a free-trade system, at twenty dollars. Assume also that a ton of American pig iron will cost twenty-five dollars. Assume further, that the demand for the trade of New York is a million tons annually. If the duty be fixed at $4.50 per ton, a revenue of four and a half million dollars may be realized, and not one ton of American iron can be sold except at a loss.

If otherwise the duty be laid at six dollars per ton the American producer would have an advantage over the English producer, and in time the English article would be driven from the market, except for two or three circumstances. The English maker might have the means of reducing his labor and expense account to the extent of a dollar per ton, or an excess of product in England might compel him to seek this market, or he might occasionally avail himself of a sudden demand in America, which the home producer could not meet. Thus incidentally a system of protection will yield a revenue, but the same process of reasoning shows that a revenue system can not give protection as an incident.

Upon the question of protection the Republican party is a unit substantially. Any movement by that party, when in power, is accepted by the country as a friendly proceeding. Consequently, business is not disturbed. The organization of the Democratic party is hostile to the system of protection. Its measures, therefore, awaken apprehensions, disturb business, put capital in peril, and diminish the opportunities for labor. Nearly three thousand million dollars are embarked in manufactures. About two and three-fourths million operatives are employed at an annual aggregate sum in wages of nearly one thousand million dollars. These vast interests of labor and capital cannot be touched by a hostile hand without disturbing every other interest, nor without affecting unfavorably every branch of industry.

While it would not be just to say that the members of the Republican party are agreed in support of what is known as the system of Civil Service Reform, it is just to claim that there is a very general opinion in the party that there shall be a full and fair trial of the undertaking, and that at the end the results shall be accepted as the basis of a public policy. For the Democratic party no corresponding claim can be made. If its history be considered in connection with the declarations of leading Democrats, and the neglect of the national organization to commit itself to the new policy, it is reasonable to assume that the existing law would either be repealed or its purpose would be avoided in administration should the Democratic party attain power in the country.

But these issues, one and all, are insignificant when compared or contrasted with the issue raised by the systematic and continuous suppression of the votes of half a million citizens in the States of the South. The fact of such suppression is proved conclusively and often it is admitted by those who profit by the proceeding. The records of Congress in regard to the conduct of elections in Louisiana, Mississippi, and South Carolina so sustain the allegation that the justice of the charge is outside of the region of controversy. For excuse and defense it is pleaded that it is impossible to live under negro government. If this plea be allowed as matter for justification or defense, then it follows that the minority may usurp the government of a State or of the United States whenever the rule of the majority is disagreeable or burdensome. The rule of the majority, when its authority is both derived and exercised by constitutional processes, is the law of our political life. If the rule of the majority may be overturned whenever the minority is dissatisfied, the government ceases to be a government of laws and becomes a government of men. If a minority may dispossess the majority, then a minority of the usurping minority may seize power, and the process may go on until a single person becomes supreme and absolute. It is thus that the government of an usurping minority runs rapidly into despotic sway.

The vital element of Republican institutions is in the right and the recognition of the right of every citizen, who is duly qualified to vote, to have his vote counted, and in the consequent proposition that the government, as constituted by the majority vote, shall be recognized and obeyed. In the States of the South the right to vote has, in some instances, been denied; in other cases the votes cast have either not been counted or they have been counted for candidates of the opposite party; and in other cases the legally constituted governments have been overthrown by force, or abandoned through fear of force.

In 1875, the government of Mississippi was seized by force, whose incidents were murder and other brutal crimes.

In 1877, South Carolina and Louisiana were seized by the representatives of the minority party.

In all these States the Democratic party enjoyed the benefits of the political and personal crimes committed; and in all these States the rule of the Democratic party has been perpetuated, sometimes by force and sometimes by fraud. These proceedings were planned and executed systematically, and their results have been accepted by the Democratic party of the States concerned, and by the Democratic party as a national organization.

By these usurpations in the States of the South the Democrats not only wrested power from the lawful majority in those States, but they also secured a majority in the United States Senate for a time, and in the House of Representatives they have been able to command a majority in four Congresses. The Presidential elections of 1876 and 1880 were in peril from the same cause, and if now there could be free elections and an honest count and return of the votes cast in the eleven States that were engaged in the Rebellion, the pending contest would be without excitement as the result would be free from doubt.

By these usurpations the Democratic party has secured political advantages such as it did not enjoy even in the days of slavery. The former slaves are counted according to their number in the basis of representation, while under the old constitution each class of five was estimated as equal to three free persons. Upon the present basis, the South gains more than thirty representatives in Congress and an equal number of votes in the electoral colleges. In several of the States of the South the use of force, culminating in a reign of terror, has suppressed the negro vote and left the old slave masters and their adherents in full and undisputed possession of political power. Fraudulent practices at the voting places and the falsification of returns, are now for the most part adequate means for the perpetuation of the mastery first gained by force.

By these usurpations the negro race of the South and many white persons, not of the Democratic party, are deprived of the privileges and immunities to which they are entitled by the Constitution of the United States.

But this statement does not measure nor even indicate the magnitude of the evil. In a Republic there can be no baser political crime than a usurpation by which millions of men are robbed of their rightful share in the government.

By these usurpations, States have been seized by a minority and held through fear and force, both Houses of Congress have been captured and the executive department has been put in peril. If the elections in the old Slaves States were free, and the returns were honest, the Republican party could command so large a majority that the election of its candidates would be conceded from the day of their nomination. In the presence of this usurpation the votes of two Democrats in South Carolina have as much weight in the government as is given to the votes of five citizens of New York or Illinois. And never until the elections are full, free, and honest in the States of the South can the voters in the North enjoy an equality of power in the government of the country.

Thus does it appear that the voters of the North have an equal interest with the disfranchised citizens of the South in the restoration of those citizens to the enjoyment of their constitutional rights.

The reëstablishment of the Union implied the restoration of the States, recently in rebellion, to their full right of representation in the Congress of the United States. This was done, but there have been moments when many citizens of the North, compelled, as they have been compelled, to witness the outrages perpetrated by the remnant of the old slave-holding class upon the enfranchised blacks, to doubt the wisdom of the reconstruction policy.

The reëstablishment of the Union was a necessity, and when the Fifteenth Amendment to the Constitution was ratified it was assumed by the old Free States that security was taken for ultimate justice and permanent peace. That result has not been attained. The South has enjoyed the right of representation, in the fullest measure, and at the same time by force, fraud, and intimidation, a third of its inhabitants have been excluded from all part in the government of the country.

If this injustice and wrong were to continue, if there were neither remedy nor redress for this gross violation of personal and public rights, then, indeed, the reëstablishment of the Union could be regarded only as a mistake.

The acts of injustice and wrong of which the country now complains were first perpetrated upon a scale sufficiently large to attract public attention about the year 1870, and as yet no effectual remedy has been applied. This condition of things ought not longer to continue. If reformation does not come speedily from the States themselves there should be an exercise of power from without. As the Democratic party is benefited by the existing condition of things, there is no ground to anticipate any action by that party that shall tend to the restoration of the franchise to the negro population. Indeed, the success of the Democratic party in the pending election, would perpetuate the wrong for a period of four years at least.

But the nation can not be a silent and indifferent witness of the flight from their homes of thousands of citizens escaping from lawless oppression, and seeking refuge in the States that recognize the equal rights of men. The nation cannot be a silent and indifferent witness of the consequent disturbance of labor, and the injury wrought by the unnatural competition among laborers in one section of the Union, and the coincident dearth of laborers in another section, and all because the laborer is the subject of personal and political injustice. Nor can the nation remain silent and indifferent, when by fraud and force a section recently in arms, seizes, first, the government of States and then by the same means attempts the conquest of the Government of the United States. The remedy is with the Republican party; and if that party is again put in possession of the government, in all its branches, every constitutional power should be sought out, organized and made effective for the protection of the citizen against the systematized scheme of the South to destroy the equality of men and the equality of States.

If there could be a free vote and an honest count in the States of the South there would be no occasion for the Republican party to contest for New York or Indiana, except to secure a wholesome public policy in those States. Whatever of peril now menaces the civil service, the financial system, the industries and business of the country is due to the fact of a solid South.

A solid South means the rule absolute of a minority in several of the old Slave States, with the possibility of like absolute rule over the whole country. If the solidity of the South is not broken from within, and that speedily, it must be shattered from without. It will not be broken by divisions in the Democratic party either North or South.

A policy of waiting, of confidence, of negations, of blindness, will prove fatal in the end. The Republican party should declare its purpose, should frame the issue, should boldly stake everything it has or may have of fortune or power upon the effort to redeem its supporters and allies in the South from the domination of a minority.

In this campaign this one question is the paramount question to which every other is subordinate or incident. The rule of the minority must be destroyed or the Republican idea will disappear in the South, or the downtrodden will rise in arms against their oppressors and involve the States concerned in civil strife. Justice and peace alike demand the assertion of the doctrine of equality of rights in the States of the South.

CHAPTER XIV.

THE INFLUENCE OF THE UNITED STATES IN THE AFFAIRS OF THE WORLD DUE TO THE ADMINISTRATION OF THE GOVERNMENT BY THE REPUBLICAN PARTY.

When the Constitution was adopted, and during the first twenty years of our national existence, our standing was not affected seriously by the circumstance that slavery was recognized and protected in the organic law. The discussions in regard to the emancipation of the slaves in the British islands upon our coast, aroused attention to and provoked criticism upon the inconsistency of our system.

The friends of Republican institutions were ashamed to cite the United States as an example, and citizens resident or sojourning in Europe were compelled to preserve a humiliating silence when the character of their country was the subject of conversation or debate.

In countries where slavery did not exist the system had but few defenders, and none of the defenders of the system, wherever found, were friends to republican institutions.

For seventy years our example as a nation was calculated to bring the system of popular government into discredit. The theory of the government and the practice under it were inconsistent.

The ruling classes in Europe were hostile to our system for the reason that it threatened the overthrow of dynastic institutions. The existence of slavery tended to alienate the masses. In that condition of public sentiment it was always possible for the governments of Europe to command a popular support in any controversy that might arise with the United States.

Our peril during the first eighteen months of the Rebellion was due to that cause; but when the emancipation of the slaves was proclaimed it was no longer possible for the government of England or France to command a popular majority in any undertaking prejudicial to the United States. The fear and the danger of foreign intervention then disappeared.

When the Thirteenth Amendment was ratified our institutions became republican, and a harmony was established between our theories and our practice which silenced criticism and enabled our friends and the friends of freedom everywhere to cite our example as a model for imitation.

Our protective system has been, it now is, and for a long time to come it will continue to be, a disturbing influence in the policies of European States.

Aside from the spirit of conquest in barbarous and semi-barbarous tribes and nations, and the fury of religious zeal in more advanced peoples and communities, the controlling inducements which lead men to migrate from one country to another are preferences for institutions, civil and political, and hopes for a higher condition of domestic and social life. These hopes include the prospect of wealth or competency as the means by which a higher condition of domestic and social life is to be secured. The more ignorant classes of society are moved by the single consideration of their physical conditions. Others, more advanced in knowledge and more considerate as to probable advantages for themselves and their families and descendants, even for a distant and unknown future, will estimate the quality of the institutions and the nature of the government of the country to which they propose to migrate. In the nature of things this latter class must constitute a body of good citizens.

The abolition of slavery, the protective system by which the wages of labor have been advanced, and the homestead laws by which direct encouragement has been given to agricultural industry, have led tens of thousands of intelligent men to forsake their homes in Germany and the Scandinavian nations and to become citizens of the United States.

Their presence is a source of wealth and an element of power. Having chosen this country as their home, and upon high ideas of its character and destiny, they will aid in the realization of those ideas. Nor is there occasion for apprehension in the minds of any that the population of the country is approaching its capacity to furnish employment and subsistence.

If the inhabitants of all the States and Territories of this Union were transferred to the State of Texas, the number of persons to the square mile would be one hundred and ninety-one. Rhode Island now maintains a population of two hundred and fifty-four, and

Massachusetts a population of two hundred and twenty-one to the square mile.

The migration of masses of men from the States of Europe diminishes the supply of laborers and tends to raise the wages of those who remain.

This advance in wages increases the cost of manufactures and the prices of agricultural products, and all to the advantage of the United States.

As European manufactures increase in cost our ability to compete with them in the markets of the world improves, and the opportunities for export to the United States diminish. The advance in the price of agricultural products gives a better market for our surplus, and adds relatively to the profits of agriculture.

The larger part of the male emigrants are of the military age, and their expatriation may in the end cripple the power of Germany for military operations. The time is not far distant, probably, when that government will enter upon a policy of discouragement to emigration. Cheap lands and high wages in America have raised the wages of labor in England and on the Continent.

The tendency, and in a large degree the effect, of the measures of the Republican party has been to reduce the value of money in America to its value in Europe, and to advance the wages of labor in Europe to the rate of wages realized in America.

These movements foreshow the near approach of the day when we shall be able to compete with European countries in every branch of industry for which we have equal natural advantages.

At the close of the war our military power was established and our military capacity was recognized by every nation of the globe. This not alone from the conduct and success of the armies of the North; the skill, courage, and endurance of the armies of the South commanded almost equal respect.

The reunion of forces that had carried on gigantic, hostile contests for four years was accepted as an assurance that the armies of the Republic were adequate to every exigency that could arise in the life of a nation.

As a consequence we are now in a situation so fortunate that we are at once the wonder and the envy of other nations, and for ourselves we are relieved of all apprehensions as to the conduct of foreign governments in their relations to us. As long as we grant what is just and without debate, and claim only what is our proper due, there will be no occasion for controversy. Moreover, we have shown our disposition to submit matters of doubt to the arbitration of peace, rather than to the arbitrament of war.

At the close of the war our debt, in proportion to our population, was equal to the debts of the most heavily burdened nations of Europe. In less than twenty years that debt has been so reduced that its too speedy liquidation threatens the derangement of the finances and business of the country.

This result is due to the public prosperity as it has been promoted by the measures of the Republican party. At any time between 1840 and 1860 a debt of one thousand or even five hundred million dollars would have destroyed the credit of the country. The lesson taught by our experience is that the weight of a public debt is not to be estimated by its magnitude as reported in dollars, but rather by the condition of the people on whom the burden is laid. It is also to be observed that the ability of a people to pay taxes can not be measured by the natural resources which they possess. The endowments granted by nature yield little or nothing until the interest of the possessor is awakened and there is an application of intelligent labor to the development of those resources.

The United States were as rich in the gifts of nature in 1850 as in 1880, and yet the results were not half as great.

The abolition of slavery, the homestead laws, the system of protection to labor in America, have encouraged migration, and at the same time so developed the resources and added to the prosperity of the country that our example commands attention in the States of Europe, in India, in China, and in Japan.

Under the old form of government the institution of slavery, recognized as it was in the Constitution, and justified or tolerated by a majority of American citizens, was everywhere a hindrance to the progress of republican ideas and an obstacle to the emigration of the more intelligent classes of European society.

America is now open to European capital and skill, and Europe is open to American ideas in all that concerns the structure and administration of government.

Thus is America becoming more and more powerful, and thus is Europe tending to republicanism.

These twenty years of Republican rule have been sufficient to extort from the "London Times," that was never our friend, this tribute to our character, position, and destiny:

"THE UNIQUE POSITION OF THE UNITED STATES.—As yet the North American republic stands alone. With the conscious power to carve its own destinies belonging to perfect national independence, it combines the Roman peace enjoyed privately and commercially by subject provinces of the ancient Roman empire. No country in the world has any interest in molesting it. None would dare gratuitously to offer it an affront or do it an injustice. Its standing army is the minutest in existence, and Gen. Sherman, who would like it enlarged, did not desire that it should be more than minute. Except for the fear of wild Indians or native desperadoes, it might disband the whole to-morrow and be perfectly secure. Its citizens are free to play with politics or to abstain at discretion. Their happy fortune has left it for the time with no more difficult problem to settle than how to avoid accumulating so enormous a reserve of public wealth as not to know what to do with its taxes. Favorable geographical circumstances must be thanked in part for its immunity from many national burdens and national alarms. Unquiet and strong neighbors compel precautions generally. The United States cannot be said to have more than two real neighbors, one too weak to be harmful; the other, which is great enough, possessed by the most ardent determination never to be otherwise than friendly. If even its neighbors had been among the most aggressive, its territory and its population make a solid mass which would have insured it against attack."

If the statements of facts as set forth in these pages are received as truthful, and the arguments based thereon are accepted as trustworthy, two important conclusions must be accepted also: That the Democratic party is not a safe custodian of political power, and that the administration of the government for nearly a quarter of a century by the Republican party is without a precedent in our history for its wisdom, its patriotism, and for the degree of success that has crowned its undertakings. Indeed, the Republican party may safely challenge all nations, all times, and all history, for a parallel of its successes.

When it entered upon the administration of the government the Union was broken in fact, though not in law, by the treasonable doings of one wing of the Democratic party. Of the other wing of that party one portion accepted the result as an accomplished fact. Consequently, the Republican party was the basis of the force, whether political or military, by which the contest was prosecuted for the reëstablishment of the government over all the territory that had been embraced in the Union previous to the passage of the ordinances of secession.

If Mr. Buchanan had asserted the right of the Union to maintain its existence, and had he summoned the country to the support of that position, it is not only probable but certain that the scheme for the secession of States would have been arrested previous to the secession of Virginia. Buchanan's position was an assurance that States might secede without incurring the peril of war.

The intelligent men of the South lost all hope of success when they were convinced that the resources and powers of the North would be devoted to the overthrow of the Confederacy, unless at times they may have indulged the delusion that the Democratic party would obtain control of the government.

Upon this view it was that Alexander H. Stevens came to the conclusion, in 1862, that the cause of the Confederacy was hopeless.

A party is responsible for its policy and for the conduct of its leaders, and this assuredly, unless the earliest and an early opportunity be taken to repudiate leaders and policy. The Democratic party of the North accepted Mr. Buchanan's position, and their platform of 1864 was in substance a recognition of that position.

If the Democratic party now maintain that in 1860, the general government, under the Constitution, had no right to coerce a State or the people of a State to remain in the Union, then their view of the relations of States to the general government has been overruled by the country, by the executive and legislative branches of the government and by the courts. If the party does not now so claim, it confesses that the position of Mr. Buchanan in 1860, and of the Chicago Convention in 1864, was an error in law and consequently an unwise position in fact.

Admitting, what is true, that the Democratic party is now free from any element of secession, and certainly free of any purpose to encourage the doctrine of secession, it is yet true that the party is composed largely, both North and South, of the men who are responsible for the grave errors of the dark years of 1860 to 1865. Those errors may not be repeated, but a party whose principles, opinions, and traditions, culminated in such fatal consequences of treason and blood, is not a safe depository of political power. The possibility of error remains, and wrong principles in regard to government are sure to yield unwise or dangerous policies in administration.

Not less gross have been the errors of the Democratic party upon the subject of protection to the industries of the country. From 1840 to 1860 it advocated a free-trade policy or a tariff for revenue only. During that period our manufactures struggled against adverse influences, and the country enjoyed only a limited degree of prosperity. And even now, in the presence of the results secured through a system of protection, the Democratic party is divided in opinion and destitute of a definite policy. The policy of the Republican party is clearly set forth in the platform of 1884.

It is declared also, in the platform, that the Republican party will use the power with which it may be entrusted to secure for the citizens of the South their just rights under the Constitution.

A party is to be judged by the application of one or both of two tests. Either by its history, by what it has done, or by its pledges for the future. Of the Republican party it can be asserted truthfully that it has kept the pledges which it has heretofore made, and that in the keeping of those pledges the safety and prosperity of the country have been secured. The country may therefore wisely trust in the pledges now made.

8

ADDRESSES, PLATFORMS, ETC.

ABRAHAM LINCOLN'S SPEECH AT SPRINGFIELD, ILL., JUNE 17, 1858.

GENTLEMEN OF THE CONVENTION:

IF we could first know where we are, and whither we are tending, we could then better judge what to do, and how to do it. We are now far on into the fifth year since a policy was initiated with the avowed object and confident promise of putting an end to slavery agitation. Under the operation of that policy, that agitation had not only not ceased, but has constantly augmented. In my opinion, it will not cease until a crisis shall have been reached and passed. "A house divided against itself cannot stand." I believe this Government cannot endure permanently half slave and half free. I do not expect the Union to be dissolved,—I do not expect the house to fall; but I do expect it will cease to be divided. It will become all one thing, or all the other. Either the opponents of slavery will arrest the farther spread of it, and place it where the public mind shall rest in the belief that it is in course of ultimate extinction, or its advocates will push it forward till it shall become alike lawful in all the States,—old as well as new, North as well as South.

Have we no tendency to the latter condition? Let any one who doubts carefully contemplate that now almost complete legal combination,—piece of machinery, so to speak,—compounded of the Nebraska doctrine and the Dred Scott Decision. Let him consider, not only what work the machinery is adapted to do, and how well adapted, but also let him study the history of its construction, and trace, if he can, or rather fail, if he can, to trace, the evidences of design and concert of action among its chief master-workers from the beginning.

But so far Congress only had acted; and an indorsement by the people, real or apparent, was indispensable, to save the point already gained, and give chance for more. The New Year of 1854 found slavery excluded from more than half the States by State constitutions, and from most of the national territory by congressional prohibition. Four days later commenced the struggle which ended in repealing that congressional prohibition. This opened all the national territory to slavery, and was the first point gained.

This necessity had not been overlooked, but had been provided for, as well as might be, in the notable argument of "*squatter sovereignty*," otherwise called "*sacred right of self-government;*" which latter phrase, though expressive of the only rightful basis of any government, was so perverted in this attempted use of it as to amount to just this: that, if any one man choose to enslave another, no third man shall be allowed to object. That argument was incorporated into the Nebraska Bill itself, in the language which follows: "It being the true intent and meaning of this act not to legislate slavery into any Territory or State, nor exclude it therefrom, but to leave the people thereof perfectly free to form and regulate their domestic institutions in their own way, subject only to the Constitution of the United States."

Then opened the roar of loose declamation in favor of "squatter sovereignty" and "sacred right of self-government."

"But," said opposition members, "let us be more specific,—let us *amend* the bill so as to expressly declare that the people of the Territory *may* exclude slavery." "Not we," said the friends of the measure; and down they voted the amendment.

While the Nebraska Bill was passing through Congress, a law-case involving the question of a negro's freedom, by reason of his owner having voluntarily taken him first into a Free State, and then a Territory covered by the congressional prohibition, and held him as a slave,—for a long time in each,—was passing through the United States Circuit Court for the District of Missouri; and both the Nebraska Bill and lawsuit were brought to a decision in the same month of May, 1854. The negro's name was Dred Scott, which name now designates the decision finally made in the case.

Before the then next Presidential election, the law-case came to, and was argued in, the Supreme Court of the United States; but the decision of it was deferred until *after* the election. Still, *before* the election, Senator Trumbull, on the floor of the Senate, requests the leading advocate of the Nebraska Bill to state *his opinion* whether a people of a Territory can constitutionally exclude slavery from their limits; and the latter answers, "That is a question for the Supreme Court."

The election came. Mr. Buchanan was elected, and the *indorsement*, such as it was, secured. That was the *second* point gained. The indorsement, however, fell short of a clear popular majority by nearly four hundred thousand votes; and so, perhaps, was not overwhelmingly reliable and satisfactory. The outgoing President, in his last annual Message, as impressively as possible echoed back upon the people the weight and authority of the indorsement.

The Supreme Court met again; did not announce their decision, but ordered a re-argument. The Presidential inauguration came, and still no decision of the court; but the incoming President, in his inaugural address, fervently exhorted the people to abide by the forthcoming decision, *whatever it might be*. Then, in a few days, came the decision.

This was the third point gained.

The reputed author of the Nebraska Bill finds an early occasion to make a speech at this Capitol indorsing the Dred Scott Decision, and vehemently denouncing all opposition to it. The new President, too, seizes the early occasion of the Silliman letter to indorse and strongly construe that decision, and to express his astonishment that any different view had ever been entertained. At length a squabble springs up between the President and the author of the Nebraska Bill, on the mere question of fact whether the Lecompton Constitution was, or was not, in any just sense, made by the people of Kansas; and, in that squabble, the latter declares that all he wants is a fair vote for the people, and that he cares not whether slavery be voted down or voted up. I do not understand his declaration, that he cares not whether slavery be voted down or voted up, to be intended by him other than as an apt definition of the policy he would impress upon the public mind,—the principle for which he declares he has suffered much, and is ready to suffer to the end.

And well may he cling to that principle! If he has any parental feeling, well may he cling to it! That principle is the only shred left of his original Nebraska doctrine. Under the Dred Scott Decision, squatter sovereignty squatted out of existence,—tumbled down like temporary scaffolding; like the mould at the foundry, served through one blast, and fell back into loose sand; helped to carry an election, and then was kicked to the winds. His late joint struggle with the Republicans against the Lecompton Constitution involves nothing of the original Nebraska doctrine. That struggle was made on a point —the right of a people to make their own constitution—upon which he and the Republicans have never differed.

The several points of the Dred Scott Decision, in connection with Senator Douglas's "care-not" policy, constitute the piece of machinery in its present state of advancement. The working-points of that machinery are:

First, That no negro slave, imported as such from Africa, and no descendant of such, can ever be a citizen of any State, in the sense of that term as used in the Constitution of the United States.

This point is made in order to deprive the negro, in every possible event, of the benefit of this provision of the United States Constitution which declares that "The citizens of each State shall be entitled to all the privileges and immunities of citizens in the several States."

Secondly, That, "subject to the Constitution of the United States," neither Congress nor a Territorial Legislature can exclude slavery from any United States Territory.

This point is made in order that individual men may fill up the Territories with slaves, without danger of losing them as property, and thus to enhance the chances of permanency to the institution through all the future.

Thirdly, That whether the holding a negro in actual slavery in a Free State makes him free, as against the holder, the United States courts will not decide, but will leave it to be decided by the courts of any Slave State the negro may be forced into by the master.

This point is made, not to be pressed immediately; but if acquiesced in for a while, and apparently indorsed by the people at an election, then to sustain the logical conclusion, that, what Dred Scott's master might lawfully do with Dred Scott in the Free State of Illinois, every other master may lawfully do with any other one or one thousand slaves in Illinois, or in any other Free State.

Auxiliary to all this, and working hand in hand with it, the Nebraska doctrine, or what is left of it, is to educate and mould public opinion, at least Northern public opinion, not to care whether slavery is voted down or voted up.

This shows exactly where we now are, and partially, also, whither we are tending.

It will throw additional light on the latter to go back and run the mind over the string of historical facts already stated. Several things will now appear less dark and mysterious than they did when they were transpiring. The people were to be left "perfectly free," "subject only to the Constitution." What the Constitution had to do with it, outsiders could not then see. Plainly enough now, it was an exactly fitted niche for the Dred Scott Decision afterward to come in, and declare that perfect freedom of the people to be just no freedom at all.

Why was the amendment expressly declaring the right of the people to exclude slavery voted down? Plainly enough now; the adoption of it would have spoiled the niche for the Dred Scott Decision.

Why was the court decision held up? Why even a senator's individual opinion withheld till after the Presidential election? Plainly enough now; the speaking out then would have damaged the "*perfectly free*" argument upon which the election was to be carried.

Why the outgoing President's felicitation on the indorsement? Why the delay of a re-argument? Why the incoming President's advance exhortation in favor of the decision? These things look like the cautious patting and petting of a spirited horse preparatory to mounting him, when it is dreaded that he may give the rider a fall. And why the hasty after-indorsements of the decision by the President and others?

We cannot absolutely know that all these exact adaptations are the result of preconcert. But when we see a lot of framed timbers, different portions of which we know have been gotten out at different times and places, and by different workmen,—Stephen, Franklin, Roger, and James, for instance,—and when we see these timbers joined together, and see they exactly make the frame of a house or a mill, all the tenons and mortises exactly fitting, and all the lengths and proportions of the different pieces exactly adapted to their respective places, and not a piece too many or too few,—not omitting even scaffolding—or, if a single piece be lacking, we can see the place in the frame exactly fitted and prepared to yet bring such piece in,—in such a case, we find it impossible not to believe that Stephen, and Franklin, and Roger, and James all understood one another from the beginning, and all worked upon a common plan or draft drawn up before the first blow was struck.

It should not be overlooked, that, by the Nebraska Bill, the people of a State as well as Territory were to be left "*perfectly free*," "*subject only to the Constitution.*" Why mention a State? They were legislating for Territories, and not for or about States. Certainly the people of a State are and ought to be subject to the Constitution of the United States; but why is mention of this lugged into this merely territorial law? Why are the people of a Territory and the people of a State therein lumped together, and their relation to the Constitution therein treated as being precisely the same?

While the opinion of the court by Chief Justice Taney, in the Dred Scott case, and the separate opinions of all the concurring judges, expressly declare that the Constitution of the United States neither permits Congress nor a Territorial Legislature to exclude slavery from any United States Territory, they all omit to declare whether or not the same Constitution permits a State, or the people of a State, to exclude it. *Possibly*, this was a mere *omission;* but who can be quite sure, if McLean or Curtis had sought to get into the opinion a declaration of unlimited power in the people of a State to exclude slavery from their limits, just as Chase and Mace sought to get such declaration, in behalf of the people of a Territory, into the Nebraska Bill,—I ask, who can be quite sure that it would not have been voted down in the one case as it had been in the other?

The nearest approach to the point of declaring the power of a State over slavery is made by Judge Nelson. He approaches it more than once, using the precise idea, and almost the language too, of the Nebraska Act. On one occasion his exact language is, "Except in cases where the power is restrained by the Constitution of the United States, the law of the State is supreme over the subject of slavery within its jurisdiction."

In what cases the power of the State is so restrained by the United States Constitution is left an open question, precisely as the same question, as to the restraint on the power of the Territories, was left open in the Nebraska Act. Put that and that together, and we have another nice little niche, which we may ere long see filled with another Supreme Court decision, declaring that the Constitution of the United States does not permit a State to exclude slavery from its limits. And this may especially be expected if the doctrine of "care not whether slavery be voted down or voted up" shall gain upon the public mind sufficiently to give promise that such a decision can be maintained when made.

Such a decision is all that slavery now lacks of being alike lawful in all the States. Welcome or unwelcome, such decision is probably coming, and will soon be upon us, unless the power of the present political dynasty shall be met and overthrown. We shall lie down pleasantly dreaming that the people of Missouri are on the verge of making their State free; and we shall awake to the reality, instead, that the Supreme Court has made Illinois a Slave State.

To meet and overthrow the power of that dynasty is the work now before all those who would prevent that consummation. That is what we have to do. But how can we best do it?

There are those who denounce us openly to their own friends, and yet whisper softly, that Senator Douglas is the *aptest* instrument there is with which to effect that object. They do not tell us, nor has he told us, that he wishes any such object to be effected. They wish us to infer all, from the facts that he now has a little quarrel with the present head of the dynasty; and that he has regularly voted with us, on a single point, upon which he and we have never differed.

They remind us that *he* is a very *great man*, and that the largest of us are very small ones. Let this be granted. But "a *living dog* is better than a *dead lion*." Judge Douglas, if not a *dead* lion for this work, is at least a *caged* and *toothless one*. How can he oppose the advances of slavery? He don't care any thing about it. His avowed mission is impressing the "public heart" to care nothing about it.

A leading Douglas Democrat newspaper thinks Douglas's superior talent will be needed to resist the revival of the African slave-trade. Does Douglas believe an effort to revive that trade is approaching? He has not said so. Does he *really* think so? But, if it is, how can he resist it? For years he has labored to prove it a *sacred right* of white men to take negro slaves into the new Territories. Can he possibly show that it is less a sacred right to buy them where they can be bought cheapest? And unquestionably they can be bought cheaper in Africa than in Virginia.

He has done all in his power to reduce the whole question of slavery to one of a mere right of property; and as such, how can he oppose the foreign slave-trade,—how can he refuse that trade in that "property" shall be "perfectly free,"—unless he does it as a *protection* to the home production? And, as the home *producers* will probably not ask the protection, he will be wholly without a ground of opposition.

Senator Douglas holds, we know, that a man may rightfully be wiser to-day than he was yesterday; that he may rightfully change when he finds himself wrong. But can we for that reason run ahead, and infer that he will make any particular change, of which he himself has given no intimation? Can we safely base our action upon any such vague inferences?

Now, as ever, I wish not to misrepresent Judge Douglas's position, question his motives, or do aught that can be personally offensive to him. Whenever, *if ever*, he and we can come together, on *principle*, so that our great cause may have assistance from his great ability, I hope to have interposed no adventitious obstacle.

But clearly he is not now with us; he does not pretend to be; he does not promise ever to be. Our cause, then, must be intrusted to, and conducted by, its own undoubted friends,—those whose hands are free, whose hearts are in the work, who do care for the result.

Two years ago the Republicans of the nation mustered over thirteen hundred thousand strong. We did this under the single impulse of resistance to a common danger, with every external circumstance against us. Of strange, discordant, and even hostile elements, we gathered from the four winds, and formed and fought the battle through, under the constant hot fire of a disciplined, proud, and pampered enemy. Did we brave all then to falter now?—*now*, when that same enemy is wavering, dissevered, and belligerent?

The result is not doubtful. We shall not fail,—if we stand firm, we shall not fail. *Wise counsels* may *accelerate* or *mistakes delay* it; but, sooner or later, the victory is *sure* to come.

ABRAHAM LINCOLN'S INAUGURAL ADDRESS,
March 4, 1861.

Fellow-Citizens of the United States: In compliance with a custom as old as the Government itself, I appear before you to address you briefly, and to take in your presence the oath prescribed by the Constitution of the United States to be taken by the President "before he enters on the execution of his office."

I do not consider it necessary at present for me to discuss those matters of administration about which there is no special anxiety or excitement.

Apprehension seems to exist among the people of the Southern States that by the accession of a Republican administration their property and their peace and personal security are to be endangered. There has never been any reasonable cause for such apprehension. Indeed, the most ample evidence to the contrary has all the while existed and been open to their inspection. It is found in nearly all the published speeches of him who now addresses you. I do but quote from one of those speeches when I declare that "I have no purpose, directly or indirectly, to interfere with the institution of slavery in the States where it exists. I believe I have no lawful right to do so, and I have no inclination to do so." Those who nominated and elected me, did so with full knowledge that I had made this and many similar declarations, and have never recanted them. And more than this, they placed in the platform for my acceptance, and as a law to themselves and to me, the clear and emphatic resolution which I now read:

"*Resolved*, That the maintenance inviolate of the rights of the States, and especially the right of each State to order and control its own domestic institutions according to its own judgment exclusively, is essential to the balance of power on which the perfection and endurance of our political fabric depend, and we denounce the lawless invasion by armed force of the soil of any State or Territory, no matter under what pretext, as among the gravest of crimes."

I now reiterate these sentiments; and, in doing so, I only press upon the public attention the most conclusive evidence of which the case is susceptible, that the property, peace, and security of no section are to be in anywise endangered by the now incoming administration. I add, too, that all the protection which, consistently with the Constitution and the laws, can be given, will be cheerfully given to all the States when lawfully demanded, for whatever cause—as cheerfully to one section as to another.

There is much controversy about the delivering up of fugitives from service or labor. The clause I now read is as plainly written in the Constitution as any other of its provisions:

"No person held to service or labor in one State, under the laws thereof, escaping into another, shall, in consequence of any law or regulation therein, be discharged from such service or labor, but shall be delivered up on claim of the party to whom such service or labor may be due."

It is scarcely questioned that this provision was intended by those who made it for the reclaiming of what we call fugitive slaves; and the intention of the law-giver is the law. All members of Congress swear their support to the whole Constitution—to this provision as much as any other. To the proposition, then, that slaves, whose cases come within the terms of this clause, "shall be delivered up," their oaths are unanimous. Now, if they would make the effort in good temper, could they not, with nearly equal unanimity, frame and pass a law by means of which to keep good that unanimous oath?

There is some difference of opinion whether this clause should be enforced by national or by State authority; but surely that difference is not a very material one. If the slave is to be surrendered, it can be of but little consequence to him, or to others, by which authority it is to be done. And should any one, in any case, be content that his oath shall go unkept, on a merely unsubstantial controversy as to *how* it shall be kept?

Again, in any law upon this subject, ought not all the safeguards of liberty known in civilized and humane jurisprudence to be introduced, so that a free man be not, in any case, surrendered as a slave? And might it not be well at the same time to provide by law for the enforcement of that clause in the Constitution which guarantees that "the citizens of each State shall be entitled to all privileges and immunities of citizens in the several States?"

I take the official oath to-day with no mental reservations, and with no purpose to construe the Constitution or laws by any hypercritical rules. And while I do not choose now to specify particular acts of Congress as proper to be enforced, I do suggest that it will be much safer for all, both in official and private stations, to conform to and abide by all those acts which stand unrepealed, than to violate any of them, trusting to find impunity in having them held to be unconstitutional.

It is seventy-two years since the first inauguration of a President under our National Constitution. During that period fifteen different and greatly distinguished citizens have, in succession, administered the executive branch of the Government. They have conducted it through many perils, and generally with great success. Yet, with all this scope for precedent, I now enter upon the same task for the brief constitutional term of four years under great and peculiar difficulty. A disruption of the Federal Union, heretofore only menaced, is now formally attempted.

I hold that, in contemplation of universal law, and of the Constitution, the Union of these States is perpetual. Perpetuity is implied, if not expressed, in the fundamental law of all national governments. It is safe to assert that no government proper ever had a provision in its organic law for its own termination. Continue to execute all the express provisions of our National Constitution, and the Union will endure forever—it being impossible to destroy it, except by some action not provided for in the instrument itself.

Again, if the United States be not a Government proper, but an association of States in the nature of the contract merely, can it, as a contract, be peaceably unmade by less than all the parties who made it? One party to a contract may violate it—break it, so to speak; but does it not require all to lawfully rescind it?

Descending from these general principles, we find the proposition that, in legal contemplation, the Union is perpetual, confirmed by the history of the Union itself. The Union is much older than the Constitution. It was formed in fact by the Articles of Association in 1774. It was matured and continued by the Declaration of Independence in 1776. It was further matured, and the faith of all the then thirteen States expressly plighted and engaged that it should be perpetual, by the Articles of Confederation in 1778. And, finally, in 1787, one of the declared objects for ordaining and establishing the Constitution was "*to form a more perfect union.*"

But if destruction of the Union, by one, or by a part only, of the States, be lawfully possible, the Union is *less* perfect than before, the Constitution having lost the vital element of perpetuity.

It follows, from these views, that no State, upon its own mere notion, can lawfully get out of the Union; that *resolves* and *ordinances* to that effect are legally void, and that acts of violence within any

State or States, against the authority of the United States, are insurrectionary or revolutionary, according to circumstances.

I therefore consider that, in view of the Constitution and the laws, the Union is unbroken, and, to the extent of my ability, I shall take care, as the Constitution itself expressly enjoins upon me, that the laws of the Union be faithfully executed in all the States. Doing this I deem to be only a simple duty on my part; and I shall perform it, so far as practicable, unless my rightful masters, the American people, shall withhold the requisite means, or, in some authoritative manner, direct the contrary. I trust this will not be regarded as a menace, but only as a declared purpose of the Union that it *will* constitutionally defend and maintain itself.

In doing this there need be no bloodshed or violence; and there shall be none, unless it be forced upon the national authority. The power confided to me will be used to hold, occupy, and possess the property and places belonging to the Government, and to collect the duties and imposts; but, beyond what may be necessary for these objects, there will be no invasion; no using of force against or among the people anywhere. Where hostility to the United States, in any interior locality, shall be so great and universal as to prevent competent resident citizens from holding the Federal offices, there will be no attempt to force obnoxious strangers among the people for that object. While the strict legal right may exist in the Government to enforce the exercise of these offices, the attempt to do so would be so irritating, and so nearly impracticable withal, that I deem it better to forego, for the time, the uses of such offices.

The mails, unless repelled, will continue to be furnished in all parts of the Union. So far as possible, the people everywhere shall have that sense of perfect security which is most favorable to calm thought and reflection. The course here indicated will be followed, unless current events and experience shall show a modification or change to be proper, and in every case and exigency my best discretion will be exercised, according to circumstances actually existing, and with a view and a hope of a peaceful solution of the national troubles and the restoration of fraternal sympathies and affections.

That there are persons in one section or another who seek to destroy the Union at all events, and are glad of any pretext to do it, I will neither affirm nor deny ; but if there be such I need address no word to them. To those, however, who really love the Union, may I not speak?

Before entering upon so grave a matter as the destruction of our national fabric, with all its benefits, its memories, and its hopes, would it not be wise to ascertain precisely why we do it? Will you hazard so desperate a step while there is any possibility that any portion of the ills you fly from have no real existence? Will you, while the certain ills you fly to are greater than all the real ones you fly from—will you risk the commission of so fearful a mistake?

All profess to be content in the Union, if all constitutional rights can be maintained. Is it true, then, that any right, plainly written in the Constitution, has been denied? I think not. Happily, the human mind is so constituted that no party can reach to the audacity of doing this. Think, if you can, of a single instance in which a plainly-written provision of the Constitution has ever been denied. If, by the mere force of numbers, a majority should deprive a minority of any clearly-written constitutional right, it might, in a moral point of view, justify revolution—certainly would if such right were a vital one. But such is not our case. All the vital rights of minorities and of individuals are so plainly assured to them by affirmations and negations, guarantees and prohibitions, in the Constitution, that controversies never arise concerning them. But no organic law can ever be framed with a provision specifically applicable to every question which may occur in practical administration. No foresight can anticipate, nor any document of reasonable length contain express provisions for all possible questions. Shall fugitives from labor be surrendered by National or by State authority? The Constitution does not expressly say. *May* Congress prohibit slavery in the Territories? The Constitution does not expressly say. *Must* Congress protect slavery in the Territories? The Constitution does not expressly say.

From questions of this class spring all our constitutional controversies, and we divide upon them into majorities and minorities. If the minority will not acquiesce the majority must, or the Government must cease. There is no other alternative; for continuing the Government is acquiescence on one side or the other. If a minority in such case will secede rather than acquiesce they make a precedent which, in turn, will divide and ruin them; for a minority of their own will secede from them whenever a majority refuses to be controlled by such minority. For instance, why may not any portion of a new confederacy, a year or two hence, arbitrarily secede again, precisely as portions of the present Union now claim to secede from it? All who cherish disunion sentiments are now being educated to the exact temper of doing this.

Is there such perfect identity of interests among the States to compose a new union, as to produce harmony only, and prevent renewed secession?

Plainly, the central idea of secession is the essence of anarchy. A majority held in restraint by constitutional checks and limitations, and always changing easily with deliberate changes of popular opinions and sentiments, is the only true sovereign of a free people. Whoever rejects it, does, of necessity, fly to anarchy or to despotism. Unanimity is impossible; the rule of a minority, as a permanent arrangement, is wholly inadmissible; so that, rejecting the majority principle, anarchy or despotism in some form is all that is left.

I do not forget the position assumed by some, that constitutional questions are to be decided by the Supreme Court; nor do I deny that such decision must be binding, in any case, upon the parties to a suit, as to the object of that suit, while they are also entitled to very high respect and consideration in all parallel cases by all other departments of the Government. And while it is obviously possible that such decision may be erroneous in any given case, still the evil effect following it, being limited to that particular case, with the chance that it may be overruled, and never become a precedent for other cases, can better be borne than could the evils of a different practice. At the same time the candid citizen must confess that if the policy of the Government upon vital questions, affecting the whole people, is to be irrevocably fixed by decision of the Supreme Court, the instant they are made in ordinary litigation between parties in personal actions the people will have ceased to be their own rulers, having to that extent practically resigned their government into the hands of that eminent tribunal.

Nor is there in this view any assault upon the court or the judges. It is a duty from which they may not shrink to decide cases properly brought before them, and it is no fault of theirs if others seek to turn their decisions to political purposes. One section of our country believes slavery is *right*, and ought to be extended, while the other believes it is *wrong*, and ought not to be extended. This is the only substantial dispute. The fugitive slave clause of the Constitution, and the law for the suppression of the foreign slave trade, are each as well enforced, perhaps, as any law can ever be in a community where the moral sense of the people imperfectly supports the law itself. The great body of the people abide by the dry legal obligation in both cases, and a few break over in each. This, I think, cannot be perfectly cured; and it would be worse in both cases *after* the separation of the sections than before. The foreign slave trade, now imperfectly suppressed, would be ultimately revived without restriction in one section; while fugitive slaves, now only partially surrendered, would not be surrendered at all by the other.

Physically speaking, we cannot separate. We cannot remove our respective sections from each other, nor build an impassable wall between them. A husband and wife may be divorced, and go out of the presence and beyond the reach of each other; but the different parts of our country cannot do this. They cannot but remain face to face; and intercourse, either amicable or hostile, must continue between them. Is it possible, then, to make that intercourse more advantageous or more satisfactory *after* separation than *before?* Can aliens make treaties easier than friends can make laws? Can treaties be more faithfully enforced between aliens than laws can among friends? Suppose you go to war, you cannot fight always; and when after much loss on both sides, and no gain on either, you cease fighting, the identical old questions, as to terms of intercourse, are again upon you.

This country, with its institutions, belongs to the people who inhabit it. Whenever they shall grow weary of the existing Government, they can exercise their *constitutional* right of amending it, or their *revolutionary* right to dismember or overthrow it. I cannot be ignorant of the fact that many worthy and patriotic citizens are desirous of having the National Constitution amended. While I make no recommendation of amendments, I fully recognize the rightful authority of the people over the whole subject, to be exercised in either of the modes prescribed in the instrument itself; and I should, under existing circumstances, favor rather than oppose a fair opportunity being afforded the people to act upon it. I will venture to add that to me the convention mode seems preferable, in that it allows amendments to originate with the people themselves, instead of only permitting them to take or reject propositions originated by others, not especially chosen for the purpose, and which might not be precisely such as they would wish either to accept or refuse. I understand a proposed amendment to the Constitution — which amendment, however, I have not seen — has passed Congress, to the effect that the Federal Government shall never interfere with the domestic institutions of the States, including that of persons held to service. To avoid misconstruction of what I have said, I depart from my purpose not to speak of particular amendments so far as to say that, holding such a provision now to be implied constitutional law, I have no objection to its being made express and irrevocable.

The Chief Magistrate derives all his authority from the people, and they have conferred none upon him to fix terms for the separation of the States. The people themselves can also do this if they choose; but the Executive, as such, has nothing to do with it. His duty is to administer the present Government, as it came to his hands, and to transmit it, unimpaired by him, to his successor.

Why should there not be a patient confidence in the ultimate justice of the people? Is there any better or equal hope in the world? In our present differences is either party without faith of being in the right? If the Almighty Ruler of Nations, with His eternal truth and justice, be on your side of the North, or on yours of the South, that truth and that justice will surely prevail, by the judgment of this great tribunal of the American people.

By the frame of the Government under which we live, this same people have wisely given their public servants but little power for mischief; and have, with equal wisdom, provided for the return of that little to their own hands at very short intervals. While the people retain their virtue and vigilance, no administration, by any extreme of weakness or folly, can very seriously injure the Government in the short space of four years.

My countrymen, and all, think calmly and *well* upon this whole subject. Nothing valuable can be lost by taking time. If there be an object to hurry any of you, in hot haste, to a step which you would never take *deliberately*, that object will be frustrated by taking time; but no good object can be frustrated by it. Such of you as are now dissatisfied, still have the old Constitution unimpaired, and, on the sensitive point, the laws of your own framing under it; while the new administration will have no immediate power, if it would, to change either. If it were admitted that you who are dissatisfied hold the right side in the dispute, there still is no single good reason for precipitate action. Intelligence, patriotism, Christianity, and a firm reliance in Him who has never yet forsaken this favored land, are still competent to adjust, in the best way, all our present difficulty.

In *your* hands, my dissatisfied fellow-countrymen, and not in *mine*, is the momentous issue of civil war. The Government will not assail *you*. You can have no conflict without being yourselves the aggressors. *You* have no oath registered in Heaven to destroy the Government, while I shall have the most solemn one to "preserve, protect, and defend it."

I am loath to close. We are not enemies, but friends. We must not be enemies. Though passion may have strained, it must not break our bonds of affection. The mystic chords of memory, stretching from every battle-field and patriot grave to every living heart and hearth-stone, all over this broad land, will yet swell the chorus of the Union, when again touched, as surely they will be, by the better angels of our nature.

PROCLAMATION OF EMANCIPATION.
September 22, 1862.

I, Abraham Lincoln, President of the United States of America, and Commander-in-Chief of the army and navy thereof, do hereby proclaim and declare that hereafter, as heretofore, the war will be prosecuted for the object of practically restoring the constitutional relation between the United States and each of the States and the people thereof, in which States that relation is or may be suspended or disturbed.

That it is my purpose, upon the next meeting of Congress, to again recommend the adoption of a practical measure tendering pecuniary aid to the free acceptance or rejection of all Slave States, so called, the people whereof may not then be in rebellion against the United States, and which States may then have voluntarily adopted, or thereafter may voluntarily adopt, immediate or gradual abolishment of slavery within their respective limits; and that the effort to colonize persons of African descent, with their consent, upon this continent or elsewhere, with the previously obtained consent of the governments existing there, will be continued.

That on the first day of January, in the year of our Lord one thousand eight hundred and sixty-three, all persons held as slaves within any State, or designated part of a State, the people whereof shall then be in rebellion against the United States, shall be then, thenceforward, and forever free; and the Executive Government of the United States, including the military and naval authority thereof, will recognize and maintain the freedom of such persons, and will do no act or acts to repress such persons, or any of them, in any efforts they may make for their actual freedom.

That the Executive will, on the first day of January aforesaid, by proclamation, designate the States, and parts of States, if any, in which the people thereof, respectively, shall then be in rebellion against the United States; and the fact that any State, or the people thereof, shall on that day be, in good faith, represented in the Congress of the United States by members chosen thereto at elections wherein a majority of the qualified voters of such State shall have participated, shall, in the absence of strong countervailing testimony, be deemed conclusive evidence that such State, and the people thereof, are not in rebellion against the United States.

That attention is hereby called to an act of Congress entitled, "An Act to make an additional article of war," approved March 3, 1862, and which act is in the words and figures following:

Be it enacted by the Senate and House of Representatives of the United States of America in Congress assembled, That hereafter the following shall be promulgated as an additional article of war, for the government of the army of the United States, and shall be obeyed and observed as such:

"ARTICLE —. All officers or persons in the military or naval service of the United States are prohibited from employing any of the forces under their respective commands for the purpose of returning fugitives from service or labor who may have escaped from any persons to whom such service or labor is claimed to be due; and any officer who shall be found guilty by a court-martial of violating this article shall be dismissed from the service.

"SEC. 2. *And be it further enacted,* That this act shall take effect from and after its passage."

Also to the ninth and tenth sections of an act entitled, "An Act to suppress insurrection, to punish treason and rebellion, to seize and confiscate property of rebels, and for other purposes," approved July 17, 1862, and which sections are in the words and figures following:

"SEC. 9. *And be it further enacted,* That all slaves of persons who shall hereafter be engaged in rebellion against the Government of the United States, or who shall in any way give aid or comfort thereto, escaping from such persons and taking refuge within the lines of the army; and all slaves captured from such persons or deserted by them, and coming under the control of the Government of the United States; and all slaves of such person found *on* [or] being within any place occupied by rebel forces and afterwards occupied by the forces of the United States, shall be deemed captives of war, and shall be forever free of their servitude, and not again held as slaves.

"SEC. 10. *And be it further enacted,* That no slave escaping into any State, Territory, or the District of Columbia, from any other State, shall be delivered up, or in any way impeded or hindered of his liberty, except for crime, or some offense against the laws, unless the person claiming said fugitive shall first make oath that the person to whom the labor or service of such fugitive is alleged to be due is his lawful owner, and has not borne arms against the United States in the present rebellion, nor in any way given aid and comfort thereto; and no person engaged in the military or naval service of the United States shall, under any pretense whatever, assume to decide on the validity of the claim of any person to the service or labor of any other person, or surrender up any such person to the claimant, on pain of being dismissed from the service."

And I do hereby enjoin upon and order all persons engaged in the military and naval service of the United States to observe, obey, and enforce, within their respective spheres of service, the act and sections above recited.

And the Executive will in due time recommend that all citizens of the United States who shall have remained loyal thereto throughout the rebellion shall (upon the restoration of the constitutional relations between the United States and their respective States and people, if that relation shall have been suspended or disturbed) be compensated for all losses by acts of the United States, including the loss of slaves.

In witness whereof, I have hereunto set my hand, and caused the seal of the United States to be affixed.

Done at the city of Washington this twenty-second day of September, in the year of our Lord one thousand eight hundred and sixty-two, and of the independence of the United States the eighty-seventh.

  By the President,   ABRAHAM LINCOLN.
WILLIAM H. SEWARD, *Secretary of State.*

JANUARY 1, 1863.

WHEREAS, On the twenty-second day of September, in the year of our Lord one thousand eight hundred and sixty-two, a proclamation was issued by the President of the United States, containing, among other things, the following, to wit:

"That on the first day of January, in the year of our Lord one thousand eight hundred and sixty-three, all persons held as slaves within any State, or designated part of a State, the people whereof shall be in rebellion against the United States, shall be then, thenceforward, and forever, free; and the Executive Government of the United States, including the military and naval authority thereof, will recognize and maintain the freedom of such persons, and will do no act or acts to repress such persons, or any of them, in any efforts they may make for their actual freedom.

"That the Executive will, on the first day of January aforesaid, by proclamation, designate the States, and parts of States, if any, in which the people thereof, respectively, shall then be in rebellion against the United States; and the fact that any State, or the people thereof, shall on that day be in good faith represented in the Congress of the United States, by members chosen thereto at elections wherein a majority of the qualified voters of such States shall have participated, shall, in the absence of strong countervailing testimony be deemed conclusive evidence that such State, and the people thereof, are not then in rebellion against the United States."

Now, therefore, I, ABRAHAM LINCOLN, President of the United States, by virtue of the power in me vested as Commander-in-Chief of the Army and Navy of the United States, in time of actual armed rebellion against the authority and Government of the United States, and as a fit and necessary war measure for suppressing said rebellion, do, on this first day of January, in the year of our Lord one thousand eight hundred and sixty-three, and in accordance with my purpose so to do, publicly proclaimed for the full period of one hundred days from the day first above mentioned, order and designate as the States, and parts of States, wherein the people thereof, respectively, are this day in rebellion against the United States, the following, to wit:

Arkansas, Texas, Louisiana (except the parishes of St. Bernard, Plaquemines, Jefferson, St. John, St. Charles, St. James, Ascension, Assumption, Terre Bonne, Lafourche, St. Mary, St. Martin, and Orleans, including the city of New Orleans), Mississippi, Alabama, Florida, Georgia, South Carolina, North Carolina, and Virginia (except the forty-eight counties designated as West Virginia, and also the counties of Berkeley, Acomac, Northampton, Elizabeth City, York, Princess Ann, and Norfolk, including the cities of Norfolk and Portsmouth), and which excepted parts are for the present left precisely as if this proclamation were not issued.

And by virtue of the power and for the purpose aforesaid, I do order and declare that all persons held as slaves within said designated States, and parts of States, are, and henceforward shall be, free; and that the Executive Government of the United States, including the military and naval authorities thereof, will recognize and maintain the freedom of such persons.

And I hereby enjoin upon the people so declared to be free to abstain from all violence, unless in necessary self-defense; and I recommend to them that in all cases when allowed, they labor faithfully for reasonable wages.

And I further declare and make known that such persons, of suitable condition, will be received into the armed service of the United States to garrison forts, positions, stations, and other places, and to man vessels of all sorts in said service.

And upon this act, sincerely believed to be an act of justice, warranted by the Constitution upon military necessity, I invoke the considerate judgment of mankind and the gracious favor of Almighty God.

In witness whereof, I have hereunto set my hand and caused the seal of the United States to be affixed.

Done at the city of Washington this first day of January, in the year of our Lord one thousand, eight hundred and sixty-three, and of the independence of the United States of America the eighty-seventh.

By the President, ABRAHAM LINCOLN.

WILLIAM H. SEWARD, *Secretary of State.*

ABRAHAM LINCOLN'S ORATION AT GETTYSBURG.

NOVEMBER 19, 1863.

Fourscore and seven years ago our fathers brought forth upon this continent a new nation, conceived in liberty, and dedicated to the proposition that all men are created equal.

Now we are engaged in a great civil war, testing whether that nation, or any nation so conceived and so dedicated, can long endure. We are met on a great battle-field of that war. We are met to dedicate a portion of it as the final resting-place of those who here gave their lives that that nation might live. It is altogether fitting and proper that we should do this.

But in a larger sense we cannot dedicate, we cannot consecrate, we cannot hallow this ground. The brave men, living and dead, who struggled here, have consecrated it far above our power to add or detract. The world will little note nor long remember what we say here, but it can never forget what they did here. It is for us, the living, rather to be dedicated here to the unfinished work that they have thus far so nobly carried on. It is rather for us to be here dedicated to the great task remaining before us,—that from these honored dead we take increased devotion to the cause for which they here gave the last full measure of devotion,—that we here highly resolve that the dead shall not have died in vain, that the nation shall, under God, have a new birth of freedom, and that the government of the people, by the people, and for the people, shall not perish from the earth.

ABRAHAM LINCOLN'S SECOND INAUGURAL ADDRESS.
MARCH 4, 1865.

Fellow-Countrymen: At this second appearing to take the oath of the Presidential office, there is less occasion for an extended address than there was at the first. Then, a statement, somewhat in detail, of a course to be pursued, seemed fitting and proper. Now, at the expiration of four years, during which public declarations have been constantly called forth on every point and phase of the great contest which still absorbs the attention and engrosses the energies of the nation, little that is new could be presented. The progress of our arms, upon which all else chiefly depends, is as well known to the public as to myself; and it is, I trust, reasonably satisfactory and encouraging to all. With high hope for the future, no prediction in regard to it is ventured.

On the occasion corresponding to this four years ago, all thoughts were anxiously directed to an impending civil war. All dreaded it—all sought to avert it. While the inaugural address was being delivered from this place, devoted altogether to *saving* the Union without war, insurgent agents were in this city seeking to *destroy* it without war—seeking to dissolve the Union, and divide the effects, by negotiation. Both parties deprecated war; but one of them would *make* war rather than let the nation survive; and the other would *accept* war rather than let it perish. And the war came.

One-eighth of the whole population were colored slaves, not distributed generally over the Union, but localized in the southern part of it. These slaves constituted a peculiar and powerful interest. All knew that this interest was, somehow, the cause of the war. To strengthen, perpetuate, and extend this interest was the object for which the insurgents would rend the Union, even by war; while the Government claimed no right to do more than restrict territorial enlargement of it. Neither party expected for the war the magnitude or the duration which it has already attained. Neither anticipated that the *cause* of the conflict might cease with, or even before, the conflict itself should cease. Each looked for an easier triumph, and a result less fundamental and astounding. Both read the same Bible and prayed to the same God; and each invoked His aid against the other. It may seem strange that any men should dare to ask a just God's assistance in wringing their bread from the sweat of other men's faces; but let us judge not, that we be not judged. The prayers of both could not be answered—that of neither has been answered fully. The Almighty has His own purposes. "Woe unto the world because of offenses! for it must needs be that offenses come; but woe to that man by whom the offense cometh." If we shall suppose that American slavery is one of those offenses which, in the providence of God, must needs come, but which, having continued through His appointed time, He now wills to remove, and that He gives to both North and South this terrible war, as the woe due to those by whom the offense came, shall we discern therein any departure from those divine attributes which the believers in a living God always ascribe to Him? Fondly do we hope—fervently do we pray—that this mighty scourge of war might speedily pass away. Yet, if God wills that it continue until all the wealth piled up by the bondman's two hundred and fifty years of unrequited toil shall be sunk, and until every drop of blood drawn with the lash shall be paid by another drawn with the sword, as was said three thousand years ago, so still it must be said, "The judgments of the Lord are true and righteous altogether."

With malice toward none; with charity for all; with firmness in the right, as God gives us to see the right, let us strive on to finish the work we are in; to bind up the nation's wounds, to care for him who shall have borne the battle, and for his widow and his orphan—to do all which may achieve and cherish a just and lasting peace among ourselves, and with all nations.

REPUBLICAN PLATFORM, ADOPTED AT PHILADELPHIA, JUNE 17, 1856.

This convention of delegates, assembled in pursuance of a call addressed to the people of the United States, without regard to past political differences or divisions, who are opposed to the repeal of the Missouri Compromise, to the policy of the present administration, to the extension of slavery into Free Territory; in favor of admitting Kansas as a Free State, of restoring the action of the Federal Government to the principles of Washington and Jefferson; and who purpose to unite in presenting candidates for the offices of President and Vice-President, do resolve as follows:

Resolved, That the maintenance of the principles promulgated in the Declaration of Independence, and embodied in the Federal Constitution, is essential to the preservation of our Republican institutions, and that the Federal Constitution, the rights of the States, and the Union of the States, shall be preserved.

Resolved, That with our Republican fathers we hold it to be a self-evident truth that all men are endowed with the inalienable rights to life, liberty, and the pursuit of happiness, and that the primary object and ulterior design of our Federal Government were, to secure these rights to all persons within its exclusive jurisdiction; that as our Republican fathers, when they had abolished slavery in all our national territory, ordained that no person should be deprived of life, liberty, or property, without due process of law, it becomes our duty to maintain this provision of the Constitution against all attempts to violate it for the purpose of establishing slavery in any Territory of the United States, by positive legislation, prohibiting its existence or extension therein. That we deny the authority of Congress, of a territorial legislature, of any individual or association of individuals, to give legal existence to slavery in any Territory of the United States, while the present Constitution shall be maintained.

Resolved, That the Constitution confers upon Congress sovereign power over the Territories of the United States for their government, and that in the exercise of this power it is both the right and the imperative duty of Congress to prohibit in the Territories those twin relics of barbarism—polygamy and slavery.

Resolved, That while the Constitution of the United States was ordained and established, in order to form a more perfect Union, establish justice, insure domestic tranquility, provide for the common defense, promote the general welfare, and secure the blessings of liberty, and contains ample provisions for the protection of the life, liberty, and property of every citizen, the dearest constitutional rights of the people of Kansas have been fraudulently and violently taken from them; their territory has been invaded by an armed force; spurious and pretended legislative, judicial, and executive officers have been set over them, by whose usurped authority, sustained by the military power of the government, tyrannical and unconstitutional laws have been enacted and enforced; the rights of the people to keep and bear arms have been infringed; test oaths of an extraordinary and entangling nature have been imposed, as a condition of exercising the right of suffrage and holding office; the right of an accused person to a speedy and public trial by an impartial jury has been denied; the right of the people to be secure in their persons, houses, papers, and effects against unreasonable searches and seizures, has been violated; they have been deprived of life, liberty, and property, without due process of law; that the freedom of speech and of the press has been abridged; the right to choose their representatives has been made of no effect; murders, robberies, and arsons, have been instigated or encouraged, and the offenders have been allowed to go unpunished; that all these things have been done with the knowledge, sanction, and procurement of the present national administration; and that for this high crime against the Constitution, the Union, and humanity, we arraign the administration, the President, his advisers, agents, supporters, apologists, and accessories, either before or after the facts, before the country and before the world; and that it is our fixed purpose to bring the actual perpetrators of these atrocious outrages, and their accomplices, to a sure and condign punishment hereafter.

Resolved, That Kansas should be immediately admitted as a State of the Union with her present free constitution, as at once the most effectual way of securing to her citizens the enjoyment of the rights and privileges to which they are entitled, and of ending the civil strife now raging in her territory.

Resolved, That the highwayman's plea that "might makes right," embodied in the Ostend circular, was in every respect unworthy of American diplomacy, and would bring shame and dishonor upon any government or people that gave it their sanction.

Resolved, That a railroad to the Pacific ocean, by the most central and practical route, is imperatively demanded by the interests of the whole country, and that the Federal Government ought to render immediate and efficient aid in its construction, and, as an auxiliary thereto, the immediate construction of an emigrant route on the line of the railroad.

Resolved, That appropriations of Congress for the improvement of rivers and harbors of a national character, required for the accommodation and security of our existing commerce, are authorized by the Constitution, and justified by the obligation of government to protect the lives and property of its citizens.

Resolved, That we invite the affiliation and coöporation of the men of all parties, however differing from us in other respects, in support of the principles herein declared; and believing that the spirit of our institutions, as well as the constitution of our country, guarantees liberty of conscience and equality of rights among citizens, we oppose all proscriptive legislation affecting their security.

REPUBLICAN PLATFORM, CHICAGO,
May 17, 1860.

Resolved, That we, the delegated representatives of the Republican electors of the United States, in convention assembled, in discharge of the duty we owe to our constituents and our country, unite in the following declarations:

1. That the history of the nation, during the last four years, has fully established the propriety and necessity of the organization and perpetuation of the Republican party, and that the causes which called it into existence are permanent in their nature, and now, more than ever before, demand its peaceful and constitutional triumph.

2. That the maintenance of the principles promulgated in the Declaration of Independence, and embodied in the Federal Constitution, "That all men are created equal; that they are endowed by their Creator with certain inalienable rights; that among these are life, liberty, and the pursuit of happiness; that to secure these rights, governments are instituted among men, deriving their just powers from the consent of the governed," is essential to the preservation of our Republican institutions; and that the Federal Constitution, the

rights of the States, and the Union of the States, must and shall be preserved.

3. That to the Union of the States this nation owes its unprecedented increase in population, its surprising development of material resources, its rapid augmentation of wealth, its happiness at home and its honor abroad; and we hold in abhorrence all schemes for disunion, come from whatever source they may; and we congratulate the country that no Republican member of Congress has uttered or countenanced the threats of disunion so often made by Democratic members, without rebuke and with applause from their political associates; and we denounce those threats of disunion, in case of a popular overthrow of their ascendency, as denying the vital principles of a Free Government, and as an avowal of contemplated treason, which it is the imperative duty of an indignant people sternly to rebuke and forever silence.

4. That the maintenance inviolate of the rights of the States, and especially the right of each State to order and control its own domestic institutions according to its own judgment exclusively, is essential to that balance of powers on which the perfection and endurance of our political fabric depends; and we denounce the lawless invasion, by armed force, of the soil of any State or Territory, no matter under what pretext, as among the gravest of crimes.

5. That the present Democratic administration has far exceeded our worst apprehensions, in its measureless subserviency to the exactions of a sectional interest, as especially evinced in its desperate exertions to force the infamous Lecompton constitution upon the protesting people of Kansas; in construing the personal relations between master and servant to involve an unqualified property in persons; in its attempted enforcement, everywhere, on land and sea, through the intervention of Congress and of the federal courts, of the extreme pretensions of a purely local interest; and in its general and unvarying abuse of the power entrusted to it by a confiding people.

6. That the people justly view with alarm the reckless extravagance which pervades every department of the Federal Government; that a return to rigid economy and accountability is indispensable to arrest the systematic plunder of the public treasury by favored partisans; while the recent startling developments of frauds and corruptions at the federal metropolis, show that an entire change of administration is imperatively demanded.

7. That the new dogma, that the constitution, of its own force, carries slavery into any or all of the territories of the United States, is a dangerous political heresy, at variance with the explicit provisions of that instrument itself, with contemporaneous exposition, and with legislative and judicial precedent—is revolutionary in its tendency, and subversive of the peace and harmony of the country.

8. That the normal condition of all the territory of the United States is that of freedom; that as our Republican fathers, when they had abolished slavery in all our national territory, ordained that "no person shall be deprived of life, liberty, or property, without due process of law," it becomes our duty, by legislation, whenever such legislation is necessary, to maintain this provision of the Constitution against all attempts to violate it; and we deny the authority of Congress, of a territorial legislature, or of any individuals, to give legal existence to slavery in any territory of the United States.

9. That we brand the recent re-opening of the African slave trade, under the cover of our national flag, aided by perversions of judicial power, as a crime against humanity and a burning shame to our country and age; and we call upon Congress to take prompt and efficient measures for the total and final suppression of that execrable traffic.

10. That in the recent vetoes, by their federal governors, of the acts of the legislatures of Kansas and Nebraska, prohibiting slavery in those territories, we find a practical illustration of the boasted Democratic principles of non-intervention and popular sovereignty, embodied in the Kansas-Nebraska bill, and a demonstration of the deception and fraud involved therein.

11. That Kansas should, of right, be immediately admitted as a State under the constitution recently formed and adopted by her people, and accepted by the House of Representatives.

12. That, while providing revenue for the support of the General Government by duties upon imports, sound policy requires such an adjustment of these imports as to encourage the development of the industrial interest of the whole country; and we commend that policy of national exchanges which secures to the working-men liberal wages, to agriculture remunerative prices, to mechanics and manufacturers an adequate reward for their skill, labor, and enterprise, and to the nation commercial prosperity and independence.

13. That we protest against any sale or alienation to others of the public lands held by actual settlers, and against any view of the

homestead policy which regards the settlers as paupers or suppliants for public bounty; and we demand the passage by Congress of the complete and satisfactory homestead measure which has already passed the House.

14. That the Republican party is opposed to any change in our naturalization laws, or any State legislation by which the rights of citizenship hitherto accorded to immigrants from foreign lands shall be abridged or impaired; and in favor of giving a full and efficient protection to the rights of all classes of citizens, whether native or naturalized, both at home and abroad.

15. That appropriations by Congress for river and harbor improvements of a national character, required for the accommodation and security of an existing commerce, are authorized by the Constitution and justified by the obligations of government to protect the lives and property of its citizens.

16. That a railroad to the Pacific ocean is imperatively demanded by the interest of the whole country; that the Federal Government ought to render immediate and efficient aid in its construction; and that as preliminary thereto, a daily overland mail should be promptly established.

17. Finally, having thus set forth our distinctive principles and views, we invite the coöperation of all citizens, however differing on other questions, who substantially agree with us in their affirmance and support.

REPUBLICAN PLATFORM, BALTIMORE,
June 7, 1864.

Resolved, That it is the highest duty of every American citizen to maintain, against all their enemies, the integrity of the Union and the paramount authority of the Constitution and laws of the United States; and that, laying aside all differences of political opinions, we pledge ourselves, as Union men, animated by a common sentiment and aiming at a common object, to do everything in our power to aid the Government in quelling, by force of arms, the Rebellion now raging against its authority, and in bringing to the punishment due to their crimes the rebels and traitors arrayed against it.

Resolved, That we approve the determination of the Government of the United States not to compromise with rebels, nor to offer them any terms of peace, except such as may be based upon an "unconditional surrender" of their hostility, and a return to their just allegiance to the Constitution and laws of the United States; and that we call upon the Government to maintain this position, and to prosecute the war with the utmost possible vigor to the complete suppression of the Rebellion, in full reliance upon the self-sacrificing patriotism, the heroic valor, and the undying devotion of the American people to the country and its free institutions.

Resolved, That, as slavery was the cause, and now constitutes the strength, of this Rebellion, and as it must be always and everywhere hostile to the principles of Republican government, justice and the national safety demand its utter and complete extirpation from the soil of the Republic; and that we uphold and maintain the acts and proclamations by which the Government, in its own defense, has aimed a death-blow at this gigantic evil. We are in favor, furthermore, of such an amendment to the Constitution, to be made by the people in conformity with its provisions, as shall terminate and forever prohibit the existence of slavery within the limits or the jurisdiction of the United States.

Resolved, That the thanks of the American people are due to the soldiers and sailors of the army and navy, who have periled their lives in defense of their country and in vindication of the honor of its flag; that the nation owes to them some permanent recognition of their patriotism and their valor, and ample and permanent provision for those of their survivors who have received disabling and honorable wounds in the service of the country; and that the memories of those who have fallen in its defense shall be held in grateful and everlasting remembrance.

Resolved, That we approve and applaud the practical wisdom, the unselfish patriotism, and the unswerving fidelity to the Constitution and the principles of American liberty with which Abraham Lincoln has discharged, under circumstances of unparalleled difficulty, the great duties and responsibilities of the presidential office; that we approve and indorse, as demanded by the emergency and essential to the preservation of the nation, and as within the provisions of the Constitution, the measures and acts which he has adopted to defend the nation against its open and secret foes; that we approve, especcially, the Proclamation of Emancipation, and the employment, as Union soldiers, of men heretofore held in slavery; and that we have full confidence in his determination to carry these, and all other constitutional measures essential to the salvation of the country, into full and complete effect.

Resolved, That we deem it essential to the general welfare that harmony should prevail in the national councils, and we regard as worthy of public confidence and official trust those only who cordially indorse the principles proclaimed in these resolutions, and which should characterize the administration of the government.

Resolved, That the Government owes to all men employed in its armies, without regard to distinction of color, the full protection of the laws of war; and that any violation of these laws, or of the usages of civilized nations in the time of war, by the rebels now in arms, should be made the subject of prompt and full redress.

Resolved, That foreign immigration, which in the past has added so much to the wealth, development of resources, and increase of power to this nation—the asylum of the oppressed of all nations—should be fostered and encouraged by a liberal and just policy.

Resolved, That we are in favor of the speedy construction of the railroad to the Pacific coast.

Resolved, That the national faith, pledged for the redemption of the public debt, must be kept inviolate; and that, for this purpose, we recommend economy and rigid responsibility in the public expenditures, and a vigorous and just system of taxation; and that it is the duty of every loyal State to sustain the credit and promote the use of the national currency.

Resolved, That we approve the position taken by the government, that the people of the United States can never regard with indifference the attempt of any European power to overthrow by force, or to supplant by fraud, the institutions of any Republican government on the western continent, and that they will view with extreme jealousy, as menacing to the peace and independence of this, our country, the efforts of any such power to obtain new footholds for monarchical governments, sustained by a foreign military force, in near proximity to the United States.

REPUBLICAN PLATFORM—CHICAGO,
May 20, 1868.

1. We congratulate the country on the assured success of the reconstruction policy of Congress, as evidenced by the adoption, in the majority of the States lately in rebellion, of Constitutions securing

equal civil and political rights to all; and it is the duty of the Government to sustain those institutions, and to prevent the people of such States from being remitted to a state of anarchy.

2. The guarantee by Congress of equal suffrage to all loyal men at the South was demanded by every consideration of public safety, of gratitude, and of justice, and must be maintained; while the question of suffrage in all the loyal States properly belongs to the people of those States.

3. We denounce all forms of repudiation as a national crime; and the national honor requires the payment of the public indebtedness in the uttermost good faith to all creditors at home and abroad, not only according to the letter, but the spirit, of the laws under which it was contracted

4. It is due to the labor of the nation that taxation should be equalized and reduced as rapidly as the national faith will permit.

5. The national debt, contracted as it has been for the preservation of the Union for all time to come, should be extended over a fair period for redemption; and it is the duty of Congress to reduce the rate of interest thereon whenever it can be honestly done.

6. That the best policy to diminish our burden of debt is to so improve our credit that capitalists will seek to loan us money at lower rates of interest than we now pay, and must continue to pay, so long as repudiation, partial or total, open or covert, is threatened or suspected.

7. The Government of the United States should be administered with the strictest economy; and the corruptions which have been so shamefully nursed and fostered by Andrew Johnson call loudly for radical reform.

8. We profoundly deplore the tragic death of Abraham Lincoln, and regret the accession to the Presidency of Andrew Johnson, who has acted treacherously to the people who elected him and the cause he was pledged to support; who has usurped high legislative and judicial functions; who has refused to execute the laws; who has used his high office to induce other officers to ignore and violate the laws; who has employed his executive powers to render insecure the property, the peace, liberty, and life of the citizens; who has abused the pardoning power; who has denounced the national legislature as unconstitutional; who has persistently and corruptly resisted, by every means in his power, every proper attempt at the reconstruction of the States lately in rebellion; who has perverted the public pa-

tronage into an engine of wholesale corruption; and who has been justly impeached for high crimes and misdemeanors, and properly pronounced guilty thereof by a vote of thirty-five Senators.

9. The doctrine of Great Britain and other European powers, that because a man is once a subject he is always so, must be resisted at every hazard by the United States, as a relic of feudal times, not authorized by the laws of nations, and at war with our national honor and independence. Naturalized citizens are entitled to protection in all their rights of citizenship as though they were native born; and no citizen of the United States, native or naturalized, must be liable to arrest and imprisonment by any foreign power for acts done or words spoken in this country; and, if so arrested and imprisoned, it is the duty of the Government to interfere in his behalf.

10. Of all who were faithful in the trials of the late war, there were none entitled to more especial honor than the brave soldiers and seamen who endured the hardships of campaign and cruise, and imperiled their lives in the service of the country. The bounties and pensions provided by the laws for these brave defenders of the nation are obligations never to be forgotten; the widows and orphans of the gallant dead are the wards of the people—a sacred legacy bequeathed to the nation's protecting care.

11. Foreign immigration, which in the past has added so much to the wealth, development, and resources, and increase of power to this Republic, the asylum of the oppressed of all nations, should be fostered and encouraged by a liberal and just policy.

12. This convention declares itself in sympathy with all oppressed people who are struggling for their rights.

13. That we highly commend the spirit of magnanimity and forbearance with which men who have served in the Rebellion, but who now frankly and honestly coöperate with us in restoring the peace of the country and reconstructing the Southern State Governments upon the basis of impartial justice and equal rights, are received back into the communion of the loyal people; and we favor the removal of the disqualifications and restrictions imposed upon the late rebels, in the same measure as the spirit of disloyalty shall die out, and as may be consistent with the safety of the loyal people.

14. That we recognize the great principles laid down in the immortal Declaration of Independence, as the true foundation of democratic government; and we hail with gladness every effort toward making these principles a living reality on every inch of American soil.

REPUBLICAN PLATFORM—PHILADELPHIA,
June 5, 1872.

The Republican party of the United States, assembled in National Convention in the city of Philadelphia, on the 5th and 6th days of June, 1872, again declares its faith, appeals to its history, and announces its position upon the questions before the country.

1. During eleven years of supremacy it has accepted, with grand courage, the solemn duties of the times. It suppressed a gigantic Rebellion, emancipated four millions of slaves, decreed the equal citizenship of all, and established universal suffrage. Exhibiting unparalleled magnanimity, it criminally punished no man for political offenses, and warmly welcomed all who proved their loyalty by obeying the laws and dealing justly with their neighbors. It has steadily decreased, with firm hand, the resultant disorders of a great war, and initiated a wise and humane policy toward the Indians. The Pacific railroad and similar vast enterprises have been generously aided and successfully conducted, the public lands freely given to actual settlers, immigration protected and encouraged, and a full acknowledgment of the naturalized citizen's rights secured from European powers. A uniform national currency has been provided, repudiation frowned down, the national credit sustained under the most extraordinary burdens, and new bonds negotiated at lower rates. The revenues have been carefully collected and honestly applied. Despite annual large reductions of the rates of taxation, the public debt has been reduced during General Grant's Presidency at the rate of a hundred millions a year, great financial crises have been avoided, and peace and plenty prevail throughout the land. Menacing foreign difficulties have been peacefully and honorably compromised, and the honor and power of the nation kept in high respect throughout the world. This glorious record of the past is the party's best pledge for the future. We believe the people will not intrust the Government to any party or combination of men composed chiefly of those who have resisted every step of this beneficent progress.

2. The recent amendments to the National Constitution should be cordially sustained because they are right, not merely tolerated because they are law, and should be carried out according to their spirit by appropriate legislation, the enforcement of which can safely be intrusted only to the party that secured those amendments.

3. Complete liberty and exact equality in the enjoyment of all civil, political, and public rights should be established and effectually maintained throughout the Union by efficient and appropriate State and Federal legislation. Neither the law nor its administration should admit any discrimination in respect to citizens by reason of race, creed, color, or previous condition of servitude.

4. The National Government should seek to maintain honorable peace with all nations, protecting its citizens everywhere, and sympathizing with all peoples who strive for greater liberty.

5. Any system of civil service under which the subordinate positions of the Government are considered rewards for mere party zeal is fatally demoralizing; and we, therefore, favor a reform of the system, by laws which shall abolish the evils of patronage, and make honesty, efficiency, and fidelity the essential qualifications for public positions, without practically creating a life tenure for office.

6. We are opposed to further grants of the public lands to corporations and monopolies, and demand that the national domain be set apart for free homes for the people.

7. The annual revenue, after paying current expenditures, pensions, and the interest on the public debt, should furnish a moderate balance for the reduction of the principal; and that revenue, except so much as may be derived from a tax upon tobacco and liquors, should be raised by duties upon importations, the details of which should be so adjusted as to aid in securing remunerative wages to labor, and promote the industries, prosperity, and growth of the whole country.

8. We hold in undying honor the soldiers and sailors whose valor saved the Union. Their pensions are a sacred debt of the nation, and the widows and orphans of those who died for their country are entitled to the care of a generous and grateful people. We favor such additional legislation as will extend the bounty of the Government to all our soldiers and sailors who were honorably discharged, and who in the line of duty became disabled, without regard to the length of service or cause of such discharge.

9. The doctrine of Great Britain and other European powers concerning allegiance—"once a subject, always a subject"—having at last, through the efforts of the Republican party, been abandoned, and the American idea of the individual's right to transfer allegiance having been accepted by European nations, it is the duty of our Government to guard with jealous care the rights of adopted citizens

against the assumption of unauthorized claims by their former governments, and we urge continued careful encouragement and protection of voluntary immigration.

10. The franking privilege ought to be abolished, and a way prepared for a speedy reduction in the rates of postage.

11. Among the questions which press for attention is that which concerns the relations of capital and labor; and the Republican party recognizes the duty of so shaping legislation as to secure full protection and the amplest field for capital, and for labor, the creator of capital, the largest opportunities and a just share of the mutual profits of these two great servants of civilization.

12. We hold that Congress and the President have only fulfilled an imperative duty in their measures for the suppression of violence and treasonable organizations in certain lately rebellious regions, and for the protection of the ballot-box; and, therefore, they are entitled to the thanks of the nation.

13. We denounce repudiation of the public debt, in any form or disguise, as a national crime. We witness with pride the reduction of the principal of the debt, and of the rates of interest upon the balance, and confidently expect that our excellent national currency will be perfected by a speedy resumption of specie payment.

14. The Republican party is mindful of its obligations to the loyal women of America for their noble devotion to the cause of freedom. Their admission to wider fields of usefulness is viewed with satisfaction; and the honest demand of any class of citizens for additional rights should be treated with respectful consideration.

15. We heartily approve the action of Congress in extending amnesty to those lately in rebellion, and rejoice in the growth of peace and fraternal feeling throughout the land.

16. The Republican party proposes to respect the rights reserved by the people to themselves as carefully as the powers delegated by them to the States and to the Federal Government. It disapproves of the resort to unconstitutional laws for the purpose of removing evils, by interference with rights not surrendered by the people to either the State or National Government.

17. It is the duty of the general Government to adopt such measures as may tend to encourage and restore American commerce and ship-building.

18. We believe that the modest patriotism, the earnest purpose, the sound judgment, the practical wisdom, the incorruptible integ-

rity, and the illustrious services of Ulysses S. Grant have commended him to the heart of the American people; and with him at our head, we start to-day upon a new march to victory.

19. Henry Wilson, nominated for the Vice-Presidency, known to the whole land from the early days of the great struggle for liberty as an indefatigable laborer in all campaigns, an incorruptible legislator and representative man of American institutions, is worthy to associate with our great leader and share the honors which we pledge our best efforts to bestow upon them.

REPUBLICAN PLATFORM—CINCINNATI,

June 14, 1876.

When, in the economy of Providence, this land was to be purged of human slavery, and when the strength of the Government of the people, by the people, and for the people, was to be demonstrated, the Republican party came into power. Its deeds have passed into history, and we look back to them with pride. Incited by their memories to high aims for the good of our country and mankind, and looking to the future with unfaltering courage, hope, and purpose, we, the representatives of the party, in National Convention assembled, make the following declaration of principles:

1. The United States of America is a nation, not a league. By the combined workings of the National and State Governments, under their respective Constitutions, the rights of every citizen are secured, at home and abroad, and the common welfare promoted.

2. The Republican party has reserved these governments to the hundredth anniversary of the nation's birth, and they are now embodiments of the great truths spoken at its cradle—"That all men are created equal; that they are endowed by their Creator with certain inalienable rights, among which are life, liberty, and the pursuit of happiness; that for the attainment of these ends governments have been instituted among men, deriving their just powers from the consent of the governed." Until these truths are cheerfully obeyed, or, if need be, vigorously enforced, the work of the Republican party is unfinished.

3. The permanent pacification of the Southern section of the Union, and the complete protection of all its citizens in the free enjoyment of all their rights, is a duty to which the Republican party

stands sacredly pledged. The power to provide for the enforcement of the principles embodied in the recent constitutional amendments is vested, by those amendments, in the Congress of the United States; and we declare it to be the solemn obligation of the legislative and executive departments of the Government to put into immediate and vigorous exercise all their constitutional powers for removing any just causes of discontent on the part of any class, and for securing to every American citizen complete liberty and exact equality in the exercise of all civil, political, and public rights. To this end we imperatively demand a Congress and a Chief Executive whose courage and fidelity to these duties shall not falter until these results are placed beyond dispute or recall.

4. In the first act of Congress signed by President Grant the National Government assumed to remove any doubt of its purpose to discharge all just obligations to its creditors, and "solemnly pledged its faith to make provision at the earliest practicable period for the redemption of the United States notes in coin." Commercial prosperity, public morals, and national credit demand that this promise be fulfilled by a continuous and steady progress to specie payment.

5. Under the Constitution, the President and heads of departments are to make nominations for office, the Senate is to advise and consent to appointments, and the House of Representatives is to accuse and prosecute faithless officers. The best interest of the public service demands that these distinctions be respected; that Senators and Representatives who may be judges and accusers should not dictate appointments to office. The invariable rule in appointments should have reference to honesty, fidelity, and capacity of the appointees, giving to the party in power those places where harmony and vigor of administration require its policy to be represented, but permitting all others to be filled by persons selected with sole reference to the efficiency of the public service, and the right of all citizens to share in the honor of rendering faithful service to the country.

6. We rejoice in the quickened conscience of the people concerning political affairs, and will hold all public officers to a rigid responsibility, and engage that the prosecution and punishment of all who betray official trusts shall be swift, thorough, and unsparing.

7. The Public-School System of the several States is the bulwark of the American Republic; and, with a view to its security and

permanence, we recommend an amendment to the Constitution of the United States, forbidding the application of any public funds or property for the benefit of any schools or institutions under sectarian control.

8. The revenue necessary for current expenditures, and the obligations of the public debt, must be largely derived from duties upon importations which, so far as possible, should be adjusted to promote the interests of American labor and advance the prosperity of the whole country.

9. We reaffirm our opposition to further grants of the public lands to corporations and monopolies, and demand that the national domain be devoted to free homes for the people.

10. It is the imperative duty of the Government so to modify existing treaties with European governments, that the same protection shall be afforded to the adopted American citizen that is given to the native born; and that all necessary laws shall be passed to protect emigrants in the absence of power in the States for that purpose.

11. It is the immediate duty of Congress to fully investigate the effect of the immigration and importation of Mongolians upon the moral and material interests of the country.

12. The Republican party recognizes, with approval, the substantial advances recently made towards the establishment of equal rights for women by the many important amendments effected by the Republican legislatures in the laws which concern the personal and property relations of wives, mothers, and widows, and by the appointment and election of women to the superintendence of education, charities, and other public trusts. The honest demands of this class of citizens for additional rights, privileges, and immunities, should be treated with respectful consideration.

13. The Constitution confers upon Congress sovereign power over the Territories of the United States for their government; and in the exercise of this power it is the right and duty of Congress to prohibit and extirpate, in the Territories, that relic of barbarism—polygamy; and we demand such legislation as shall secure this end and the supremacy of American institutions in all the Territories.

14. The pledges which the nation has given to her soldiers and sailors must be fulfilled, and a grateful people will always hold those who imperiled their lives for the country's preservation in the kindest remembrance.

15. We sincerely deprecate all sectional feeling and tendencies. We, therefore, note with deep solicitude that the Democratic party counts, as its chief hope of success, upon the electoral vote of a united South, secured through the efforts of those who were recently arrayed against the nation; and we invoke the earnest attention of the country to the grave truth that a success thus achieved would reopen sectional strife, and imperil national honor and human rights.

16. We charge the Democratic party with being the same in character and spirit as when it sympathized with treason; with making its control of the House of Representatives the triumph and opportunity of the nation's recent foes; with reasserting and applauding, in the national capitol, the sentiments of unrepentent rebellion; with sending Union soldiers to the rear, and promoting Confederate soldiers to the front; with deliberately proposing to repudiate the plighted faith of the Government; with being equally false and imbecile upon the overshadowing financial questions; with thwarting the ends of justice by its partisan mismanagement and obstruction of investigation; with proving itself, through the period of its ascendency in the lower house of Congress, utterly incompetent to administer the Government; and we warn the country against trusting a party thus alike unworthy, recreant, and incapable.

17. The national administration merits commendation for its honorable work in the management of domestic and foreign affairs, and President Grant deserves the continued hearty gratitude of the American people for his patriotism and his eminent service in war and in peace.

18. We present, as our candidates for President and Vice-President of the United States, two distinguished statesmen, of eminent ability and character, and conspicuously fitted for those high offices, and we confidently appeal to the American people to entrust the administration of their public affairs to Rutherford B. Hayes and William A. Wheeler.

REPUBLICAN PLATFORM—CHICAGO,
June 2, 1880.

The Republican party, in National Convention assembled, at the end of twenty years since the Federal Government was first committed to its charge, submits to the people of the United States its brief report of its administration:

It suppressed a rebellion which had armed nearly a million of men to subvert the national authority. It reconstructed the Union of the States with freedom, instead of slavery, as its corner-stone. It transformed four million of human beings from the likeness of things to the rank of citizens. It relieved Congress from the infamous work of hunting fugitive slaves, and charged it to see that slavery does not exist.

It has raised the value of our paper currency from thirty-eight per cent. to the par of gold. It has restored, upon a solid basis, payment in coin for all the national obligations, and has given us a currency absolutely good and equal in every part of our extended country. It has lifted the credit of the nation from the point where six per cent. bonds sold at eighty-six to that where four per cent. bonds are eagerly sought at a premium.

Under its administration railways have increased from 31,000 miles in 1860, to more than 82,000 miles in 1879.

Our foreign trade has increased from $700,000,000 to $1,150,000,000 in the same time; and our exports, which were $20,000,000 less than our imports in 1860, were $264,000,000 more than our imports in 1879.

Without resorting to loans, it has, since the war closed, defrayed the ordinary expenses of government, besides the accruing interest on the public debt, and disbursed, annually, over $30,000,000 for soldiers' pensions. It has paid $888,000,000 of the public debt, and, by refunding the balance at lower rates, has reduced the annual interest charge from nearly $151,000,000 to less than $89,000,000.

All the industries of the country have revived, labor is in demand, wages have increased, and throughout the entire country there is evidence of a coming prosperity greater than we have ever enjoyed.

Upon this record, the Republican party asks for the continued confidence and support of the people; and this Convention submits for their approval the following statement of the principles and purposes which will continue to guide and inspire its efforts:

1. We affirm that the work of the last twenty years has been such as to commend itself to the favor of the nation, and that the fruits of the costly victories which we have achieved, through immense difficulties, should be preserved; that the peace regained should be cherished; that the dissevered Union, now happily restored, should be perpetuated, and that the liberties secured to this generation should be transmitted, undiminished, to future generations; that the

order established and the credit acquired should never be impaired; that the pensions promised should be paid; that the debt so much reduced should be extinguished by the full payment of every dollar thereof; that the reviving industries should be further promoted; and that the commerce, already so great, should be steadily encouraged.

2. The Constitution of the United States is a supreme law, and not a mere contract; out of Confederate States it made a sovereign nation. Some powers are denied to the nation, while others are denied to States; but the boundary between the powers delegated and those reserved is to be determined by the national and not by the State tribunals.

3. The work of popular education is one left to the care of the several States, but it is the duty of the national government to aid that work to the extent of its constitutional ability. The intelligence of the nation is but the aggregate of the intelligence of the several States; and the destiny of the nation must be guided, not by the genius of any one State, but by the average genius of all.

4. The Constitution wisely forbids Congress to make any law respecting an establishment of religion; but it is idle to hope that the nation can be protected against the influence of sectarianism while each State is exposed to its domination. We, therefore, recommend that the Constitution be so amended as to lay the same prohibition upon the Legislature of each State, to forbid the appropriation of public funds to the support of sectarian schools.

5. We reaffirm the belief, avowed in 1876, that the duties levied for the purpose of revenue should so discriminate as to favor American labor; that no further grant of the public domain should be made to any railway or other corporation; that slavery having perished in the States, its twin barbarity—polygamy—must die in the territories; that everywhere the protection accorded to citizens of American birth must be secured to citizens of American adoption; that we esteem it the duty of Congress to develop and improve our water-courses and harbors, but insist that further subsidies to private persons or corporations must cease; that the obligations of the republic to the men who preserved its integrity in the day of battle are undiminished by the lapse of fifteen years since their final victory— to do them perpetual honor is, and shall forever be, the grateful privilege and sacred duty of the American people.

6. Since the authority to regulate immigration and intercourse between the United States and foreign nations rests with the Con-

gress of the United States and its treaty-making powers, the Republican party, regarding the unrestricted immigration of the Chinese as an evil of great magnitude, invoke the exercise of that power to restrain and limit that immigration by the enactment of such just, humane, and reasonable provisions as will produce that result.

7. That the purity and patriotism which characterized the early career of Rutherford B. Hayes in peace and war, and which guided the thoughts of our immediate predecessor to select him for a presidential candidate, have continued to inspire him in his career as chief executive, and that history will accord to his administration the honors which are due to an efficient, just, and courteous discharge of the public business, and will honor his interposition between the people and proposed partisan laws.

8. We charge upon the Democratic party the habitual sacrifice of patriotism and justice to a supreme and insatiable lust for office and patronage. That to obtain possession of the National and State Governments, and the control of place and position, they have obstructed all efforts to promote the purity and to conserve the freedom of suffrage; have devised fraudulent certifications and returns; have labored to unseat lawfully-elected members of Congress, to secure, at all hazards, the vote of a majority of the States in the House of Representatives; have endeavored to occupy, by force and fraud, the places of trust given to others by the people of Maine, and rescued by the courageous action of Maine's patriotic sons; have, by methods vicious in principle and tyrannical in practice, attached partisan legislation to appropriation bills, upon whose passage the very movements of governments depend; have crushed the rights of the individual; have advocated the principle and sought the favor of rebellion against the nation, and have endeavored to obliterate the sacred memories of the war, and to overcome its inestimably valuable results of nationality, personal freedom, and individual equality. Equal, steady, and complete enforcement of the laws, and protection of all our citizens in the enjoyment of all privileges and immunities guaranteed by the Constitution, are the first duties of the nation. The danger of a solid South can only be averted by the faithful performance of every promise which the nation made to the citizen. The execution of the laws, and the punishment of all those who violate them, are the only safe methods by which an enduring peace can be secured, and genuine prosperity established throughout the South. Whatever promises the nation

makes, the nation must perform; and the nation cannot with safety relegate this duty to the States. The solid South must be divided by the peaceful agencies of the ballot, and all opinions must there find free expression: and to this end honest voters must be protected against terrorism, violence, or fraud. And we affirm it to be the duty and the purpose of the Republican party to use all legitimate means to restore all the States of this Union to the most perfect harmony which may be practicable; and we submit to the practical, sensible people of the United States to say whether it would not be dangerous to the dearest interests of our country, at this time to surrender the administration of the National Government to a party which seeks to overthrow the existing policy, under which we are so prosperous, and thus bring distrust and confusion where there is now order, confidence, and hope.

9. The Republican party, adhering to a principle affirmed by its last National Convention, of respect for the Constitutional rule covering appointments to office, adopts the declaration of President Hayes, that the reform of the civil service should be thorough, radical, and complete. To this end it demands the coöperation of the legislative with the executive department of the Government, and that Congress shall so legislate that fitness, ascertained by proper practical tests, shall admit to the public service; and that the power of removal for cause, with due responsibility for the good conduct of subordinates, shall accompany the power of appointment.

REPUBLICAN PLATFORM—CHICAGO,
June 3, 1884.

The Republicans of the United States, in National Convention assembled, renew their allegiance to the principle upon which they have triumphed in six successive Presidential elections, and congratulate the American people on the attainment of so many results in legislation and administration by which the Republican party has, after saving the Union, done so much to render its institutions just, equal, and beneficent—the safeguard of liberty and the embodiment of the best thought and highest purposes of our citizens.

The Republican party has gained its strength by quick and faithful response to the demands of the people for the freedom and the equality of all men, for a united nation assuring the rights of all citizens, for the elevation of labor, for an honest currency, for purity in legislation, and for integrity and accountability in all departments of the Government; and it accepts anew the duty of leading in the work of progress and reform.

We lament the death of President Garfield, whose sound statesmanship, long conspicuous in Congress, gave promise of a strong and successful Administration, a promise fully realized during the short period of his office as President of the United States. His distinguished success in war and in peace has endeared him to the hearts of the American people.

In the Administration of President Arthur we recognize a wise, conservative, and patriotic policy, under which the country has been blessed with remarkable prosperity, and we believe his eminent services are entitled to, and will receive, the hearty approval of every citizen.

It is the first duty of a good government to protect the rights and promote the interests of its own people. The largest diversity of industry is most productive of general prosperity and of the comfort and independence of the people. We therefore demand that the imposition of duties on foreign imports shall be made, not for revenue only, but that, in raising the requisite revenues for the Government, such duties shall be so levied as to afford security to our diversified industries and protection to the rights and wages of the laborer, to the end that active and intelligent labor, as well as capital, may have its just reward and the laboring man his full share in the national prosperity. Against the so-called economic system of the Democratic party, which would degrade our labor to the foreign standard, we enter our earnest protest. The Democratic party has failed completely to relieve the people of the burden of unnecessary taxation by a wise reduction of the surplus. The Republican party pledges itself to correct the inequalities of the tariff and to reduce the surplus, not by the vicious and indiscriminate process of horizontal reduction, but by such methods as will relieve the tax-payer without injuring the labor or the great productive interests of the country. We recognize the importance of sheep husbandry in the United States, the serious depression which it is now experiencing, and the danger threatening its future prosperity; and we therefore respect the demands of the representative of this important agricultural interest for a readjustment of duty upon foreign wool, in order that such industry shall have full and adequate protection.

We have always recommended the best money known to the civilized world, and we urge that an effort be made to unite all commercial nations in the establishment of an international standard which shall fix for all the relative value of gold and silver coinage.

The regulation of commerce with foreign nations and between the States is one of the most important prerogatives of the General Government, and the Republican party distinctly announces its purpose to support such legislation as will fully and efficiently carry out the constitutional power of Congress over inter-State commerce. The principle of the public regulation of railway corporations is a wise and salutary one for the protection of all classes of the people, and we favor legislation that shall prevent unjust discrimination and excessive charges for transportation, and that shall secure to the people and to the railways alike the fair and equal protection of the laws.

We favor the establishment of a national bureau of labor, the enforcement of the eight-hour law, a wise and judicious system of general education by adequate appropriation from the national revenues wherever the same is needed.

We believe that everywhere the protection to a citizen of American birth must be secured to citizens by American adoption, and we favor the settlement of national differences by international arbitration.

The Republican party having its birth in a hatred of slave labor, and in a desire that all men may be free and equal, is unalterably opposed to placing our workingmen in competition with any form of servile labor, whether at home or abroad. In this spirit we denounce the importation of contract labor, whether from Europe or Asia, as an offense against the spirit of American institutions, and we pledge ourselves to sustain the present law restricting Chinese immigration and to provide such further legislation as is necessary to carry out its purposes.

The reform of the civil service, auspiciously begun under Republican administration, should be completed by the further extension of the reformed system already established by law to all the grades of the service to which it is applicable. The spirit and purpose of the reform should be observed in all executive appointments, and all laws at variance with the objects of existing reformed legislation should be repealed, to the end that the dangers to free institutions which lurk in the power of official patronage may be wisely and effectively awarded.

The public lands are the heritage of the people of the United States, and should be reserved as far as possible, for small holdings by actual settlers. We are opposed to the acquisition of large tracts of these lands by corporations or individuals, especially where such holdings are in the hands of non-resident aliens, and we will endeavor to obtain such legislation as will tend to correct this evil.

We demand of Congress the speedy forfeitures of all land grants which have lapsed by reason of non-compliance with acts of incorporation in all cases where there has been no attempt in good faith to perform the conditions of such grants.

The grateful thanks of the American people are due to the Union soldier and sailors of the late war, and the Republican party stands pledged to suitable pensions for all who were disabled, and for the widows and orphans of those who died in the war. The Republican party also pledged itself to the repeal of the limitations contained in the arrears act of 1879, so that all invalid soldiers shall share alike, and their pensions shall begin with the date of disability or discharge, and not with the date of the application.

The Republican party favors a policy which shall keep us from entangling alliance with foreign nations, and which shall give the right to expect that foreign nations shall refrain from meddling in American affairs. The policy which seeks peace and can trade with all powers, but especially with those of the Western Hemisphere.

We demand the restoration of our navy to its old-time strength and efficiency, that it may in any sea protect the rights of American citizens and the interests of American commerce, and we call upon Congress to remove the burdens under which American shipping has been depressed, so that it may again be true that we have a commerce which leaves no sea unexplored, and a navy which takes no law from superior force.

Resolved, That appointments by the President to offices in the Territories should be made from the *bona fide* citizens and residents of the Territories which they are to serve.

Resolved, That it is the duty of Congress to enact such laws as shall promptly and effectually suppress the system of polygamy within our Territory and divorce the political from the ecclesiastical power from the so-called Mormon Church, and that the law so enacted should be rigidly enforced by the civil authorities if possible, and by the military if need be.

The people of the United States, in their organized capacity, constitute a nation, and not a mere confederacy of States. The National Government is supreme within its sphere of national duty, but the States have reserved rights which should be faithfully maintained; each should be guarded with jealous care, so that the harmony of our system of government may be preserved and the Union kept inviolate. The perpetuity of our institutions rests upon the maintenance of a free ballot, an honest count, and correct returns. We denounce the fraud and violence practiced by the Democracy in Southern States, by which the will of the voter is defeated, as dangerous to the preservation of free institutions, and we solemnly arraign the Democratic party as being the guilty recipient of the fruits of such fraud and violence.

We extend to the Republicans of the South, regardless of their former party affiliations, our cordial sympathy, and pledge to them our most earnest efforts to promote the passage of such legislation as will secure to every citizen, of whatever race or color, the full and complete recognition, possession, and exercise of all civil and political rights.

DEMOCRATIC PLATFORM—CHICAGO.
August 29, 1864.

Resolved, That in the future, as in the past, we will adhere with unswerving fidelity to the Union under the Constitution, as the only solid foundation of our strength, security, and happiness as a people, and as a frame-work of government equally conducive to the welfare and prosperity of all the States, both Northern and Southern.

Resolved, That this convention does explicitly declare, as the sense of the American people, that after four years of failure to restore the Union by the experiment of war, during which, under the pretense of a military necessity of a war power higher than the Constitution, the Constitution itself has been disregarded in every part, and public liberty and private right alike trodden down, and the material prosperity of the country essentially impaired, justice, humanity, liberty, and the public welfare demand that immediate efforts be made for a cessation of hostilities, with a view to an ultimate convention of all the States, or other peaceable means, to the end that, at the earliest practicable moment, peace may be restored on the basis of the Federal Union of all the States.

Resolved, That the direct interference of the military authority of the United States in the recent elections held in Kentucky, Maryland, Missouri, and Delaware, was a shameful violation of the Constitution; and the repetition of such acts in the approaching election will be held as revolutionary, and resisted with all the means and power under our control.

Resolved, That the aim and object of the Democratic party is to preserve the Federal Union and the rights of the States unimpaired; and that they hereby declare that they consider the administrative usurpation of extraordinary and dangerous powers not granted by the Constitution, the subversion of the civil by the military law in States not in insurrection, the arbitrary military arrest, imprisonment, trial, and sentence of American citizens in States where civil law exists in full force, the suppression of freedom of speech and of the press, the denial of the right of asylum, the open and avowed disregard of State rights, the employment of unusual test-oaths, and the interference with and denial of the right of the people to bear arms in their defense, as calculated to prevent a restoration of the Union and the perpetuation of a government deriving its just powers from the consent of the governed.

Resolved, That the shameful disregard of the administration to its duty in respect to our fellow-citizens who now are, and long have been, prisoners of war, in a suffering condition, deserves the severest reprobation, on the score alike of public policy and common humanity.

Resolved, That the sympathy of the Democratic party is heartily and earnestly extended to the soldiers of our army and the sailors of our navy, who are and have been in the field and on sea under the flag of their country; and, in the event of our attaining power, they will receive all the care and protection, regard and kindness, that the brave soldiers of the Republic have so nobly earned.

PUBLIC SERVICES OF JAMES G. BLAINE.

THE nomination of Mr. Blaine was not an accident, nor was it due to a systematic organization of political force. Indeed, the friends of other candidates were more active than were the friends of Mr. Blaine.

Opposing candidates were presented in each of six States, New York, Ohio, Indiana, Illinois, Connecticut, and Vermont. These candidates were not only strong within the States where they resided, respectively, but they commanded confidence, and were entitled to support in all parts of the Union.

In several of those States delegates were elected who were friendly to Mr. Blaine, and he was the second choice of a majority of those who preferred other candidates.

Hence, at Chicago, the fact was disclosed at an early stage of the Convention that it was impossible to unite the delegates who prefered other candidates upon any one of the candidates named. This circumstance was not due to any want of confidence in or respect for those candidates, but to the fact that Mr. Blaine was the second choice of many whose first preference was for other persons. It is thus apparent that Mr. Blaine's nomination was acceptable to a large majority of the Convention.

Mr. Blaine's popularity in the country is not due to a sudden and unreasoning impulse on the part of the people. The period of its growth extends over many years, and the events of those years demonstrate the depth and strength of the public feeling. He was the leading candidate in the Convention of 1876; he was a formidable candidate in the Convention of 1880; and he is the successful candidate of the Republican party in 1884. Neither his candidacy nor his nomination can be treated as a surprise.

Nor can it be assumed with any degree of justice that his nomination is due to the machinations of leaders. A candidacy might be advanced, and a nomination even might be secured by the organized efforts of friends, but such agencies are quite inadequate to give to a man a continuing and increasing support in three successive presidential contests. And especially must this be true when the candidate is without office, without patronage, and destitute of all extraneous means of advancing himself in the public esteem.

Therefore his standing among the people is not due to agencies or to extraneous influences, but to the presence of personal qualities constantly and through many years exhibited. In the elements and characteristics of leadership in public, political affairs, he has not been surpassed by any one in America and equaled only by Mr. Clay. In Mr. Blaine are combined, as was the case also in Mr. Clay, the power of controlling deliberative assemblies by the exhibition of courage, tact, and skill in debate, with personal qualities which inspire confidence and promote lasting attachments in those persons to whom a leader is known only by a casual introduction or temporary acquaintance.

By the possession and exhibition of this combination of rare qualities, Mr. Blaine rose rapidly to the position of a leader in the House of Representatives, while at the same time he gained the confidence and enlisted the support of the majority of those in the country who agreed with him in political opinions.

It is a significant fact that Mr. Blaine's strongholds in the country are in the States and districts where the Republican party can command majorities. This fact precludes the suggestion or the thought that the nomination of Mr. Blaine was due to the schemes of partisans. It was in fact due to the opinion of the Republican masses that he was the fittest man in the party for the post of leader in a great national contest.

His nomination was an act of submission to the will of the majority and as the will of the majority it is entitled to respect.

The rule of the minority in parties can only end in the overthrow of Free States. If parties are ruled by minorities, then, as a consequence, the States themselves will be ruled by minorities. Dissatisfied minorities are justifiable when they change their party allegiance; but unsatisfied minorities are not to be justified in demanding the submission of the majority to their will, and when such demands are made a wise majority will decline to accede to them and at the hazard of whatever consequences may follow. It was only that, that the South demanded as the price of peace.

The entire period of Mr. Blaine's public life has been devoted to the support of the principles of the Republican party. In two most important ways he has earned the right to represent that party.

First, as a brilliant, bold, and skillful leader in the House of Representatives, and then as an aggressive, eloquent, and convincing campaign speaker.

In successive presidential contests he advanced the cause and defended the positions of the Republican party in a manner to satisfy his friends and to command the respect and excite the fears of his opponents.

Mr. Blaine was elected a member of the thirty-eighth Congress and he took his seat in December, 1863. His career as a public man then opened before him and at the first session he achieved a national reputation. He was then thirty-three years of age.

That House of Representatives was the first House elected under the pressure and the responsibilities of the war. "Fortunate is that country whose annals are uninteresting," is a maxim whose reason is found in the fact that in peaceful times men of moderate abilities rise to places of distinction and thus the times neither show forth eminent talents in rulers nor extraordinary events in affairs. The Thirty-eighth Congress contained many able men and in American history it is only surpassed by the Thirty-ninth Congress. The House of Representatives numbered among its members Stevens, Kelley, Randall, and Schofield of Pennsylvania; Schenck, Garfield, Cox, Ashley, and Pendleton, from Ohio; Winter Davis, Francis Thomas, and Creswell from Maryland; Wilson, Allison, and Kasson, from Iowa; E. B. Washburne, and Owen Lovejoy from Illinois, and Voorhees, Julian, Orth, and Colfax from Indiana. Many of these men, and others their equals from other States, had had long experience in public affairs. In such an assembly it was no easy undertaking for a new member to rise to a position of recognized equality with old leaders and trained parliamentarians. The House of Representatives always possesses a large share of ability, and the judgment pronounced upon its own members is always a just judgment. Mediocrity and pretense may find favor occasionally, but for a brief period only at most, while capacity to deal with questions and affairs is early recognized and the possessor is accorded his true position freely and without delay. The House is usually just to its own members.

It is a noticeable fact, that of the eminent men who were members of the House of Representatives of the Thirty-eighth Congress, and especially of those who were members for the first time, a large number were under forty years of age. Of those mentioned, neither Garfield, Blaine, Cox, Ashley, Randall, Pendleton, Creswell, Wilson, Allison, or Voorhees had reached that age. Some of these men had then acquired a national reputation, and others gained that distinction without delay. Mr. Conkling had been elected to the Thirty-sixth Congress when he was only thirty years of age, and at an earlier period in our history Webster, Clay, Calhoun and others were known to the country before they had reached that period of life, and their qualities were as well understood, and appreciated as justly as they were in their maturer years.

It is a singular fact, that at this moment there is not one man in the country, and who is less than forty years of age, that has achieved a national reputation in politics or law. The same remarks may be made of England, France, and Germany. If there are exceptions, knowledge of the gifted persons has not reached this country.

The first important debate in which Mr. Blaine took a part related to the tariff, and his speech was called out by an attack made by Mr. Cox of Ohio, upon the system of protection, and consequently upon New England as at once responsible for the wrong and the chief beneficiary of it.

After an elaborate review of the tariff, Mr. Cox said: "I never was afraid of buying in the cheapest market and selling in the dearest market I could find." . . . "The tendency of the present tariff system, and, in fact, of all tariffs, revenue or protective, more or less, is to drain wealth from the unprotected States and accumulate it in the protected States. It can now be understood why New England accumulates wealth so much more rapidly than the Western States."

To these assertions and doctrines Mr. Blaine replied, and in his reply he exhibited the qualities which have rendered him efficient in controversial debate and conspicuous before the country. He spoke for Maine as a State, but as a member of the Union, rather than as a State of the New England group. His mode of defense was a system of attack also. Ohio was arraigned as a State that derived more benefit from the system of protection than fell to the State of Maine.

Mr. Cox's speech was prepared with great care, and it was stuffed with statistics, designed to prove that the doctrine of protection was an error, that its application in this country divided the States into two classes—the protected and non-protected,—and that the Eastern States, and the States of New England especially, were protected, while the States of the West were the non-protected class. In his view, taxation without benefits was imposed upon one set of States, and bounties, which yielded no consideration in return, were distributed to other States. The argument was based upon the census of 1860, supported by writers upon political economy, from Adam Smith to Dr. Wayland, and elaborated through twenty-five columns of the *Congressional Globe*. Mr. Blaine's reply was made without preparation, and it illustrates, therefore, his ability to command his resources upon the instant—a quality indispensable in a leader.

An inexorable law of parliamentary life assigns to the leader the task of meeting every opponent upon the ground that he may choose, and that without delay. For this task Mr. Blaine was ever ready, and he accepted it not so much as a necessity or a duty as a pleasure which he coveted. If his reply to Mr. Cox does not present him at his best, it illustrates his readiness in debate, his system of defense by attack, and his power to marshal the facts and events in history in support of his views and position.

"It has grown to be a habit in this House, Mr. Chairman, to speak of New England as a unit, and in assailing the New England States to class them together, as has been done to-day by the gentleman from Ohio (Mr. Cox) throughout his entire speech. In response to such attacks, each particular Representative from a New England State might feel called upon to defend the whole section. For myself, sir, I take a different view. I have the honor to represent in part only one State, the State of Maine, and I have no more to do with the local and particular interests of the rest of New England than with any other State in the Union. The other New England States are ably represented upon this floor, and it would be officious and arrogant in me to attempt to speak for them. But when the gentleman from Ohio presumes to charge here that the State I represent receives from Federal legislation any undue protection to her local interests, he either ignorantly or willfully misrepresents the case so grossly, that for ten minutes I will occupy the attention of the House in correcting him.

"If the gentleman from Ohio who has given us such a learned lecture on political economy were at all well posted in regard to the industrial pursuits of the people of Maine, he would know that the great and leading interests are lumber and navigation. Now will the gentleman be good enough to tell the House what protection is extended by the laws of the United States to the lumber interest? At no time in our history, sir, did lumber receive more than a feeble protection, and even that was taken away ten years ago by the gentleman's political associates when they formed the reciprocity treaty, and thus broke down the only barrier we had, and threw in the whole lumber product of the British Provinces to compete with us. And in regard to our great interest of navigation, will the gentleman be good enough to tell the House when a ship is launched from a Maine ship-yard to engage in the commerce of the world, what protection is given by the United States laws against competition with foreign bottoms? Not a particle, sir. These two great leading interests of my State derive no advantage from Federal legislation, while one of them has been very greatly damaged by the treaty-making power of the Federal Government. I do not hesitate to declare here to-day that the State of Ohio has upon her products and her manufactures ten dollars of protection from Federal legislation where Maine has twenty-five cents.

"But, sir, let us take another view of this matter. The State of Maine consumes every year five hundred thousand barrels of flour, all of which, with a very trifling exception, is brought from the West, and a large proportion, I presume, from the State of Ohio. Now, if the gentleman's logic be good, it would be a very admirable idea for this country to so change its domestic industry as to detach the six hundred thousand people of Maine from their present pursuits and convert them into producers instead of consumers of bread-stuffs and provisions. And let this change be made throughout all the manufacturing and commercial districts of the Union, converting the five million consumers into producers of grain and meats, and the withering effect on the gentleman's State and on the entire West would be too apparent to require a speech of an hour and a half to demonstrate it. Sir, I am tired of such talk as the gentleman from Ohio has indulged in to-day, and in so far that it includes my own State as being a pensioner upon the General Government, or being dependent upon the bounty of any other State, I hurl back the charge with scorn. If there be a State in this Union that can say with truth that her Federal connection confers no special benefit of a material character, that State is Maine. And yet, sir, no State is more attached to the Federal Union than Maine. Her affection and her pride are centered in the Union, and God knows that she has contributed of her best blood and treasure without stint in supporting the war for the Union; and she will do so to the end. But she resents, and I, speaking for her, resent the insinuation that she derives any undue advantage from Federal legislation or that she gets a single dollar that she does not pay back. As compared with Ohio, whence this slander comes, I repeat, sir, that Maine receives from the Federal legislation no protection worth reckoning.

* * * * * * * * *

"No, sir; but the gentleman comes up here and classifies the States of the Union as 'protected' and 'unprotected' States, and he puts my State in the 'protected' class, while the most youthful page on this floor who has studied Mitchell's Geography knows that the gentleman's own State derives from the General Government an immeasurably larger degree of protection for her local interests than the State of Maine does. And I tell the gentleman that he shall not with impunity include my State in his wholesale slander.

"I observe, sir, that a great deal has been said, recently, in the other end of the Capitol in regard to the fishing bounties, a portion of which is paid to Maine. I have a word to say on that matter, and I may as well say it here. According to the records of the Navy Department, the State of Maine has sent into the naval service since the beginning of this war six thousand skilled seamen, to say nothing of the trained and invaluable officers she has contributed to the same sphere of patriotic duty. For these men the State has received no credit whatever on her quotas for the army. If you will calculate the amount of bounty that would have been paid to that number of men had they enlisted in the army instead of entering the navy, as they did, without bounty, you will find it will foot up a larger sum than Maine has received in fishing bounties for the past twenty years. Thus, sir, the original proposition on which fishing bounties were granted—that they would build up a hardy and skillful class of mariners for the public defense in time of public danger—has been made good a hundred and a thousand-fold by the experience and the developments of this war.

"Thus much, sir, I have felt called upon to say in response to the elaborate and carefully prepared speech of the gentleman from Ohio. I have spoken in vindication of a State that is as independent and as proud as any within the limits of the Union. I have spoken for a people as high-toned and as honorable as can be found in the wide world. I have spoken for a particular class—many of them my constituents—who are as manly and as brave as ever faced the ocean's storms. And so long, sir, as I have a seat on this floor the State of Maine shall not be slandered by the gentleman from Ohio, or by gentlemen from any other State."

When the bill to amend the act for enrolling and calling out the national forces was pending in the House of Representatives (February, 1865), Mr. Blaine proposed an amendment designed to remedy the injustice of allowing credits to towns and cities for men not furnished by such cities and towns. In support of the amendment Mr. Blaine said, "nothing so discourages and disheartens the brave men at the front as the belief that proper measures are not adopted at home for reënforcing and sustaining them. Even a lukewarmness or a backwardness is enough; but when you add to that the suspicion that unfair devices have been resorted to by those charged with filling quotas, you naturally inflame the prejudices and passions of our veterans in the field in a manner calculated to lessen their personal zeal and generally to weaken the discipline of the army. After four years of such patriotic and heroic effort for national unity as the world has never witnessed before, we cannot now afford to have the great cause injured, or its fair fame darkened by a single unworthy incident connected with it. The improper practices of individuals cannot disgrace or degrade the nation; but after these practices are brought to the attention of Congress we shall assuredly be disgraced and degraded if we fail to apply the requisite remedy when that remedy is in our power.

Let us then in this hour of triumph to the national arms do our duty here, our duty to the troops in the field, our duty to our constituents at home, and our duty, above all, to our country, whose existence has been in such peril in the past, but whose future of greatness and glory seems now so assured and so radiant."

At the commencement of the first session of the thirty-ninth Congress, Mr. Blaine introduced a bill to reimburse the loyal States for the expenses incurred and debts contracted in support of the war for the preservation of the Union. The proposition involved an appropriation of about one hundred and eighteen million dollars. He supported the measure in an elaborate speech in which he reviewed the scheme of Mr. Hamilton for the assumption of the State debts in the administration of Gen. Washington, and he cited also the opinions of many eminent men who favored the act. In that speech Mr. Blaine had a field for the use of his knowledge of American political history, extensive, minute, and accurate, a knowledge for which he has found a large field in his great work, TWENTY YEARS IN CONGRESS.

That speech, however, presents Mr. Blaine at his best as a parliamentary speaker. It is not an oration, and the day has passed for the delivery of orations in deliberative assemblies. Henceforth, orations are reserved for anniversary days and commemorative occasions. Argument is every where acceptable; a clear, chaste, forcible style is demanded; and when the cause or the occasion justifies or requires that elevated quality of speech which we call eloquence, but which no one can describe, and which only a favored few can create, the charm is for all, the rustic and the noble, the ignorant and the learned, the generation that is and the generations, successive, that are to come.

Interest in the subject of Mr. Blaine's speech has passed away; but if the speech itself can now attract the reader, its quality is thus shown to be above the reach of disparaging criticism.

Closing his review of the history of the country in regard to the assumption of State debts, he says:

"The precedents, then, for such legislation as is contemplated in the pending bill are ample and uniform in our congressional history. The principles on which this legislation is based are so plain as to scarcely need any argument in support of them, and yet, with your leave, I will proceed to point out some reasons of peculiar force, as it seems to me, why the State debts incurred in the war for the Union should be made a common charge on the national treasury. If such reimbursement was just and equitable in former wars, it is so now in a far more enlarged and imperative sense.

"I need not remind the House, Mr. Chairman, that during the past five years all the loyal States have been compelled to raise large sums of money in aid and support of the war for the Union. The statistics of expenditure have been gathered with all practicable exactness by the special committee which reported the pending bill, and the aggregate in the loyal States reached well-nigh five hundred million dollars. Nor was this vast sum of money expended fruitlessly, needlessly, or wastefully. I do not state the case too strongly when I assert that without it the war would not and could not have succeeded. Had not volunteering been stimulated and sustained by the State and local bounties we should have been thrown back on the "rough and perilous edge" of the draft in its naked, indiscriminate, and most repulsive form. At several of the most critical junctures of the war, when reverses had been experienced, when popular ardor and hope were chilled, and when the administration felt weak and timid, the revival of patriotism and courage throughout the land had its origin in the stimulus imparted to fresh volunteering by the large inducement of the local bounties. The most that can be said in favor of the conscription law is that it operated as an incentive to enlistments, being held *in terrorem* over the people, and inducing thousands to volunteer for bounties in order to avoid the possible alternative of being drafted into the service without other pecuniary reward than the monthly pay. It is not discreditable to American patriotism that our people have a deep prejudice against conscriptions, and it was therefore wise, nay, it was absolutely necessary, for the strength, harmony, and success of the Union cause, that the loyal States, counties, cities, and towns, should offer bounties sufficient to fill the ranks of our army without a ruthless resort to the draft. The money thus expended for bounties was, I repeat, wisely, and in the main economically, expended; far more carefully, indeed, than the average of Federal disbursements during the war. Though raised by local effort, every dollar of it was designed for the good of the national cause; and hence every dollar is fairly reimbursable from the national treasury.

And this great effort on the part of the loyal States was not made for themselves only. Success of the Union cause was really of no more importance to them than to the revolted States, to the States yet to grow up on our vast western domain, and, indeed, to all the generations that are to follow us as American citizens and the inheritors of Republican Government and constitutional liberty. The contest was not local, but general; not for ourselves, but for mankind; not merely for to-day, but for all time. The twenty-five loyal States derive no more advantage from the victorious issue of the war than do the eleven revolted States which were thereby saved from anarchy and destruction, or the forty new States that are yet to be added to the Union, and which would never have had an opportunity to reach an organized existence but for the successful struggle which has assured to them the fostering care and protecting ægis of the great Republic.

The contest, then, was one in which all the States, both now existing and hereafter to be organized, were equally interested; and what justice, what semblance even of fair dealing is there in leaving a heavy burden of debt on Maine, while Nevada has not paid a dollar in the struggle; or in asking Michigan to pour out her money and her credit like water, while Colorado escapes without the cost of a penny? Nevada and Colorado were as much interested prospectively in the result of the contest as Maine and Michigan, and the burden should be proportionally and impartially shared between them.

Some gentlemen, with a tender sympathy which I fail to appreciate, argue that the Southern States have suffered so severely in their abortive rebellion that they ought not to be called on to bear anything more than their part of the national debt already contracted. What those States expended in their wicked effort to destroy this Union is not, in my judgment, to be reckoned to their credit on the national ledger, nor is the exhaustion to which they were reduced by their insane persistence in the war, to be made the basis of an appeal to our sympathy, much less to our reason. They were kept back from suicide and redeemed with a great price, and it is but fair and honest that they should pay their full proportion of the cost, even to the uttermost farthing. But as a matter of fact let it be asserted that the lately revolted States are not burdened or embarrassed with debt. Their obligations incurred in supporting the rebellion have been or will be repudiated, so that however much certain speculative traitors may lose, the political communities are free from debt and will enjoy light local taxation. They are not therefore in a position to decline their fair share of the national burden, and as the tax to support that burden is raised wholly by impost and excise, it cannot fall heavily on any community until the revival of business and the development of trade shall provide the means of meeting and sustaining it.

And in this connection let me remark, Mr. Chairman, that it is not only for the interest of the loyal States to adopt this measure, but it is preëminently for their interest to adopt it *now*. The subject is a dangerous one to leave open, and unless definitely and finally closed at this time it may reappear in a future Congress in a form most embarrassing and detrimental to the national treasury and the national credit. Whenever the Representatives are readmitted on this floor from the Southern States you will find a series of propositions introduced for the relief of their constituents from losses entailed by the war. These schemes will embrace compensation for slaves emancipated for the benefit of the Union; restitution for property seized for the use of the Federal army; payment for losses inflicted by the march of our troops, and the nameless and numberless other claims which the extraordinary events of the past five years will so readily suggest. Let us beware how we leave open a class of meritorious claims from the loyal States with which the southern jobs may be combined and coalesced into a gigantic onslaught upon the Federal treasury. Pass the present measure and you at once remove the opportunity and the temptation for such a dangerous coalition. Pledge the one hundred and eighteen millions embraced in this bill, and you will thereby escape the danger of paying twelve hundred millions in the future. The whole matter is subject to our control to-day. It may not always remain so.

For many years to come, Mr. Chairman, the loyal States will in any event inevitably bear the principal burden in sustaining the national credit. In addition to this, unless the pending measure prevails, they will each be called upon to bear a large local debt whose interest is provided by direct, merciless, and I had almost said, ruinous taxation. Throughout the States represented on this floor to-day the direct tax on property, real and personal, will annually average more than two per cent. of its value, while in many communities it reaches the staggering rate of three to three and a half and even four per cent. Such taxation may be endured, and has been patiently and patriotically endured during our great struggle for national existence, but as a permanent charge upon the property of the country, ina ddition to all the Federal taxes, it is more than can be borne without grievous affliction. Let it be remembered that the local tax of which I am speaking comes in the most oppressive form. It is not disguised by any excise system, nor lightened by any indirection. It is so many dollars out of the earnings of the farmer, the gains of the merchant, the wages of the mechanic, and the savings of the humblest. It embarrasses every enterprise, is felt as a hardship at every fireside, and shrouds the business and commercial future with doubt and despondency. The communities that are thus suffering have never thought and will never think of resorting to repudiation as a remedy, but their high sense of honor on this point and their determination to meet all their obligations should not be taken, as I am sorry to say it is by some, as an argument for leaving them to struggle unaided against their onerous and crushing burdens.

But the financial question involved in this measure is not of pressing interest merely to the States that are so sorely burdened with debt and taxation. I maintain that it is of equal importance to the General Government that these debts be assumed, and my fear is that if this policy should be rejected serious embarrassment may result to the Treasury of the United States. When Mr. Hamilton originally recommended the policy of assumption with regard to the revolutionary debt, he did not view it simply from the stand-point of justice to the States, but quite as much from motives of sound policy touching the interests of the Federal Treasury. To quote his own language, he declared that "the assumption of the State debts was no less a measure of sound policy than of substantial justice, and that it would contribute in an eminent degree to an orderly, stable, and satisfactory arrangement of the national finances." The communities that are oppressed with these local debts are the same that pay almost the entire national revenue collected under the excise law, and the latter is felt as an infinitely greater burden because of its coming in addition to the heavy direct tax levied by the local authorities. Could this local tax be relieved to the extent which this bill would relieve it, the Federal tax could be paid with great ease, even if largely increased beyond its present rate. To illustrate my position by pertinent figures, let me say that the pending bill if adopted would add some one hundred and eighteen millions to the national debt, or, in other words, it would increase it a trifle more than four per cent., and would call for a corresponding increase in the amount raised to pay interest. But the immense relief that would be experienced throughout the loyal States by the removal of these enormous direct taxes would enable them to pay the increased excise with comparative case. And in this way the General Government would have the field to itself, and could regulate its system of taxation with far greater efficiency and far greater equity. Competing and conflicting systems of taxation can but produce mutual injury, and if the power can be lodged wholly or mainly in one, a larger amount of money can be raised with less burden to the people than where each is compelled to make the utmost exaction to meet the demands upon it.

If there be any correctness in the view just suggested, the assumption of the State debts would make a nominal rather than a real addition to the national debt. The States and communities which owe these debts are precisely the same States and communities upon which must rest the maintenance of the national credit during the entire period that it may be said to be on trial before the world. While this oppressive burden of local indebtedness is upon them, it impairs their resources and their ability to carry the national debt by even a larger amount. And if the national debt is increased by refunding to the States, the local burdens are, to say the least, correlatively and proportionally reduced. This fact is so palpable and undeniable that it is only a waste of time to repeat it. Bankers and money-lenders would everywhere recognize it; and the tendency of such a policy would be to strengthen the national credit throughout the world. The change of securities does not change the amount to be raised by taxation, it only simplifies the mode of obtaining it. And this phase of the case presents another striking parallel to the first assumption as proposed and accomplished by Mr. Hamilton. In discussing the identical point to which I have just referred, that great master of finance dismissed it summarily with the following brief and conclusive comment:

"Admitting that a provision must be made in some way or other for the entire debt, it will certainly follow that no greater revenues will be required, whether that provision be made wholly by the United States or partly by them and partly by the States separately."

Another point, Mr. Chairman, in this connection, for the special attention of those gentlemen who fear that the adoption of the pending measure would injure the national credit. Nothing is so injurious to credit as uncertainty. It is the apprehension to-day of what our debt may be rather than the knowledge of what it is that prevents our bonds selling at a premium in gold, both at home and abroad. One source of uncertainty is found in this very question of the war debts of the States. Will they be assumed, or will they not, and if assumed, to what amount? are questions asked at all financial centers, with anxious concern. So long as nothing is done the worst is feared, and the anticipated amount of assumption will expand with the agitation of the question. It is natural to exaggerate the unknown. *Omne ignotum pro magnifico.* We can put an end to injurious surmises as to what may be done, by adopting at once the very moderate and well-guarded proposition now under discussion. Refusing to pass this bill will not quiet agitation nor remove alarm. Agitation will go on and injury to our national credit will be the inevitable result.

Should the policy of assuming these debts be rejected, an act of injustice would be done entirely without precedent thus far in the dealings between the General Government and the States. The strange spectacle would be presented of less than one-third of the prospective number of States bearing in its most oppressive form an enormous debt, every dollar of which was contracted as much for the benefit of the other two thirds of the Union as for themselves.

The prejudicial effect which this would have on the States subjected to the burden need not be described. It would in a great degree cripple their energies and retard their growth, and the climax of its baleful influence would be made odiously and cruelly manifest in the emigration from the old to the new States, and from the North to the South, for the purpose of escaping the very tax which was incurred that the new States might be born and that the South might be saved from suicide. I could not, by any reasoning, enhance the force of such a fact as this, nor strengthen the plea which it makes for the equalization of the entire debt created by the war.

If further argument were needed to show the justice of reimbursing the States for their advances in support of the war, it would be found in the fact that Congress, in devising a system of taxation for the Union, has deprived the States of all the means of raising money except through the instrumentality of a direct levy on real and personal property. Many of the States had previously enjoyed the advantage of certain forms of excise, tolls, and other indirect taxes, which enabled them to lighten, if not entirely remove, the burden of local government. In Massachusetts, I believe, the tax derived from the State banks for a long series of years almost supported the State government; and other States had similar sources of revenue, if not proportionally so large; but the General Government, through its constitutional right to levy impost and excise, has absorbed all the easy and ready available channels of taxation, throwing back the States, as I have said, to the severest form of raising revenue. It is an inevitable hardship that, for necessary local purposes, the States must procure revenue by direct tax, but it is a hardship rendered almost unendurable by its injustice when the States have in this way to raise a large sum to pay the interest and principal of a debt contracted for the good of the whole Union. The power to meet the burden having been taken from the States, common equity demands that the burden should be taken away also.

And the burden to which I have just referred, Mr. Chairman, falls with increased severity on the farmers and other holders of real estate, from the fact that so vast a proportion of the personal property in many communities has sought investment in Government securities, which are specially exempt from State and municipal taxation. I should certainly be among the last to countenance a breach of the national faith in the slightest degree. We must stand by the terms "nominated in the bond," no matter how onerous and oppressive they may be. No hardship can arise to any of us from observing good faith on the part of the Government, at all comparable with the hardship that would ensue to all of us by violating that faith even by the remotest hint. But while we all agree, I trust, on this point, I submit that as the policy of the Government has made the war debt of the States bear unequally on different classes of the community, and most oppressively on the specially meritorious class, it is the imperative duty of the Government to equalize the burden by assuming an equitable share of the debt.

I am not willing, Mr. Chairman, to be understood as making in these remarks a supplicating appeal for relief on behalf of my own State, or the other loyal Commonwealths that have "borne the heat and burden of the day" throughout the great contest that has resulted so auspiciously for all the interests of humanity. Supplication is the language of those who have no right to use a stronger phrase. But standing here to-day as one of the Representatives of the people, I have a right to demand that equal and exact justice be done to all the States of the Union, and that the Government of the Union should without cavil or hesitation pay the debts which were contracted on its own account and for its own benefit. Justice is all that the loyal States ask, and in the grand language of Mr. Hamilton, already quoted, "justice is not completely fulfilled until the entire debt of every State contracted in relation to the war is embraced in one general and comprehensive plan of payment."

In a speech delivered the 7th of March, 1868, Mr. Blaine discussed the subject of the currency in connection with the finances of the country. A statement had been made that the Republican party, or the Republican leaders, designed to pay the five-twenty bonds in gold. This statement he refuted. As none of those bonds were due and payable previous to the year 1882, he counseled delay, and upon the ground that long before that time the United States notes would be as valuable as coin, and that the bonds would be paid in the currency then used in business. But he denounced the scheme of paying the bonds in greenbacks. These are his words:

"Does any sane man doubt that the inflation of the currency would speedily result in its depreciation? If so, he shuts his eyes to the prominent facts of history, to our own experience as a nation, and to the plainest deductions of common sense. An excess of irredeemable money at once raises the price of all commodities necessary for daily consumption. Clothing becomes higher and food becomes higher, without a corresponding increase of those of limited means to purchase these articles. The rich can stand it, but what would become of the poor? The man who lives by his daily toil would find the necessaries of life run up in price far beyond any increase he could hope to secure for his labor; and it would soon become a struggle for existence with him and his family. I do not think any imagination can picture or foretell the misery that would be inflicted on this country if the currency should be inflated to the extent necessary to pay the five-twenties in greenbacks, as advocated by the gentleman from Massachusetts (Mr. Butler), and the gentleman from Ohio, not now a member of this House (Mr. Pendleton). And in this connection I desire further to say that it is an immense delusion to attribute any of the dullness now prevalent in business circles to a scarcity of money. We have over seven hundred million dollars of paper money now in circulation—nearly three times as much as the entire bank circulation of the United States prior to 1861, while it is quite notorious that the money markets in our business centers were rarely known to be easier, or more abundantly supplied than during the whole of this winter. Moreover, business of all kinds in France and England at this time is far duller than with us; and yet in both these countries the plethora of money is in excess of what was ever known before. The Bank of France alone holds a surplus of $200,000,000, and a corresponding amount is held in the Bank of England, and by the large banking-houses at Frankfort-on-the-Main. In view of these facts, it seems to me that no delusion is so absurd as to suppose that any relief could come from an inflation of the currency. Misery, wide-spread and hopeless, would be its only and inevitable result.

"Nor do I see how any gentleman can consistently propose an inflation of the currency in the face of an express and solemn pledge to the contrary by Congress. When the Government was very hard pressed for money, and when the great fear was that our whole financial fabric, like the continental system of our Revolutionary ancestors, might be utterly and hopelessly ruined by a deluge of paper money, Congress, by deliberate enactment of June 30, 1864, pledged to all the public creditors that 'the total amount of treasury notes *issued or to be issued* should never exceed $400,000,000.' We are now within $40,000,000 of that amount, and if we were ever so eager to pay off our five-twenties in greenbacks, we are absolutely estopped by the $400,000,000 pledge. If we disregard that pledge we might as well trample on others, and take a short cut at once to repudiation and national bankruptcy. A government that will disregard one solemn pledge cannot expect to be trusted on other pledges."

That Mr. Blaine possessed the full confidence of President Garfield there can be no doubt. Their relations were not official merely; they were bound to each other by the ties of sincere friendship. Mr. Blaine's eulogy on President Garfield was received by the country as the tribute of a friend; but it was received also as a wise and just analysis of the President's character and career. Only a friend could have written the closing passages of the eulogy:

"On the morning of July 2d, the President was a contented and happy man—not in an ordinary degree, but joyfully, almost boyishly happy. On his way to the railroad station, to which he drove slowly, in conscious enjoyment of the beautiful morning, with an unwonted sense of leisure and a keen anticipation of pleasure, his talk was all in the grateful and gratulatory vein. He felt that after four months of trial his administration was strong in its grasp of affairs, strong in popular favor, and destined to grow stronger; that grave difficulties confronting him at his inauguration had been safely passed; that trouble lay behind him and not before him; that he was soon to meet the wife whom he loved, now recovering from an illness which had but lately disquieted, and at times almost unnerved him; that he was going to his Alma Mater to renew the most cherished associations of his young manhood, and to exchange greetings with those whose deepening interest had followed every step of his upward progress from the day he entered upon his college course until he had attained the loftiest elevation in the gift of his countrymen.

"Surely, if happiness can ever come from the honors or triumphs of this world, on that quiet July morning James A. Garfield may well have been a happy man. No foreboding of evil haunted him; no slightest premonition of danger clouded his sky. His terrible fate was upon him in an instant. One moment he stood erect, strong, confident in the years stretching peacefully out before him; the next he lay wounded, bleeding, helpless, doomed to weary weeks of torture, to silence, and the grave.

"Great in life, he was surpassingly great in death. For no cause, in the very frenzy of wantonness and wickedness, by the red hand of murder, he was thrust from the full-tide of this world's interest, from its hopes, its aspirations, its victories, into the visible presence of death—and he did not quail. Not alone for the one short moment in which, stunned and dazed, he could give up life, hardly aware of its relinquishment; but through days of deadly languor, through weeks of agony, that was not less agony because silently borne, with clear sight and calm courage, he looked into his open grave. What blight and ruin met his anguished eyes, whose lips may tell—what brilliant, broken plans, what baffled, high ambitions, what sundering of strong, worn, manhood's friendships, what bitter rending of sweet household ties! Behind him a proud, expectant nation; a great host of sustaining friends; a cherished and happy mother, wearing the full, rich honors of her early toil and tears; the wife of his youth, whose whole life lay in his; the little boys not yet emerged from childhood's day of frolic; the fair young daughter; the sturdy sons, just springing into closest companionship, claiming every day and every day rewarding a father's love and care; and in his heart the eager, rejoicing power to meet all demand. Before him, desolation and great darkness! And his soul was not shaken. His countrymen were thrilled with instant, profound, and universal sympathy. Masterful in his mortal weakness, he became the center of a nation's love, enshrined in the prayers of a world. But all the love and all the sympathy could not share with him his suffering. He trod the winepress alone. With unfaltering front he faced death. With unfailing tenderness he took leave of life. Above the demoniac hiss of the assassin's bullet he heard the voice of God. With simple resignation he bowed to the Divine decree.

"As the end drew near, his early craving for the sea returned. The stately mansion of power had been to him the wearisome hospital of pain, and he begged to be taken from its prison walls, from its oppressive, stifling air, from its homelessness and its hopelessness. Gently, silently, the love of a great people bore the pale sufferer to the longed-for healing of the sea, to live or to die, as God should will, within sight of its heaving billows, within sound of its manifold voices. With wan, fevered face tenderly lifted to the cooling breeze, he looked out wistfully upon the ocean's changing wonders; on its far sails, whitening in the morning light; on its restless waves, rolling shoreward to break and die beneath the noon-day sun; on the red clouds of evening, arching low to the horizon; on the serene and shining pathway of the stars. Let us think that his dying eyes read a mystic meaning, which only the rapt and parting soul may know. Let us believe that in the silence of the receding world he heard the great waves breaking on a farther shore, and felt already upon his wasted brow the breath of the eternal morning."

Mr. Blaine's leadership on the floor of the House was interrupted by his transfer to the Speaker's chair at the commencement of the forty-first Congress. He served as Speaker during the forty-first, forty-second, and forty-third Congresses. As a presiding officer he takes a place in the small class which consists of Mr. Clay, Mr. Winthrop, and General Banks.

During the first session of the forty-fourth Congress, Mr. Blaine resigned his seat in the House upon his appointment to the Senate, where he served with distinction until he became Secretary of State in the administration of President Garfield.

It is to be said of Mr. Blaine that he has had a long, varied, and successful career in public life. He has been connected with both houses of Congress, and with the Executive department. If experience is of any value, he is well equipped for the duties of President.

There is a general and aggressive public sentiment which demands the retention of experienced officers in all the subordinate places of government, and at the same time the country indulges in the illusion that the chief place of all may be safely filled, or wisely filled, by a man who is without experience even in the forms of government.

The shafts hurled in disappointment, envy, or malice, reach every conspicuous station in life. Every representative man is a victim. Leadership awakens rivalry, and it implies hostility.

In this contest the Republican party does not seek for success in the obscurity of its candidates. It has selected men of large experience, of abilities recognized generally, and often tested.

PUBLIC SERVICES OF JOHN A. LOGAN.

OF the personages of American history, a few only have risen to distinction in more than one walk in life. General Logan belongs to the exceptionally small class who have attained eminence, a right to be known historically, in more than one department of effort and contest. The prizes in war are attractive, and the names of those who gain them are known widely. The favor of the multitude is sure to wait upon the successful soldier. The victories of peace are not more easily won than the victories of war; but when won, they do not so readily command the applause of mankind.

General Logan has been a successful leader in peace and in war.

It was his fortune to be born into a family of attainments in professional and general knowledge, and therefore he enjoyed advantages in his childhood and youth that were not common to frontier life in America a half a century ago. His mother was of Scottish ancestry, and of a family which numbered among its members some who were lawyers and others who were entrusted with public duties. His father was an Irishman in nationality, and a physician by profession. He had the means to command a private tutor for the education of his children, and their opportunities for gaining knowledge were superior to the opportunities of others in the vicinity. General Logan shared and improved these advantages; but he was also trained and disciplined for the stern duties of a soldier and a statesman as a sharer in the hardships of frontier life. He was prepared for the profession of the law by a course of three years at college, and by a full course at the Louisville Law School.

Leaving college in his twentieth year, he volunteered as a private in a regiment raised for the Mexican war. He served as a lieutenant of Company H, First Illinois Infantry. In Mexico he acquired some knowledge of the art of war, some acquaintance with its perils and duties, and a speaking knowledge of the Spanish language.

Upon his return, he was elected clerk of Jackson county in 1849, but he resigned the position that he might pursue his studies in the Law Department of the Louisville University.

He commenced his professional life at Murphysboro', Illinois, in partnership with his uncle, Ex-Governor Jenkins.

The childhood and youth of eminent men are subjects of interest; but the events and surroundings of childhood and youth do not demonstrate, and usually they do not foreshow the future of the man. There are failures in life where the early advantages were many; and there have been successes when the early advantages were few. The educational advantages enjoyed and improved by General Logan were greater than were possessed by Washington, Jackson, Harrison, Taylor, or Lincoln. The fact that General Logan enjoyed the means for acquiring knowledge does not demonstrate his fitness for public employment; but he is not to be excluded from the roll of soldiers and statesmen upon the ground that he did not have the benefit of teachers or schools, or that he neglected to improve his opportunities.

The fastidiousness in politics of men who are mere scholars, and the claim indirectly made that the country should be governed by scholars, will yet receive a rebuke at the hands of the people. There is a general opinion that the means of education should be furnished to all the children and youth of the country, but there is an opinion equally general and equally sound that mere scholarship is not a guarantee for wisdom in the administration of governments.

In 1852 General Logan was elected to the House of Representatives of the State of Illinois. His legal attainments were recognized, especially in criminal jurisprudence; and upon the expiration of his term of service in the Legislature he was chosen prosecuting attorney for the judicial district in which he resided.

In 1858, at the age of thirty-two, General Logan was elected a Representative in the Thirty-sixth Congress. He was a Democrat—a Douglas Democrat—and his majority was greater than any Democratic majority previously given in the district.

At the session of December, 1860, General Logan supported the "Crittenden Compromise," and he strove to avert a war, but always as a Union man. He voted for the resolution approving the President's action in support of the laws and for the preservation of the Union. In December, 1860, he voted for a resolution introduced by Mr. Morris, his colleague. That resolution was in these words:

"*Resolved by the House of Representatives*, That we are unalterably and immovably attached to the Union of the States; that we recognize in that union the primary cause of our present greatness and prosperity as a nation; that we have yet seen nothing, either in the election of Abraham Lincoln to the Presidency of the United States, or from any other source, to justify its dissolution, and that we pledge to each other 'our lives, our fortunes, and our sacred honors' to maintain it."

This vote should end all controversy as to General Logan's position upon the subject, and it should silence the groundless calumny that he had any sympathy, even the least, either with the Secessionists or with the doctrines of secession. While he was yet a member of the House of Representatives he carried a musket and served as a private soldier in the first battle of Bull Run. Thus at an early day he redeemed the pledge that he had given by his vote in favor of the Morris resolution.

A majority of General Logan's constituents were immigrants from the Slave States, or descendants of immigrants from those States, and the weight of public sentiment was in favor of the South. This sentiment General Logan met and overcame by his personal influence and by public addresses. Upon his return to his district in the early summer of 1861, threats of personal violence were made frequently; but in a series of speeches he accomplished two important results. He recruited a regiment, the Thirty-first Illinois, and he changed the public sentiment of the district.

Then and thus his career as a soldier began. His first experience was at Belmont, where his horse was shot under him, and his pistol at his side was shattered by a shot from the enemy. The official report says, "Colonel Logan's admirable tactics not only foiled the frequent attempts of the enemy to flank him, but secured a steady advance towards the enemy's camp."

This was the beginning of the verification of the prophecy that he made when he canvassed his district for the Union and for a regiment of volunteers: "Should the free navigation of the Mississippi river be obstructed by force, the men of the West will hew their way through human gore to the Gulf of Mexico."

Logan's regiment formed a part of the expedition against Forts Henry and Donelson. He was the first to enter Fort Henry, and in command of a cavalry force he captured eight guns. These forts, and especially Donelson, constituted the defense of Nashville. The siege of Donelson lasted three days. Logan's regiment suffered severely. Of 606 men who were engaged in the battle 303 were killed or wounded. Logan received three wounds so severe that his life was in peril, and yet he continued in command until from loss of blood he was unable to stand.

General McClernand says: "Schwartz's battery being left unsupported by the retirement of the 29th, the 31st boldly rushed to its defense, and at the same moment received the combined attack of the forces on the right and of others in front, supposed to have been led by General Buckner. The danger was imminent, and calling for a change of disposition adapted to meet it, which Colonel Logan made by forming the right wing of his battalion at an angle with the left. In this order he supported the battery, which continued to play upon the enemy and held him in check until his regiment's supply of ammunition was entirely exhausted."

Colonel Oglesby of the 8th Illinois, commanding the First Brigade, says in his report of the battle: "Turning to the 31st, which yet held its place in line, I ordered Colonel Logan to throw back his right, so as to form a crochet on the right of the 11th Illinois. In this way Colonel Logan held in check the advancing foe for some time under the most destructive fire, whilst I endeavored to assist Colonel Cruft with his brigade in finding a position on the right of the 31st. It was now four hours since fighting began in the morning. The cartridge-boxes of the 31st were nearly empty. The Colonel had been severely wounded, and the Lieutenant-Colonel, John H. White, had, with some thirty others, fallen dead on the field and a large number wounded. In this condition Colonel Logan brought off the remainder of his regiment in good order."

General Logan was promoted to the rank of Brigadier-General for his conduct at the battle of Fort Donelson, and upon the recommendation of General Grant. Of General Logan and three others he says: "They have fully earned their positions on the field of battle."

After an absence of two months, and before he had recovered from his wounds, General Logan took command of his brigade, and was engaged in the battle of Corinth, the 28th and the 29th of May, 1862. Of his conduct in that contest General Sherman says: "And further I feel under special obligations to this officer, General Logan, who, during the two days he served under me, held critical ground on my right, extending down to the railroad."

It was at this crisis of affairs, when our arms had met with serious reverses in the Peninsula under McClellan, when Pope had been defeated before Washington, that the friends of General Logan solicited the use of his name as a candidate for election to the Thirty-eighth Congress. A weak man or a timid man might have seized the occasion to retire from the army without the reproach of resigning in the face of the enemy. General Logan declined the opportunity in a letter filled with patriotic sentiments:

"In reply, I would most respectfully remind you that a compliance with your request on my part would be a departure from the settled resolution with which I resumed my sword in defense and for the perpetuity of a government, the like and blessings of which no other nation or age shall enjoy, if once suffered to be weakened or destroyed.

"In making this reply, I feel that it is unnecessary to enlarge as to what were, or may hereafter be, my political views, but would simply state that politics of every grade and character whatsoever are now ignored by me, since I am convinced that the Constitution and life of this Republic—which I shall never cease to adore—are in danger. I express my views and politics when I assert my attachment for the Union. I have no other politics now, and consequently no aspirations for civil place and power. . . . . I have entered the field, to die if need be, for this government, and I never expect to return to peaceful pursuits until the object of this war of preservation has become a fact established. . . . . If the South by her malignant treachery has imperiled all that made her great and wealthy, and it were to be lost, I would not stretch forth my hand to save her from destruction, if she will not be saved by a restoration of the Union."

To these pledges General Logan was faithful. He returned to peaceful pursuits only when the authority of the Union was reëstablished in every State.

He was commissioned Major-General of Volunteers, November 29, 1862, and he and his command were in the advance in all the movements of the autumn of 1862 and of the winter and spring of 1863, which terminated in the fall of Vicksburg, the 4th day of July in that year.

The winter of 1862 and 1863 was a gloomy period in the annals of the war. The elections of 1862 had resulted disastrously to the Republican party. There was discontent in the loyal States, and there was discontent in the army.

In February, 1863, General Logan issued an address to the Seventeenth Army Corps, of which he was then in command:

"*My Fellow Soldiers:* Debility from recent illness has prevented and still prevents me from appearing amongst you, as has been my custom, and is my desire. It is for this cause I deem it my duty to communicate with you now, and give you the assurance that your General still maintains unshaken confidence in your patriotism, devotion, and in the ultimate success of our glorious cause. I am aware that influences of the most discouraging and treasonable character, well calculated and designed to render you dissatisfied, have recently been brought to bear upon some of you by professed friends. Newspapers, containing treasonable articles, artfully falsifying the public sentiment at your homes, have been circulated in your camps. Intriguing political tricksters, demagogues, and time-servers, whose corrupt deeds are but a faint reflex of their more corrupt hearts, seem determined to drive our people on to anarchy and destruction. They had hoped, by magnifying the reverses of our arms, basely misrepresenting the conduct and slandering the character of our soldiers in the field, and boldly denouncing the acts of the constituted authorities of the Government as unconstitutional usurpations, to produce general demoralization in the army, and thereby reap their political reward, weaken the cause we have espoused, and aid all those arch-traitors of the South to dismember our mighty Republic, and trail in the dust the emblem of our national unity, greatness, and glory. Let me remind you, my countrymen, that we are soldiers of the Federal Union, armed for the preservation of the Federal Constitution and the maintenance of its laws and authority. Upon your faithfulness and devotion, heroism and gallantry, depend its perpetuity. To us has been committed this sacred inheritance, baptized in the blood of our fathers. We are soldiers of a government that has always blessed us with prosperity and happiness. It has given to every American citizen the largest freedom and the most perfect equality of rights and privileges. It has afforded us security in person and property, and blessed us until, under its beneficent influence, we were the proudest nation on earth.

"We should be united in our efforts to put down a rebellion, that now, like an earthquake, rocks the Nation from State to State and from center to circumference, and threatens to engulf us all in one common ruin, the horrors of which no pen can portray. We have solemnly sworn to bear true faith to this Government, preserve its Constitution, and defend its glorious flag against all its enemies and opposers.

"To our hands has been committed the liberties, the prosperity, and happiness of future generations. Shall we betray such a trust? Shall the brilliance of your past achievements be dimmed and tarnished by hesitation, discord, and dissension, whilst armed traitors menace you in front and unarmed traitors intrigue against you in the rear? We are in no way responsible for any action of the civil authorities. We constitute the military arm of the Government. That the civil power is threatened and attempted to be paralyzed, is the reason for resort to the military power. To aid the civil authorities (not to oppose or obstruct) in the exercise of their authority is our office; and shall we forget this duty, and stop to wrangle and dispute over this or that political act or measure, whilst the country is bleeding at every pore; whilst a fearful wail of anguish, wrung from the heart of a distracted people, is borne upon every breeze, and widows and orphans are appealing to us to avenge the loss of their loved ones who have fallen by our side in defense of the old blood-stained banner, and whilst the Temple of Liberty itself is being shaken to its very center by the ruthless blows of traitors, who have desecrated our flag, obstructed our national highways, destroyed our peace, desolated our firesides, and draped thousands of homes in mourning?

"Let us stand firm at our posts of duty and of honor, yielding a cheerful obedience to all orders from our superiors until, by our united efforts, the Stars and Stripes shall be planted in every city, town, and hamlet of the rebellious States. We can then return to our homes, and through the ballot-box peacefully redress all our wrongs, if any we have.

"Whilst I rely upon you with confidence and pride, I blush to confess that recently some of those who were once our comrades in arms have so far forgotten their honor, their oaths, and their country, as to shamefully desert us, and sulkily make their way to their homes, where, like culprits, they dare not look an honest man in the face. Disgrace and ignominy (if they escape the penalty of the law) will not only follow them to their dishonored graves, but will stamp their names with infamy to the latest generation. The scorn and contempt of every true man will ever follow those base men who, forgetful of their oaths, have, like cowardly spaniels, deserted their comrades in arms in the face of the foe, and their country in the hour of its greatest peril. Every true-hearted father or mother, brother, sister, or wife, will spurn the coward who could thus not only disgrace himself, but his name and his kindred. An indelible stamp of infamy should be branded upon his cheek, that all who look upon his vile countenance may feel for him the contempt his cowardice merits.

"Could I believe that such conduct found either justification or excuse in your hearts, or that you would for a moment falter in our glorious purpose of saving the nation from threatened wreck and hopeless ruin, I would invoke from Deity, as the greatest boon, a common grave to save us from such infamy and disgrace. The day is not far distant when traitors and cowards, North and South, will cower before the indignation of an outraged people. MARCH BRAVELY ON! Nerve your strong arms to the task of overthrowing every obstacle in the pathway of victory, until, with shouts of triumph, the last gun is fired that proclaims us a united people under the old flag and one government! Patriot soldiers! this great work accomplished, the reward for such services as yours will be realized! the blessings and honors of a grateful people will be yours!"

In the style of this address there may be food for critics; but in the purpose and sentiments of the address there is cheer for the patriot. It was designed to encourage war-worn veterans, who, after two years of service and of peril on many hard-fought fields, had not accomplished the great purpose of the war nor demonstrated the possibility of success.

In some States enlistments were discouraged and deserters were protected. The efficiency of the army was affected by the opinions of the troops as to the state of the public sentiment at home. General Logan's address was designed to meet the difficulties of the situation in a political as well as military point of view.

General Logan occupied responsible positions and took a leading part in all the movements under General Grant, which culminated finally in the capture of Vicksburg. The movement down the Mississippi river, across the channel, and through the State of Mississippi, was the brilliant undertaking of the war, and the most successful achievement until the final triumph at Appomattox. It decided the fate of Vicksburg, secured the free navigation of the river, and dissipated every doubt as to the final success of the Union cause. The battle of "Champion Hill" was the final and decisive battle of a brilliant series, and in that battle General Logan was a conspicuous actor.

"When our troops halted along the slopes of Champion Hill," says the Comte de Paris in his *History of the Civil War in America*, "the dead and wounded were piled together in such vast numbers, that these soldiers, although tried on many a battle-field, called the place 'The Hill of Death.'"

The same eminent and impartial authority says: "The battle of Champion Hill, considering the number of troops engaged, could not compare with the great conflicts we have already mentioned, but *it produced results far more important* than most of those great hecatombs, like Shiloh, Fair Oaks, Murfreesborough, Fredericksburg, and Chancellorsville, which left the two adversaries fronting each other, both unable to resume the fight. *It was the most complete defeat the Confederates had sustained since the commencement of the war.* They left on the field of battle from three to four thousand killed and wounded, three thousand able-bodied prisoners, and thirty pieces of artillery. But these figures can convey no idea of the magnitude of the check experienced by Pemberton, from which he could not again recover. . . . . *This battle was the crowning work* of the operations conducted by Grant with equal audacity and skill since his landing at Bruinsburg. In outflanking Pemberton's left, along the slopes of Champion Hill, he had completely cut off the latter from all retreat north. Notwithstanding the very excusable error he had committed in stopping Logan's movement for a short time, *the latter had through this manœuver secured victory to the Federal army.*"

General Grant, in his report of this battle, uses the following language: "Logan rode up at this time, and told me that if Hovey could make another dash at the enemy, *he could come up from where he then was and capture the greater part of their force; which suggestions were acted upon and fully realized.*"

The siege of Vicksburg followed.

"On the morning of the 18th," says the Comte de Paris in his history, "Pemberton, with all his troops, shut himself up inside the vast fortifications constructed around Vicksburg. His forces, including the sick and a very small number of wounded—for those of Champion Hill had all remained on the battle-field—amounted to thirty-three thousand men. . . . . On the morning of the 19th the investment of Vicksburg was complete. McClernand on the left, McPherson on the center, and Sherman on the right, surrounded the place from the Mississippi on the south to the Yazoo on the north. Pemberton had abandoned all the outer works without a fight. . . . Grant's army, reduced by fighting and rapid marching, did not reach forty thousand men."

13

General Logan's corps was engaged in the two memorable assaults on Vicksburg, and portions of his command gained and occupied positions nearest the lines of the enemy. Upon the surrender, Logan's command, with General Grant at the head, was the first to enter the city. Says the Comte de Paris: "It had fully deserved this honor."

General Logan was put in command of the city, and he was at the same time the recipient from the Board of Honor of the Seventeenth Army Corps of a gold medal, on which were inscribed the names of the nine battles in which he had been most distinguished for heroism and generalship.

General Logan spent a portion of the autumn of 1863 in Illinois, where, in a series of speeches, he gave efficient support to the administration and contributed largely to the successes of the Republican party in that year.

In November, 1863, General Logan succeeded General Sherman as commander of the Fifteenth Corps, and from that time forward he was engaged conspicuously in all the movements of the army, from the capture of Atlanta to the surrender of Johnston.

General Logan's magnanimity and sense of justice were exhibited in his treatment of General Thomas. It is known that in the autumn of 1864 General Logan was ordered to Nashville, and to the command of the Army of the Cumberland. When he arrived at Louisville he learned that General Thomas had attacked the enemy. Logan telegraphed immediately to General Grant, and suggested that Thomas should not be removed. For himself, he asked to be assigned to the command of the Fifteenth Army Corps.

General Logan's farewell address to the Army of the Tennessee was dated at Louisville, Kentucky, July 18, 1865. Thereupon he resigned his commission and turned to the pursuits of private life.

His military career was such that the officers of the regular army and the graduates of West Point assign him the first place among the volunteers. It is difficult to comprehend the reason for the distinction indicated by the form of the concessions to the military career of General Logan. If in any instance he exhibited a lack of knowledge, or if his movements had in any case been followed by disaster, there would be grounds for qualifying the words of praise used in recognition of his services.

In courage, in the ready command of his resources, in coolness of temperament in moments of peril, in ability to inspire confidence and arouse the enthusiasm of soldiers, and finally, in the degree of success that crowned all his undertakings, he deserved to be classed with the most accomplished and most successful generals of the war.

General Logan was elected to the House of Representatives of the fortieth and forty-first Congresses. He took part in the most important debates, having rank always with the leading members of the House. He was one of the managers in the impeachment of President Johnson. In all cases he sustained the policy of the Republican party in the work of reconstruction.

After four years of faithful and honorable service in the House he was elected to the Senate. He took his seat at the opening of the forty-second Congress. With the interruption of a term of two years he has continued a member of the Senate to the present time.

General Logan has been distinguished especially, both in the House and in the Senate, as the soldiers' friend. He was a witness of the hardships and sufferings met and endured by the armies of the Union; he was a sharer in the dangers of the war, and he feels, naturally, that the gratitude of the country cannot exceed the value of the services rendered by those who stood in the hot fire of battle for its defense.

His argument in the Fitz-John Porter case must be accepted as an exhaustive array of facts, and a clear presentation of the law. Its delivery occupied three whole days. It was not only listened to by a full Senate and crowded galleries, but the impression was so strong that the bill for the relief of General Porter was abandoned for the session.

There may be differences of opinion as to the merits of the appeal made to the country by Fitz-John Porter; but there can be none as to the merits of the argument of General Logan in support of the decision rendered more than twenty years ago by a competent military tribunal whose action was approved by President Lincoln.

The candidates of the Republican party represent the principles of the party, and they represent the military spirit of the country. Not the spirit of war. There is neither the wish nor the purpose to engage in new military undertakings; but there is in the Republican party an earnest wish and a fixed purpose to guard, protect and support in comfort the survivors of the armies by whose valor and sacrifices the Union was restored. There is neither arrogance nor injustice in the claim that the Republican party is the safer custodian of that duty.

The candidates of the Republican party are men of large experience in the affairs of the government. In the subordinate places of duty and trust the claim is made, and with good reasons, that experienced men should be preferred. Can it then be wise to bestow the chief posts of trusts and power and duty upon men without experience?

INDEX.

	Page.
Acquisition of the territory of Texas gave fresh consequence to slavery,	16
Act for the admission of Maine was approved March 3, 1820,	14
was passed for the admission of Missouri as a State March 6, 1820,	14
of March 6, 1820, prohibited slavery in that part of the original territory of Louisiana north of parallel 36° 30', excepting in the State of Missouri,	14
approved February 8, 1861, authorized a loan of twenty-five million dollars,	65, 66
approved March 2, 1861, increased the duties upon many articles of merchandise,	67
authorizing the issue of United States notes and for funding the public debt, was approved February 25, 1862,	68
of February 25, 1862, provisions of, relating to United States notes, issue of bonds, sinking fund, etc.,	68
establishing a national bank currency was approved February 25, 1863,	69
establishing national banks, its provisions, and the advantages derived therefrom,	69
of February 25, 1862, does not permit the issue of United States notes except upon the pledge of redemption in coin.	70
to strengthen the public credit, approved March 18, 1869, was the first legislative act of the Forty-first Congress,	71
approved March 18, 1869, provided for the payment in coin of all obligations, unless it was otherwise provided in said obligations,	71
to authorize the refunding of the national debt, was approved July 14, 1870,	72
Acts of March 2, 1861, August 5, 1861, July 14, 1862, and June 30, 1864, were for providing revenues upon a war basis, and for protection,	67, 68

(i)

INDEX.

Acts of 1816, 1828, and 1842, gave temporary encouragement to manufacturing industries,	77
Abolition views of President Lincoln in 1862,	42
Administration of Government, injustice still exists in the,	10
of President Pierce, and the country were involved in the horrors of civil war in Kansas,	20
of Mr. Tyler was controlled by the leaders of the Democratic party, in a large degree,	95
as a measure of that of Mr. Lincoln, the national bank system was adopted, but it was opposed by the Democratic members of both houses of Congress,	96
Africa, negroes found on slave-trading vessels after 1819 to be returned to,	12
the return to of captured negroes may have been just, but it was politic for the border Slave States,	13
Virginia and other border Slave States were willing that negroes found on slave-trading vessels should be returned to,	13
Agricultural Colleges, veto of grant to,	89
grants of lands to,	88
Allegiance, choice of,	92
Amalgamation, one of the fruits of slavery,	8
Amendments to the Constitution were adopted by the Republican party,	24
each of the three was opposed by the Democratic party, but it has been compelled to accept and endorse them,	96
America, had only three cotton spinning mills in 1800,	11
Annexation of Texas inured to the advantage of freedom,	6
of Texas was the policy of Southern statesmen,	15
of Texas was opposed by the Whig party of the North,	15
of Texas, Mr. Polk's election was considered an endorsement of the scheme for,	15, 16
of Texas, Congress provided for by a joint resolution approved March 1, 1845,	16
by it the United States accepted the controversy and the war then existing between Texas and Mexico,	16
of Texas in 1845, was dictated by the Democratic leaders of the South,	95
of Texas, has inured to the benefit of the country, but the scheme was designed for the advantage of slavery,	95
Arbitration, policy of,	110
Arkansas, was admitted into the Union in 1836,	14
Army, of Gen. Taylor was first termed, of observation, then of occupation, and finally of invasion,	16
of the United States, condition of in 1864,	60

INDEX.   iii

Army was only sufficient for protection against the Indians, when the Republican party came to power in March, 1861, ... 64
    could in 1862 be paid and kept in the field only by means of the United States notes, . . 70
Ashley, J. M., motion by in regard to thirteenth amendment, ... 45
Antagonism between slavery and freedom had not taken form in the colonial period or in the years of confederation, ... 22

Bank, the sum in the United States Treasury January 1, 1861, was inadequate for the safe management of a, ... 65
Beauregard, attack by, on Fort Sumter, . . . 34
Bell, John, received thirty-nine electoral votes on a popular vote of less than six hundred thousand, in 1860, ... 29
Belmont, August, speech of, at Chicago in 1864, . . 57
Bidders, the Whig and Democratic parties were, for southern support, ... 15
Bigler, Governor, speech of, at Chicago in 1864, . . 58
Bill authorizing the issue of treasury notes to the amount of ten million dollars, was approved December 17, 1860, ... 65
    for the abolition of the slave-trade in the District of Columbia was carried under the lead of Mr. Clay, ... 18
    for the surrender of fugitives from slavery, was carried under the lead of Mr. Clay, . . 18
    fugitive slave, was the most offensive of the compromise measures of 1850, . . . 19
Bills, it was claimed that those for the organization of Utah and New Mexico were an abandonment of the principles of the Missouri compromise, . . 20
Bonds, eighteen million of those authorized by the act of February 8, 1861, were sold at an average price of 89.03 per cent., ... 66
    the act authorizing the issue of six per cent., for the issue of United States notes, and for a sinking fund, was approved February 25, 1862, . . 68
    of the United States, in March, 1869, were sold at eighty-three cents on the dollar, in gold, . 71
Border States, influence of Confederacy in, . . . 44
    struggle for supremacy in, ... 41
Bounty, of land to soldiers and sailors, . . . 85
Breckinridge, J. C., was the Democratic condidate of the South, in 1860, ... 29

INDEX.

Buchanan, President, responsibility of, for the war, . 112
    veto of, on homestead bill, ... 84
    veto of bill making grants of lands to agricultural colleges, ... 89
    effect of his position in promoting secession, . 32
    opinion of in regard to secession, . . . 32
    was a minority president, . . . 29
    it was a necessity of the situation that the Confederacy should be organized during the administration of, ... 30
    in his message of December, 1860, made such declarations as justified Mr. Davis and his associates in assuming that he would not interfere, etc., . 30
    denied the right of secession as a Constitutional right, 30
    denied the right of the United States Government to prevent secession, by force, . . . 30
    upon his theory, it was competent for the smallest State to declare the Union at an end, . . 30
    upon the admission of, the Union ceased to exist on the 17th day of December, 1860, . . 30
    attempted to assert a right of property in the custom-houses and forts, which could not be visited except as an act of war, ... 30
    according to his own theory, was, from December 17, 1860 to March 4, 1861, president of a part only of the country, etc., ... 30
    if he had had two years more of official life, the Confederacy would have been firmly established, and recognized by the leading nations of the world, ... 31
Business, every branch of would be embarrassed by the financial evils that would attend the overthrow of the national banking system, . . . 98
    periods of depression in, will occur, they are inevitable, ... 99
    upon the ocean is more perilous, and the returns are more uncertain than upon land, . . 81

Calhoun, John C., the dying speech of was read in the Senate March 4, 1850, ... 17
    in his dying speech demanded an amendment to the Constitution insuring equality of political power to the South, ... 17
    is believed to have said a few months before his death, "Slavery will go down, sir; it will go down in the twinkling of an eye, sir," . . 17
    the essay of, on government, contained his plan for re-establishing the equilibrium between the Free and Slave States, ... 17
    advocated an amendment to the Constitution, which should provide for two presidents, one from the North and one from the South, . 17

INDEX.

Calhoun, John C., had, before his death, lost faith in the
  permanence of slavery, ... 17
California contained sufficient population for a State, . 16
  most of its area, and the larger part of its inhabitants were north of the line 36° 30′, . 16
  whether admitted as a Slave or Free State, would
   destroy the equilibrium of power, . . 16
  was presented for admission as a Free State, because of the annexation of Texas and the consequent war with Mexico, ... 17
  the people of, framed a Constitution without the
   authority of Congress, ... 18
  the bill for the admission of, was approved September 9, 1850, ... 18
  the real reason for the resistance to her admission
   was the exclusion of slavery, . . . 18
  the bill for the admission of, was silent upon the
   subject of slavery, ... 18
  except for slavery the admission of would have
   been considered separately, . . . 18
Campaign, in this, the question of the equality of rights
  in the South, is the paramount question, . 106
Candidates, of each party dictated by the South, . . 1
Captors, of slave-trading vessels after 1819, were required
  to deliver negroes to the President for return to
  Africa, ... 12
Census, errors of, in 1860, ... 91
  in 1850, relative representative power of the Slave
   and Free States, ... 16, 17
Cession of land to the United States, . . . 83
Chicago, Democratic convention at, in 1864, . . 57
Child, followed the condition of the mother, . . 8
Citizenship, secured by the fourteenth amendment, . . 49
  under our system, government resides in, . . 70, 71
Citizens, it is not the duty of a government to give employment to, ... 74
  the nation cannot be an indifferent witness of
   thousands of, seeking refuge in those States where
   the equal rights of men are recognized, . . 106
  of the States are citizens of the United States, . 97
Civilization, that of freedom would have triumphed in the
  end, ... 21
Civil Service, it is reasonable to assume that should the
  Democratic party attain power, the law relative
  to, would either be repealed or its purpose avoided, 102, 103
  by whatever of peril it is menaced, is due to the
   fact of a solid South, ... 106
  reform, the Democratic party can make no claim
   to friendship for, ... 102
  there is a very general opinion in the Republican
   party that there shall be a full and fair trial of
   the undertaking, ... 102

Civil War, the administration of President Pierce, and the
    country were involved in the horrors of, . 20
  the territories were made the theaters of, . . 20
Clark Thread Company, manufactories of, in Paisley, Scot-
    land, and in Newark, N. J., . . 77, 78, 79
Clay, Henry, under his lead the five compromise measures
    of 1850 were carried, ... 18
  made a public surrender of the question of the
    annexation of Texas, ... 15
  was wanting in principle or lacked the courage to
    declare his opinions, etc., . . . 15
  may have had misgivings as to slavery, . . 15
  represented the Whig party in the canvass of 1844, 15
Coin, to the redemption of all paper money in, the Repub-
    lican party is pledged, ... 99
  the act of February 25, 1862, does not permit the
    issue of United States notes, except upon a pledge
    of redemption in, ... 70
  the act approved March 18, 1869, provided for the
    payment in, of all obligations, unless it was
    otherwise provided in said obligations, . . 71
Colleges, grants to agricultural, . . . 88, 89
Colonies, of the original, seven had become free and six
    were slave in 1820, ... 13
Commerce, is the first and easiest victim of war, . . 75
Competition of the laborer in another country, . . 76
Compromise, existed for twenty years between the Free,
    Northern Slave, and Southern Slave States, upon
    the foreign slave trade, . . . 12, 13
Compromises, of and under the Constitution are alike value-
    less, ... 9
Confederacy, upon the formation of, the Democratic party
    ceased to exist in the Rebel States, . . 13
  influence of in border States, . . . 44
  its condition in 1864, ... 59
  if Jefferson Davis were to become the president of,
    he must surrender his seat in the Senate of the
    United States, ... 29, 30
  if Mr. Buchanan had had two years more of official
    life, would have been firmly established, and
    recognized by the leading nations of the world, 31
Confederate authorities, commission from, . . 35
  States, overthrow of slavery made possible by, . 38
Confederation, antagonism between slavery and freedom
    had not taken form in the years of, or during the
    colonial period, ... 22
Conflict was inevitable, because of the three provisions in
    the Constitution concerning slavery, . . 9
  when arising upon a topic that engages the thought
    of the majority, they will appropriate either ex-
    isting, or create new parties, etc., . . 9

INDEX.

Congress denied to alleged fugitives right of trial by jury,	8
in 1794 passed a penal statute against the exportation of slaves, etc.,	12
in 1794 passed a penal statute against carrying slaves between foreign countries in American vessels,	12
in 1807 proceeded to enforce the constitutional prohibition against the importation of slaves,	12
by a joint resolution, offered March 1, 1845, provided for the annexation of Texas,	16
the resolution of, guaranteed that not more than five States might be formed out of the Territory of Texas,	16
the people of California framed a Constitution without the authority of,	18
near the close of the thirty-second, a bill was introduced for the organization of the Territory of Nebraska,	19
at the opening of the thirty-third, President Pierce congratulated the country upon the settlement of the slavery controversy,	20
the question of slavery or freedom in the Territories, that should have been settled by, was the cause of a contest of arms,	20
was compelled by the exigencies of the war to assume jurisdiction of the subject of paper circulation,	97
is composed of representatives of the States and of the people,	97
anything in the nature of usurpation is impossible with,	97
the records of, fuly sustain the allegations as to the conduct of elections in Louisiana, Mississippi, and South Carolina,	103
the South gains more than thirty representatives in, by the present basis of representation, and an equal number in the electoral colleges,	104
both houses of, have been captured, and the executive department has been put in peril,	104
power of, in regard to public lands,	84
refused to pledge the public lands as security for a loan, in 1860,	65
authorized a loan of twenty-five million dollars, by an act approved February 8, 1861,	65, 66
at the extra session of, July 4, 1861, the President asked for authority to borrow four hundred million dollars,	66
was left in the control of the Republican party, by the secession of States and the resignation of Senators and Representatives,	67
the authority of, to provide for the issue of United States notes and make them a legal tender, has been sustained by the Supreme Court,	70

Congress has authority to endow United States notes with the legal tender quality or not, under an opinion of Chief Justice Marshall, etc., . . . 70
    the constitutional grant to, to borrow money, includes the power to provide for the issue of notes, either with or without interest, . . . 70
    during the administration of President Johnson, the attention of, was directed chiefly to measures of reconstruction, and to questions in controversy between the legislative and executive departments of the Government, . . . 71
    "An Act to strengthen the public credit" approved March 18, 1869, ... 71
Constitution, three provisions of which were in conflict with the principles of the founders of the Northern States, ... 7
    the provisions of, designed to protect slavery became the cause of its destruction, . . 7
    by its provisions the foreign slave-trade was tolerated for twenty years, . . . 7
    the provisions of, governing the representation of slaves, etc., ... 7, 8
    doctrine of obedience to, taught, . . . 8
    the North would concede to slavery, what was stipulated in, ... 8
    the compromises of, and under it, are alike valueless, ... 9
    the guarantees of, to slavery, were all temporary, etc., ... 9
    the three provisions therein concerning slavery, made a conflict inevitable, . . . 9
    has been reformed by the people through the Republican party, ... 9
    unjust to assume that the framers of foresaw the evils to come from slavery, . . . 11
    slavery was imbedded in, ... 12
    the pro-slavery provisions of, gave rise to the struggle for an equilibrium of political power, . 13
    the equilibrium between the Free and Slave States was destroyed by, ... 14
    required the re-distribution of political power, 14
    an act was passed March 6, 1820, authorizing the inhabitants of Missouri to frame a, . . 14
    Mr. Calhoun, in his dying speech, demanded an amendment to, insuring equality of political power to the South, ... 17
    Mr. Calhoun, in his Essay on Government, advocated an amendment to, which should provide for two Presidents, etc., ... 17
    was framed by the people of California without the authority of Congress, . . . 18

INDEX.

Constitution, the inherent antagonism between slavery and freedom was organized and developed under,	22
the amendments to, were adopted by the Republican party,	24
each of the three amendments to, was opposed by the Democratic party, but it has been compelled to accept and endorse them,	96
within the limits prescribed by, the question whether a particular power shall be exercised by the General Government, or left to the States, is for Congress,	97
the negro race and many white persons in the South are deprived of the privileges and immunities to which they are entitled under,	104
effect of thirteenth amendment to,	108
none of the provisions of, have contributed more to industrial freedom than that for the protection of authors and inventors,	75
Hamilton was an advocate of the British,	76
provision of, in regard to public lands,	83
ratification of fifteenth amendment to,	50
amendments to, the work of the Republican party,	50
fifteenth amendment of,	49
fourteenth amendment of,	49
thirteenth amendment of,	45
thirteenth amendment to, ratification of,	45
at the time of the adoption of, all the territory outside of the thirteen States was dedicated to freedom,	27
the President took the responsibility of announcing that the Government had no power under, to interfere with secession,	30
Constitutional concessions, effect of, to endow the Slave States with unequal political power,	9
effect of, to dethrone the Slave States and leave them prostrate,	9
prohibition, Congress proceeded to enforce, in 1807, against the importation of slaves,	12
Contest, bred of slavery,	10
for supremacy began when the leading men discovered that the equilibrium between the sections could not be preserved,	14
of blood occurred in Kansas,	25
Contestants, when a conflict arises that engages their thoughts they will appropriate either existing or new parties to their service,	9
Controversy, by the annexation of Texas the United States accepted, etc.,	16
over the exclusion of slavery from the Territories, effects of,	24

Cost of living in 1880 was not greater than in 1860, and the wages of the mill operatives were increased in that period by twenty per cent., . . . 80
Cotton, the export of, in 1800 was less than 90,000 bales, . 11
    the raising of, was experimental and unproductive, 11
    no domestic demand for American, in 1790, . 11
    eight bags of American, were seized in Liverpool in 1764, ... 11
    from America, neglected by English spinners in 1764, who doubted its value, . . . 11
    the culture of, was largely increased by the invention of the cotton-gin and press, . . . 11
    the cotton-gin stimulated the growth of, . . 17
    gin, enhanced the wages of labor, and added to the comfort of the laboring classes, . . . 17
    gin, stimulated the manufacture of cotton goods in the North and East, ... 17
    gin, the invention of, stimulated the importation of slaves, ... 11
    gin, stimulated the growth of cotton, . . 17
    gin, the invention of, inaugurated the slave-trade between the States of the Potomac and of the Gulf of Mexico, and added to their value, . . 11, 17
    invented by Eli Whitney of Westborough, Mass., 11
    press, invented by Jacob Marshall of Lunenburg, Mass., ... 11
Convention, Democratic, of 1864, ... 52
Conventions, Democratic State, ... 52
Country, the South subjected the political organizations of, to its will, by threats, etc., . . . 19
    the financial and commercial prosperity of, is put in jeopardy by the denial of the equality of men, 25
    was invited to the entertainment of civil war in Kansas, ... 25
    the Government of, was in the hands of the Democratic party during four of the six Presidential terms next preceding the inauguration of Mr. Lincoln, ... 95
    the annexation of Texas has inured to the benefit of, but the scheme was designed for the advantage of slavery, ... 95
    there is in, a body of men who advocate the issue of United States notes without a promise of payment in coin, ... 98, 99
    condition of, when Mr. Lincoln became President, 34
    when measures relating to human rights have been been adopted by, the Democratic party has constrained to give them, lately, approval, . . 96
    an experience of twenty years shows that our system of bank currency has never been excelled in this, or any other, ... 98

Country, not less than thirty million of the population of this, are dependent directly upon labor for means of subsistence, ... 81
Credit of the United States was impaired when the Republican party came to power in March, 1861, . 64
    the impairment of, was due to the position of the Democratic party, in reference to threats and doctrines of secession, . . . 65
Culture of cotton was largely increased by the invention of the cotton-gin and press, . . 11
Currency, that is constantly increasing in volume as compared with the increase of wealth, is a sure cause of business disaster, ... 99
    in regard to, nothing can be assured of the Democratic party, ... 99
    the power to decide the quantity and quality of, is an essential incident of sovereignty, . . 71
Customs, the gross receipts from, for the year ending June 30, 1861, were a trifle less than forty million dollars, ... 68
    the gross receipts from, for the year ending June 30, 1864, were more than one hundred and two million dollars, ... 68

Davis, Jefferson, if he were to become the President of the Confederacy, he must surrender his seat in the United States Senate, ... 29, 30
Debt, public, of the United States, ... 110
    public, guaranteed, ... 49
    was a trifle more than sixty-three million dollars at the close of the Mexican war, . . . 64
    June 30, 1860, was about two million more than it was June 30, 1849, . . . 64
    in 1860, was equal only to two dollars for each inhabitant, ... 64
    in 1791, was equal to about twenty dollars for each inhabitant, ... 64
    of the United States, in March, 1869, amounted to about two thousand six hundred million dollars, 71
    an act to authorize the refunding of the national, was approved July 14, 1870, . . . 72
    of the United States, in August, 1865, . . 72
    of the United States, June 30, 1883, . . 72
    more than three hundred and sixty million dollars of the interest-bearing, were paid during the first term of President Grant's administration, . 72
Delegates, probable that those to the Constitutional Convention from both South and North, expected the gradual extinction of slavery, . . 11
Democratic Convention of 1864, . . . 52
    Convention, platform of 1864, . . . 60

Democratic party, has always resisted, and often denounced, the measures upon which the Republican party may now rest its claim for continued confidence, 10
profited by slavery, and so resisted its overthrow, 10
now profits by intolerance and persecution, 10
now defends intolerance and persecution, 10
yielded itself to the defense of slavery, 13
subordinated its love for the Union to slavery, 13
advocated non-interference with slavery by the National Government, 13
advocated constitutional protection to slavery, 13
abandoned its principles, 13
remained passive in the North, etc., during the Rebellion, 13, 14
furnished shelter to Southern sympathizers in the North during the Rebellion, 13, 14
ceased to exist in the Rebel States upon the formation of the Confederacy, 13
was represented by Mr. Polk in the canvass of 1844, 15
achieved an easy victory in 1852, upon the declaration that the compromise measures of 1850 had secured peace, 19
of the South, the leaders of, were the leaders in nullification, 19
of the North was divided by the repeal of the Missouri compromise, 23
maintains the equality of States and denies the equality of men, 25
in power at Washington, gave its influence to making Kansas a Slave State, 25
the Government of the country was in the hands of, during four of the six Presidential terms next preceding the inauguration of Mr. Lincoln, 95
the leaders of, upon the death of General Harrison, controlled the administration of Mr. Tyler in a large degree, 95
from 1837 to 1861, there were only temporary interruptions in the domination of, 95
it is no credit to, that a scheme designed to foster slavery has been controlled for the advantage of freedom, 95
its doctrine of State rights has become odious to the people, 95, 96
in obedience to the doctrine of State rights, continued in a persistent defence of slavery, 96
the Southern half of, engaged in rebellion, 96
a portion of, in the North, either encouraged or tolerated the treasonable conduct of their Southern brethren, 96
a minority, not exceeding one-fourth of the entire organization, united with the Republican party during the Rebellion, 96

Democratic party, not exceeding one-fourth of, contributed their full share to the prosecution of the war and the destruction of slavery, . . . 96
if it is to be judged by its record from 1837 to 1861, there is no ground for belief that it would meet the demands of the present period, . . 96
when it lost power in 1860, its tariff policy and its financial ideas were alike distasteful to the people, 96
since 1860, has resisted all new measures, and more especially those relating to human rights, . 96
has been constrained to give measures relating to human rights tardy approval, after they have been adopted by the country, . . . 96
has been found each year giving assent to some measure which it had previously condemned, . 96
has uniformly resisted every new measure when it was proposed, ... 96
opposed Emancipation, but it has been compelled to accept and endorse it, ... 96
opposed each of the three Amendments to the Constitution, but it has been compelled to accept and endorse them, ... 96
opposed the homestead laws, the grants of lands to agricultural colleges, and the system of improving rivers and harbors, . . . 96
does not now avow its opposition to the homestead laws, the grants of lands to agricultural colleges, or to the system of improving rivers and harbors, ... 96
the opposition of, to the National Bank System, was due to its State rights notions, . . . 97
never admitted that a change of policy in regard to paper circulation was required, . . 97
always assumed that the war was unnecessary, and consequently that exigencies should not control the public policy, ... 97
opposed the system of bank currency at the outset, and has never exhibited friendship for it, there is no violence in assuming that it would willingly see it die, ... 98
either members of, or closely allied with, is the class of financiers who believe that the government can extemporize wealth, . . . 99
offers no assurance in regard to the currency, . 99
the policy of, in regard to the tariff is either uncertain or dangerous, ... 99
the history of from 1837 to 1860, would lead to the conclusion that it would favor free trade as a principle, ... 99
the history of from 1837 to 1860, would lead to the conclusion that it would favor a tariff for revenue only, as a wise application, etc., . . 99, 100

Democratic party, the history of, and its traditions, found expression in the platform of 1880, . . 100
the organization of, is hostile to the system of protection, ... 102
can make no claim to friendship for Civil Service Reform, ... 102
should the, attain power, it is reasonable to assume that the existing civil service law would either be repealed, or its purpose avoided, . 102, 103
the rule of has been perpetuated in South Carolina, Mississippi, and Louisiana, sometimes by force, and sometimes by fraud, . . . 103, 104
as a national organization, has accepted the results of force and fraud in Southern States, . 104
secured a majority in the United States Senate for a time, by means of usurpation in the South, . 104
has been able to command a majority in the House of Representatives during three Congresses, because of usurpation in the South, . . 104
by usurpation in the South has secured advantages such as it did not enjoy even in the days of slavery, ... 104
in the presence of this usurpation the votes of two Democrats in South Carolina, have as much weight in the government as do those of five citizens of New York, etc., . . . 105
the success of, would perpetuate the wrong in the South, for four years at least, . . . 105
being benefited by the usurpations in the South, there is no ground to anticipate any action by that party, etc., ... 105
not a safe custodian of power, . . . 111
danger from, ... 112
position of in 1864, ... 112
its reasons for supporting slavery, . . . 51
its policy in regard to the war and to slavery, . 39
votes of members of, on Proclamation of Emancipation, ... 41
alliance of, with slaveholders, . . . 52
the impairment of the public credit was due to the position of, in reference to the threats and doctrines of Secession, ... 65
Mr. Buchanan, as the representative of, transferred to Abraham Lincoln, March 4, 1861, a dissevered Union, ... 66
Mr. Buchanan, as the representative of, transferred to Abraham Lincoln, March 4, 1861, a government in form only, ... 66
Mr. Buchanan, as the representative of, transferred to Abraham Lincoln, March 4, 1861, a government whose treasury was empty, . . . 66

INDEX.

Democratic party, Mr. Buchanan, as the representative of, transferred to Abraham Lincoln, March 4, 1861, a government whose credit was broken, . . 66
    Mr. Buchanan, as the representative of, transferred to Abraham Lincoln, March 4, 1861, a government whose navy was dispersed, . . . 66
    Mr. Buchanan, as the representative of, transferred to Abraham Lincoln, March 4, 1861, a government whose army was weak in numbers, etc., . 66
    Mr. Buchanan, as the representative of, transferred to Abraham Lincoln, March 4, 1861, a government with an impending war, etc., . . 66
    was divided in 1860, ... 29
    as represented by Mr. Breckinridge, was a Secession party, ... 29
    the division of, decided the election in favor of Mr. Lincoln in 1860, ... 29
    had it supported Mr. Douglas in good faith in 1860, he would probably have been elected, . . 29
    by the aggressive acts of one wing of, and by the non-action of the representative of the whole, the Union ceased to exist, ... 31
    one wing of, said the Union had no right to exist, 31
    one wing of, said the Union had no right to maintain its existence by force, . . . 31
    the Union was dismembered and surrendered by, . 31
Democrats, in the House of Representatives, action of, in regard to the thirteenth amendment, . . 45
Department of Education, ... 90
Deposits in Savings Banks, the aggregate accumulation of, was immensely greater in 1880 than in 1860, . 80
Dictatorship, advice of McClellan to Mr. Lincoln in regard to, ... 53-54
Disabilities, under Fourteenth Amendment to the Constitution, ... 49
District of Columbia, no reference to slavery in or in the States, was made in the declaration of the Republican party of 1856, ... 23
    the Republican party was at first divided as to the abolition of slavery in, ... 23
    the bill for the abolition of the slave trade in, was carried under the lead of Mr. Clay, . . 18
Disunion, the election of Mr. Lincoln in 1860, was made the pretext for, ... 29
Dixon, Senator, from Kentucky, gave notice of an amendment to the Kansas and Nebraska bill abrogating the Missouri compromise, ... 20
Doctrine of obedience to the Constitution was taught, . 8
    the Republican party has identified itself with that of protection to domestic labor, . . . 102
Douglas, Stephen A., the champion of the repeal of the Missouri compromise, ... 20

INDEX.

Douglas, Stephen A., in the discussion in 1858, attempted in vain to prove that Mr. Lincoln was a disunionist, ... 26
    an experienced politician and a skillful debater, 27
    had, in 1858, taken a place amongst the able men of his time, ... 27
    Mr. Lincoln's mastery over, was complete, in the debate of 1858, ... 27
    received a million three hundred and seventy-five thousand of the popular, but only twelve electoral votes in 1860, ... 29
    had the Democratic party supported, in good faith in 1860, he would probably have been elected, . 29
    became the responsible author of the repeal of the Missouri Compromise, ... 20
Duties, there is a class of, that may be performed by the States, if the National Government does not assert its better right, ... 97
    customs were increased upon many articles of merchandise by an act approved March 2, 1861, 67
Duty of securing certain conceded rights rests upon the Republican party, ... 10
    to create a nation higher than to shun an evil, . 7

Education, department of, ... 90
    grants of public lands for, ... 83
    policy of Republican party in regard to, . . 88
Election of Mr. Lincoln in 1860, was made the pretext for disunion, ... 29
Elections of 1862, ... 38
    of 1864, ... 45
    if those in the old Slave States were free, and the returns honest, the republican party would command a large majority, etc., . . . 104, 105
    the records of Congress fully sustain the allegations as to the conduct of, in Louisiana, Mississippi, and South Carolina, ... 103
Electoral Colleges, at the close of every decennial period there was a new distribution of power in, . 14
    the equilibrium in, and in the House of Representatives had been destroyed, . . . 17
    the South gains more than thirty votes in, and an equal number of representatives in Congress, by the new basis of representation, . . . 104
Elements, four important, to which competition in manufactures relate, ... 101
Emancipation was opposed by the Democratic party, but it has been compelled to accept and endorse it, 96
    action of Republicans in regard to, . . . 41
    effect of the issue of proclamation of, . . 47
    justified, ... 40
    efforts of President Lincoln to secure, . . 42

INDEX   xvii

Emancipation, opposition of Democratic party to,   38
    proclamation of by Gen. Hunter,   42
    revocation of Gen. Hunter's proclamation of, 42
    views of President Lincoln,   43
    the great event of American history,   46
    the position of the Republican party as authors of, 46
    proclamation of,   38
Emigration, effects of upon Europe,   109
Encouragement, the tariff acts of 1816, 1828, and 1842, gave temporary, to manufacturing industries,   77
England, the farmers of, supply the laborers of Birmingham and Manchester,   76
Enrollment act of 1863, declared unconstitutional by the Supreme Court of Pennsylvania,   55
Equality of States, the government has been reconstructed upon this principle through the Republican party,   9
    of men, the government has been reconstructed upon this principle through the Republican party,   9
    of all men before the law, has been secured by the Republican party,   10
    of States and of representation in the Senate could not be changed, except, etc.,   14
    the old government recognized that of States, but disregarded that of men,   24
    the new government asserts that of men to be the only security for that of States,   24, 25
    of men is asserted by the Republican party as the only sure basis of the equality of States,   25
    of States is maintained by the Democratic party and that of men is denied,   25
    of States and of men is the sole surviving issue born of slavery,   25
    of States is destroyed by the denial of the right of men to vote,   25
    of rights in the South is the paramount question in this campaign,   106
Equilibrium of political power had been established in 1820,   13
    when the leading men discovered that it could not be preserved between the sections, the contest began,   14
    between the Free and Slave States was destroyed by the Constitution,   14
    of States was re-established by the admission of Michigan in 1837,   14, 15
    of representation had been destroyed, etc.,   15
    of power would be destroyed whether California were admitted as a Free or Slave State,   16
    in the House of Representatives and in the Electoral Colleges had been destroyed,   17
    the overthrow of between the Free and Slave States, was admitted in Mr. Calhoun's dying speech,   17

xviii   INDEX.

Europe, opinions of masses in, in regard to slavery, . 107
    ruling classes, views of, ... 107
    character of emigrants from, . . . 109
    migration from, effects of, ... 109
    public law of, in regard to expatriation, . . 92, 93, 94
Events, the formation of a new political party is always
    due to, ... 22
    rendered the formation of an anti-slavery party
    inevitable, ... 22
    neither men nor parties are the masters of, . 23
    were the masters of the leaders of the Revolution, 24
Exclusion of slavery from the territories was the leading
    issue in 1856, ... 24
Exigencies of the war compelled Congress to assume jurisdiction of the subject of paper circulation, . 97
Expatriation, ... 92, 93
    treaties in regard to, ... 93, 94
Expenses of the government for the year ending June 30,
    1862, ... 66
Export of cotton in 1800 was less than 90,000 bales, . 11

Farmers of England supply the laborers of Birmingham
    and Manchester, ... 76
    of the United States supply the laborers of Pittsburgh and Lowell, ... 77
Finance, a new system of, has been created by the Republican party, ... 25
    the new policy of, ... 25
Financial System, by whatever of peril it is menaced, is
    due to the fact of a solid South, . . . 106
Financiers, the class of who believe that the government
    can extemporize wealth, ... 99
Florida only remained of slave territory, . . . 15
Force, the legally constituted governments have in some
    instances been overthrown by, or abandoned
    through fear of, ... 103
    the government of Mississippi was seized by, in
    1875, ... 103
    Mr. Buchanan denied the right of the United
    States Government to prevent Secession by, . 31
    one wing of the Democratic party said that the
    Union had no right to maintain its existence by, 31
Forests, cultivation of, ... 85
Forfeiture was imposed by statute of March 2, 1807, upon
    vessels, etc., engaged in the foreign slave-trade, 12
Framers of the Constitution could not then adjust the differences between the South and North, . . 7
France, acquired Louisiana from Spain by treaty in 1763, . 14
    ceded Louisiana to the United States by treaty in
    1803, ... 14
Freedman's Bureau aid to schools, ... 90
Freedom, advanced by the struggles in Kansas, . . 9

INDEX. xix

Freedom, advanced by the Mexican war, . . . 9
    the advantage to, by the annexation of Texas, . 9
    the supporters of, and of slavery were invited to a contest of arms for the settlement of a question that should have been settled by Congress, . 20
    the civilization born of, would have triumphed in the end, ... 21
    and slavery, antagonism between had not taken form during the colonial period or in the years of confederation, ... 22
    and slavery, the inherent antagonism between, was organized and developed under the Constitution, 22
    and slavery, a struggle for the mastery between, went on for seventy years, . . . 22
    it is no credit to the Democratic party that a scheme has been controlled for the advantage of, 95
    all the territory outside of the thirteen States was dedicated to, when the Constitution was adopted, 27
Free persons, if basis of representation had been limited to, 9
Free trade and protection were not referred to in the Republican platform of 1856, ... 23
Fugitives from slavery, statutes in relation to, . . 35, 36
    right of trial by jury denied to, . . . 8
    slave laws, repeal of, ... 36

Georgia and South Carolina insisted upon their right to continue the foreign slave trade, . . . 12
Government, in its administration injustice still exists, . 10
    was organized by Texas, ... 15
    in Texas was composed largely of immigrants from the Slave States, ... 15
    Mr. Calhoun's essay on, ... 17
    was reconstructed by the Republican party upon the basis of equality of men and of States, . 24
    the new, asserts that the equality of men is the only security for the equality of States, . . 24, 25
    the question whether a particular power of, shall be exercised by the general, or left to the States, is for Congress, ... 97
    power to furnish a bank currency is now lodged with the general, ... 98
    under the defense offered for the suppression of votes, the minority may usurp the, . . 103
    ceases to be one of laws, and becomes one of men, 103
    of an usurping minority runs rapidly into despotic sway, ... 103
    that the majority vote shall be recognized and obeyed in, is a vital element in Republican institutions, ... 103
    of Mississippi seized by force in 1875, . . 103
    in a republic, usurpation of, . . . 104

Government, in the presence of usurpation, the votes of two Democrats in South Carolina have as much weight in, as do those of five citizens of New York, etc., ... 105
    never can the voters of the North enjoy an equality of power in, until elections are free in the States of the South, ... 105
    the South has enjoyed the fullest right of representation, but at the same time one-third of its inhabitants have been excluded from all part in, 105
    when those of States are seized by force and fraud, and an attempt is made upon that of the United States, the nation cannot remain indifferent, . 106
    it is not the duty of, to give employment to its citizens, ... 74
    the expenses of, for the year ending June 30, 1862, 66
    in 1861 and 1862, loans were made by, at the rate of a million dollars a day, and upon moderate terms, ... 67
    resides, under our system, in citizenship, . . 70, 71
    under the administration of by the Republican party, the Union has been restored, . . 72
    under the administration of by the Republican party, the debt has been paid, . . . 72, 73
    for the financial successes of, the country is indebted to the Republican party, . . . 73
    of the United States, the financial successes of are unexampled in the history of the world, . 73
    Mr. Buchanan denied the power of the, to prevent secession, by force, ... 30
Governments, the legally constituted, have, in some instances been overthrown, or abandoned through fear of force, ... 103
Grant, the sinking fund system was not put in operation until after the inauguration of, . . . 72
    during the first term of his administration, more than three hundred and sixty million dollars were applied to the payment of the interest-bearing debt, ... 72
Great Britain, claims in regard to citizenship, . . 93
Greatness of the Northwestern States was not foreseen, but their coming was anticipated, etc., . . 15
Guadalupe Hidalgo, by the treaty of, signed February 2, 1848, the United States acquired a vast territory of Mexico, ... 16
    the treaty of, caused California to be presented for admission as a Free State, . . . 17
Guarantees for slavery, effect of, to dethrone the Slave States and leave them prostrate, . . 9
    for slavery, effect of, to endow the Slave States with unequal political power, . . . 9
    when slavery demanded new ones, neither of the existing parties was prepared to resist, . . 9

INDEX. xxi

Habits of a people undergo great changes in a period of twenty years, ... 80
Hamilton, stated and argued the advantages of protection as well as it can now be stated, . . . 76
    was an advocate of the British Constitution, . 76
Harmony of the Republic disturbed, . . . 13
Harrison, unless his election be an exception, the South achieved a victory in every election from 1828 to 1856 inclusive, ... 15
    by the death of, in April, 1841, John Tyler succeeded to the Presidency, ... 15
    his death in 1841, made the annexation of Texas possible during his presidential term, . . 18
    upon the death of, the leaders of the Democratic party controlled the administration of Mr. Tyler in a large degree, ... 95
History of a political party furnishes better means for testing its quality, than can be deduced from its platforms or the professions of its leaders, . 95
    of the Democratic party from 1837 to 1860, would lead to the conclusion that it would favor free trade as a principle, ... 99, 100
    of the Democratic party, and its traditions, found expression in the platform of 1880, . . 100
    of the world furnishes no example for the financial successes of the government of the United States, 73
Holman, Wm. S., motion of, in regard to Thirteenth Amendment to Constitution, ... 45
Homestead bill, veto of, ... 84
    vote on, ... 84
    of 1860, ... 84
Hostilities, demand for cessation of in 1864, . . 60, 61
House of Representatives, representation of slave population in, ... 7
    at the close of every decennial period there was a new distribution of power in, . . . 14
    relative strength of South in, from 1810 to 1820, showed that it could not maintain its equality, . 14
    the equilibrium of, representation in, had been destroyed, ... 15
    the equilibrium in, and in the Electoral Colleges has been destroyed, ... 17
    the control of, was lost to the South, . . 17
    the Democratic members of, and of the Senate, opposed the adoption of the National Bank System with great unanimity, . . . 96
    the Democratic party has been able to command a majority in, ... 104
    state of parties in, in 1863, ... 38
    action of, on Emancipation, ... 41
Houses of Congress have both been captured, and the executive department has been put in peril, . 104
Hunter, General, proclamation of, in regard to slavery, . 42

INDEX.

Idleness, owners of slaves lived in,	8
Immigrants, from the Slave States largely composed the Government of Texas,	15
from Europe migrated to Free States,	17
Immigration, to the North, was encouraged because of the increased wages to laborers, brought about indirectly by the cotton gin,	17
Importation of slaves added to the political power of the South,	7, 8
of slaves was stimulated by the invention of the cotton gin,	11
Inauguration of President Lincoln,	33
Independence, Declaration of, its value,	46
Industries of the country, by whatever of peril they are menaced, is due to the fact of a solid South,	106
so long as we are the most prosperous of the nations, in our domestic, our doings upon the ocean will be insignificant as compared with our business upon land,	82
Inhabitants, the public debt in 1860, was equal only to two dollars for each,	64
the public debt in 1791, was equal to about twenty dollars for each,	64
of those in the United States in 1880, two million seven hundred thousand were employed in manufactures,	81
of those in the United States in 1880, more than thirteen million were employed in agriculture, trade, transportation, mechanics, manufactures, and mining,	81
the number of in the United States in 1880, of the age of ten years and upwards, was nearly thirty-seven million,	81
of a portion of Missouri applied for admission into the Union as a Slave State, in 1820,	14
Injustice, still exists in the administration of the government,	10
of slavery, the Democratic party has profited by,	10
Institutions, vital element of Republican, is the recognition of the right of every qualified citizen to vote, and have his vote counted,	103
a vital element in Republican, is in the proposition that the government as constituted by the majority vote, should be recognized and obeyed,	103
Interest, an average of between eleven and twelve per cent. was paid upon the loan authorized by the act of December 17, 1860,	65
Internal Revenue, the system was established by the Statute of July 1, 1862,	69
the receipts from for the year ending June 30, 1863,	69
the receipts from, for the year 1865,	69
the total collected under, up to June 30, 1883,	69

Intervention, foreign, danger from,	107
Intolerance, the Democratic party now profits by,	10
Invasion, the army of, Gen. Taylor finally became one of,	16
Invention, of the cotton gin stimulated the importation of slaves,	11
of the cotton gin added to the value of slaves in the tobacco and grain sections,	11
of the cotton gin inaugurated the slave trade between the States of the Potomac and of the Gulf of Mexico,	11
Inventions, two were made between 1788 and 1800, which increased the profits of cotton culture and the value of slave labor,	11
Inventors, if the results of the protection to were to be destroyed, the effect would be experienced by every family upon the continent,	75
Issue, of United States notes without a promise of payment in coin, advocated,	98, 99
of United States notes is the only financial measure of the war that has been assailed,	69, 70
Issues all are insignificant compared with the systematic suppression of the votes of half a million citizens,	103
Jackson, Gen., made successful resistance to nullification of the laws of the Union in 1832,	19
Jefferson and Washington were advocates of protection to domestic labor,	76
President, member of board of school trustees,	89
Johnson, Andrew, vote on homestead bill,	84
the administration of,	71
Jury, if an alleged fugitive from service had been tried by,	9
Justice, the cause of is subserved by the spirit of selfishness,	25
and peace alike demand the assertion of the doctrine of equality of rights in the States of the South,	106
Kansas, the struggles in, inured to the advantage of freedom,	9
bill for the organization of,	20
the administration of President Pierce and the country were involved in the horrors of civil war in,	20
the platform of the Republican party of 1856, demanded the admission of, as a Free State, and denounced the proceedings there,	23
became the theatre of civil war, upon the repeal of the Missouri compromise,	25
aid from the South to,	25
aid from the North to,	25
contests in,	25
ruffian raids were tolerated, if not encouraged in,	25

Kansas, towns were burned in, ... 25
    hostile legislatures assembled in, . . . 25
    antagonizing constitutional conventions met in, . 25
    vain appeals were made for the admission of as a State, ... 25
    the disorders in, strengthened the Republican party, 25
    the admission of, was postponed until January, 1861, ... 25
    settlers of, ... 88
    after the passage of the act for the organization of, all territory in the United States was open to slavery, ... 27

Labor of slaves, the value of, was largely increased by the invention of the cotton-gin and press, . . 11
    the United States had no skilled, in 1783, . . 74
    the Republican party has identified itself with the doctrine of protection to domestic, . . 25
    the nation cannot be an indifferent witness to the disturbance of, caused by the laborers going from the States of the South to those of the North, ... 106
    when the demand for, is checked, the demand for the products of, diminishes, . . . 81
    of the population of this country, not less than thirty million are dependent directly upon, for means of subsistence, ... 81
Laborer, the supplies consumed by, are largely obtained from the vicinity, ... 76
    the supplies consumed by, are, in the main, furnished by the agricultural population, . . 76
Laborers, the transfer of half a million of, from the mills to mining and agriculture, would prostrate our entire system of labor, ... 81
    competition of those in other countries, . . 76
    immigration of, to the North, was encouraged because of the increased wages, brought about indirectly by the cotton-gin, . . . 17
Land exhausted by slavery, ... 8
    because of the attractive opportunities for employment upon, the ocean was neglected, upon the return of peace, ... 82
Lands, public donation of, to agricultural colleges, . 88
    public, revenue from, ... 83
    bounties of, ... 85
    mineral, ... 85, 86
    grants to railways, ... 85
    preëmption of public, ... 85
    policy in regard to, ... 83
    grants of, ... 83
    ceded to the United States, ... 83
    slave-owners needed new, ... 8

Law, wealth, and theology had combined for the protection of slavery,	12
was enacted in Louisiana that negroes delivered under the statute of 1807 should be sold as slaves,	12
Laws, this ceases to be a government of, and becomes one of men, if the rule of the majority may be overturned whenever the minority is dissatisfied,	103
Leaders, of nullification, including Mr. Calhoun, were soon restored to public confidence,	19
Leaders of the South knew that when slavery was limited to existing territory it would begin to die,	24
Lee, General, purpose of Mr. Lincoln, when he crossed the Potomac,	
Legislation, prohibiting the exportation of slaves, etc., satisfied the North,	12
prohibiting the exportation of slaves, etc., promoted the interests of the South,	12
Liberty, love of, taught in the schools and churches,	8
Lincoln, during the four of the six Presidential terms next preceding the inauguration of, the government of the country was in the hands of the Democratic party,	95
as a measure of the administration of, the National Bank system was adopted,	96
position of, in regard to the Rebellion,	35
his nomination in 1860 was not accomplished without a severe contest,	28
the nomination of, in 1860, was made after several ballots,	28
received, in 1860, of the popular vote, one million eight hundred and sixty-six thousand,	29
received, in 1860, one hundred and eighty of the three hundred and three electoral votes,	29
was elected in 1860 because of the division in the Democratic party,	29
the election of, in 1860, was made the pretext for disunion,	29
to him more than to any one else, the Republican party is indebted for its character, its measures, and its success,	27
at every step, tested his acts by the fundamental law,	27
his mastery over Douglas was completed in the debate of 1858,	27
in the debate in 1858, claimed that the ordinance of 1787 made the institution of slavery local,	27
in the debate in 1858, characterized the repeal of the Missouri compromise a step towards making the Union all slave,	26
popular and electoral vote for, in 1860,	29
policy of, in reference to emancipation,	43
President, views of, in regard to Secession,	33

INDEX.

Lincoln, President, inauguration of, ... 32, 33
 the inaugural address of, in 1861, . . . 33
 President, character of, ... 48
 President, his place in history, . . . 47, 48
 attributes the Rebellion to slavery, . . . 43
 views of, in regard to emancipation, . . 43
 Abraham, election of 1864, ... 62
 General McClellan's letter to, of July 7, 1862, . 53
 condition of affairs when Mr. Buchanan transferred the government to, ... 66
 Abraham, was nominated for the United States Senate, in Illinois, June 17, 1858, . . 26
 Abraham, by his speech accepting the nomination for the Senate in 1858, inaugurated a discussion which has no equal in American politics, . 26
 Abraham, is the first personage in the history of the Republican party, ... 27, 28
 Abraham, is the second personage in the history of the Republic, ... 28
Liverpool, eight bags of American cotton was seized in, upon the ground that it could not have been raised in America, ... 11
Living, the cost of, in 1880 was not greater than in 1860, and the wages of the mill operatives were increased in that period 20 per cent., . . . 80
Loan, Congress refused to pledge the public lands as security for, in 1860, ... 65
 an average of between eleven and twelve per cent. interest was paid upon other, authorized by the act of December 17, 1860, . . . 65
 of twenty-five million dollars was authorized by an act approved February 8, 1861, . . 65, 66
 the passage of a law authorizing a new, was recommended by the Secretary of the Treasury in December, 1869, etc., ... 71
 authorized by act of June 22, 1860, . . . 65
 authorized by act of July 14, 1870, . . . 71, 72
Loans were made by the Government in 1861 and 1862, at the rate of a million dollars a day, and upon moderate terms, ... 67
"London Times," quotation from, ... 111
Louisiana enacted a law that negroes delivered under the statute of 1807 should be sold as slaves, . - 12
 and her associates would have made negroes found on slave-trading vessels slaves, . . . 13
 in the territory of, slavery existed, . . . 14
 it was claimed that in the territory of, included all the country west of the Mississippi, except a small region near the Gulf of Mexico, . . 14
 was acquired by France from Spain in 1763, . 14
 was ceded to the United States by France in 1803, 14
 Missouri was formed out of the territory of, . 14

INDEX. xxvii

Louisiana, all the territory of, was slave when purchased in 1803, ... 18
    and South Carolina were seized by representatives of the minority party in 1877, . . . 103
Love of political power was an inducement for the extension and defense of slavery, . . . 11, 12
Lowell, the farmers of the United States supply the laborers of, ... 76
Lunenburg, Mass., Jacob Marshall of, invented the cotton-press between 1788 and 1800, . . . 11
Lust for gain was an inducement for the extension and defense of slavery, ... 11, 12

Maine, the act for the admission of, was approved March 3, 1820, ... 14
Majority, when the thoughts of, is engaged upon a topic over which a conflict arises, the contestants will appropriate either existing or new parties to their service, ... 9
    if the rule of, may be overturned whenever the minority is dissatisfied, the government ceases to be one of laws and becomes one of men, . 103
    if the minority may dispossess, the process may go on until a single person becomes supreme, . 103
Manufactories of the United States, the operatives in, enjoy more of the comforts of life than in 1860, . 79
Manufacture of cotton goods North and East stimulated by the cotton-gin, ... 17
Manufactures, four important elements to which competition in, relate—(1) Interest on capital, (2) Wages of the operatives, (3) Perfection of machinery, (4) Skill of the operatives and mechanics, . 101
    nearly three thousand million dollars are embarked in, ... 102
    about two and three-quarter million operatives are employed in, at an annual aggregate of wages of nearly one thousand million dollars, . . 102
    at the close of the Revolutionary war, England, France, and Holland possessed all the skill, etc., 74
    the product of, aggregated not more than eight hundred and fifty-five million dollars in 1860, . 77
    employed 1,311,246 persons in 1860, . . 77
    the product of, aggregated $1,972,755,642 in 1880, 77
    employed 2,732,595 persons in 1880, . . 77
Manufacturing, the aggregate wages paid to persons employed in, in 1880, were one hundred and fifty per cent. greater than in 1860, and the increase in the number of hands was but one hundred and eight per cent., ... 77
Market, the Presidency was sold in, ... 15
Marshall, Jacob, of Lunenburg, in Worcester County, Mass., invented the cotton-press between 1788 and 1800, ... 11

INDEX.

Marshals, instructions to, in regard to valuation in 1860,	91
Mason, James M., of Virginia, read Mr. Calhoun's dying speech in the Senate, March 4, 1850,	17
Massachusetts, population of,	108, 109
property of, in 1860 and 1880,	92
McClellan, opinions of, in regard to enrollment act,	56, 57
head of the army,	53
letter of, to President Lincoln, July 7, 1862,	53
Measures, of which the Republican party may boast, have all been resisted and often denounced by the Democratic party,	10, 96
the five compromise of 1850, were carried under the lead of Mr. Clay,	18
of compromise of 1850, it was understood were opposed by General Taylor,	19
of compromise of 1850, the Fugitive Slave bill was the most offensive,	19
when those relating to human rights have been adopted by the country, the Democratic party has been constrained to give them tardy approval,	96
Men, the equality of all before the law has been secured by the Republican party,	10
the formation of a new political party is not due to the schemes of, but always to events,	22
upon the basis of the equality of, and of the equality of States, the government was reconstructed by the Republican party,	24
the new government asserts that the equality of, is the only security for the equality of States,	24, 25
the equality of, is denied by the Democratic party, and the equality of States maintained,	25
the equality of, is asserted by the Republican party as the only sure basis of the equality of States,	25
the question of the equality of, is the only surviving issue born of slavery,	25
probably more than one-half million of, are deprived of their right to vote in the Slave States, either by force of by fraud,	25
the denial of the equality of, destroys the equality of States,	25
the denial of the equality of, puts in jeopardy the financial and economical prosperity of the country,	25
and money were sent from the South into Kansas, to make it a Slave State,	25
and money were sent from the North into Kansas, to make it a Free State,	25
this government ceases to be one of laws and becomes one of, if the rule of the majority may be overturned whenever the minority is dissatisfied,	103

Men, the remedy against the systematized scheme to destroy the equality of, and the equality of the States, is with the Republican party, . . 106
Merchandise, duties were increased upon many articles of, by an act approved March 2, 1861, . . 67
Message of the President of December, 1860, justified Mr. Davis and his associates in assuming that he would not interfere, etc., ... 30
Mexican war inured to the advantage of freedom, . . 9
   at the close of, the public debt was a trifle more than sixty-three million dollars, . . . 64
Mexico, Texas declared its independence of, . 15
   claimed the territory between the Rio Grande and the Nueces, ... 16
   the war with, opened in May, 1846, . . 16
   the capture of the City of, by General Scott, ended the war, ... 16
   all the territory acquired of, was free, . . 18
   the vast territory from, has inured to the benefit of the country, but was designed for the advantage of slavery, ... 95
Michigan was admitted into the Union in 1837, . . 14, 15
Migration, incentives to, ... 86
   reasons for, ... 108
Mills, only three for cotton-spinning in America in 1800, . 11
Minority of the Democratic party not exceeding one-fourth of the entire organization, united with the Republican party during the Rebellion, . . 96
   the government of an usurping, runs rapidly into despotic sway, ... 103
   States have been held by, through fear and force, having been seized by usurpation, . . 104
   a solid South means the rule of, etc., . . 106
   the Republican party should stake everything upon the effort to redeem its supporters and allies in the South from the domination of, . . 106
   the rule of, must be destroyed, or the Republican idea will disappear in the South, or the downtrodden will rise in arms, etc., . . . 106
Mississippi, the government of, was seized by force in 1875, 103
   valley of, north of the Ohio and Missouri, taken possession of by the North, . . . 8
Missouri compromise, Senator Dixon of Kentucky gave notice of an amendment to the Kansas and Nebraska bill, abrogating the, ... 20
   Senator Douglas adopted the suggestion for the abrogation of, ... 20
   Mr. Douglas was the champion of the repeal of, . 20
   the repeal of, precipitated a contest of arms between the two forms of civilization, . . 21
   the words of repeal, ... 21
   the far-reaching results of the repeal of, . . 21

Missouri, upon the repeal of, the Democratic party of the North was divided, . . . 23
    after the repeal of, the Whig party as a national organization, ceased to exist, . . . 23
    upon the repeal of, Kansas became the theater of civil war, . . . 25
    Mr. Lincoln, in the debate of 1858, characterized the repeal of, as a step toward making the Union all slave, . . . 26
    a portion of the territory of, applied for admission into the Union as a Slave State in 1820, . 14
    was admitted as a Slave State by the act of March 6, 1820, ... 14
    the territory of, was formed out of that of Louisiana, ... 14
Money, the constitutional grant to Congress to borrow, includes the power to provide for the issue of notes, either with or without interest, . . 70
    the power to borrow, and to levy taxes is supreme, and essential to national existence, . 70
Monopoly of slave labor of the northern Slave States, Georgia and South Carolina insisted upon continuing in foreign slave-trade to check, etc., 12
Moralists, views of, upon the importation of slaves, . 12

Name, of the Republican party was only an incident, 22
Nation, to create a, a higher duty than to shun an evil, .
    cannot be an indifferent witness of the flights from their homes of thousands of citizens, etc., 106
    cannot be an indifferent witness to the disturbance of labor, caused by laborers going from the States of the South, to those of the North, . 106
    cannot remain indifferent, when by force and fraud, the governments of States are seized, and an attempt is made upon the government of the United States, ... 107
National Bank currency, the act establishing, approved February 25, 1863, . . . 69
National Banks, the act establishing it, its provisions, and the advantages derived therefrom, . . 69
National Government, duty of returning fugitives from service imposed upon it, . . . 8
    non-interference with slavery by, was the doctrine of the Democratic party, ... 13
Naturalization, ... 92, 93
Navy, scattered when the Republican party came to power in March, 1861, ... 64
Nebraska, near the close of the Thirty-Second Congress, a bill was introduced for the organization of the territory of, ... 19
Negro, in large portions of the South, his rights to vote denied, ... 24

INDEX. xxxi

Negroes, a class of moralists and theologians maintained that they were brought into civilization by the foreign slave trade, ... 12
    the statute of March 2, 1807, provided that those found on vessels in the slave trade should be delivered to the state authorities where such vessel was bought, ... 12
    delivered in Louisiana under the statute of 1807, sold as slaves, ... 12
    found on slave-trading vessels, would have been made slaves by Louisiana and her associates, . 13
    found on slave-trading vessels, would have been made free by New York and her associates, . 13
    rights of, during the war, ... 87
New Mexico, ceded to the United States by the treaty of Guadalupe Hidalgo, February 2, 1848, . 16
    a bill for the organization of the territory of, approved the same day as that for the admission of California, ... 18
    the portion of, north of parallel 36° 30′ was purchased of Texas for ten million dollars, . . 18
    the organization of the territory of, a concession to slavery, ... 18
    and Utah, by the death of President Taylor, were surrendered to the chances of slavery, . . 18, 19
    and Utah, bills for the territories of, an abandonment of the principles of the Missouri compromise, ... 20
    a part of, and all of Utah, north of the parallel 36° 30′, ... 18, 20
New York, and her associates, would have made negroes, found on slave-trading vessels, free, . 13
    and the presidency, Mr. Clay lost by his public surrender of the question of the annexation of Texas, ... 15
    statement of prices in leading articles in the market of, in 1860 and 1880, ... 80
Nomination of Mr. Lincoln in 1860, not accomplished without a severe contest, ... 28
Non-interference with slavery by the National Government, the doctrine of the Democratic party, . 13
North, the educated freemen of, were set off against the ignorant, non-voting slaves, . . . 8
    rich relatively, ... 8
    increase of population of, from 1790 to 1860, . 8
    the moral sentiment of, satisfied by the legislation prohibiting the exportation of slaves, etc., . 12
    the Democratic party of, furnished shelter to Southern sympathizers during the rebellion, . 13, 14
    vast waste in, out of which Iowa, Wisconsin, Minnesota, Oregon, Kansas, and Nebraska were formed, ... 15

North, the Whig party of the, opposed to the annexation
 of Texas, ... 15
  its excess of population due to superior civilization, ... 21
  its supremacy in commerce, in manufactures and
   in the industrial arts, due to its superior civilization, ... 21
  the Democratic party of, divided by the repeal of
   the Missouri compromise, . . . 23
  sent men and money into Kansas, to make it a free
   State, ... 25
  a portion of the Democratic party in, either encouraged or tolerated the treasonable conduct of their
   Southern brethren, ... 96
  never can the voters of, enjoy an equality of power
   in the government, until elections are free in the
   South, ... 105
Nullification, an attempt at, successfully resisted in 1832, 19
  the leaders of, restored to public confidence, . 19
  the means by which the slaveholders attempted
   to assert their power, ... 19
  the leaders in, the leaders of the Democratic party
   of the South, ... 19

Observation, the army of Gen. Taylor first termed one of, 16
Occupation, the army of Gen. Taylor termed one of, . 16
Ocean, business upon, more perilous, and returns more
   uncertain than upon land, . . . 81
  neglected upon the return of peace, . . 82
  our business upon, insignificant so long as we are
   prosperous in domestic industries, . 82
Ohio, State of, in 1860, presented Mr. Chase, . . 28
Operatives, about two and three-quarter million employed
   in manufactures, ... 102
  in the manufactories of the United States enjoy
   more of the comforts of life than in 1860, . 79
  a system which adds twenty per cent. to the wages
   of one class of, affects equally the wages of
   every other class, ... 80, 81
Opinions, Mr. Clay lacked the courage to declare his, or
   was wanting in principle, etc., . . . 15
  of Buchanan harmonized with the purposes of
   secessionists, ... 30
Ordinance of secession adopted by the State of South
   Carolina, 17th of December, 1860, . . 30
Overproduction, in foreign countries, effect of, protective
   duties upon, ... 101

Pacific Ocean, the project of a railway commended by
   Republican party of 1856, . . . 23
Parties, the Whig and Democratic, rival bidders for Southern support, ... 15
  how judged, ... 113

Party, the candidates of each usually dictated by the South,	15
the formation of a new,	22
events rendered the formation of an anti-slavery, inevitable,	22
history of a political, value of,	95
representatives of the minority, seized South Carolina and Louisiana in 1877,	103
in the United States most hostile to Great Britain, also the one most hostile to protection,	76
Peace and justice alike demanded the assertion of the doctrine of equality of rights in the States of the South,	106
upon the return of, ocean neglected,	82
Pendleton, Geo. H., nominated for Vice-President,	57
Pennsylvania, opinion of Supreme Court, in regard to Enrollment Act,	55
the votes of, in the convention of 1860, given for Gen. Cameron,	28
People, through the Republican party, destroyed slavery, reformed the Constitution, and reconstructed the government, etc.,	9
the Democratic doctrine of, has become odious to,	95, 96
when the Democratic party lost power in 1860, its tariff policy and its financial ideas were alike distasteful to,	96
Congress is composed of representatives of, and of the States,	97
the habits of, undergo great changes in a period of twenty years,	80
condition of, in 1860,	92
Persecution, the Democratic party now profits by, and defends,	10
Persons, number pecuniarily interested in slavery, increased,	7
Personage, Mr. Lincoln the first, in the history of the Republican party,	27, 28
second, in the history of the Republic,	28
Philadelphia, platform of 1856 at,	23, 24
Pierce, President, at the opening of the Thirty-third Congress, congratulated the country upon the settlement of the slavery controversy,	20
Platform, of the Republican party of 1856, condemned slavery and polygamy in the territories,	23
commended the project of a railway to the Pacific ocean,	23
commended the improvement of rivers and harbors,	23
silent on the questions of protection and free trade,	23
declared that slavery should be prohibited in all the territories, North and South,	23, 24
of the Republican party, in 1860, a contrast to that of 1856,	28

Policies of finance and protection to domestic labor can never be secure until the equality of men is recognized, ... 25
Policy of President Tyler, directed to the annexation of Texas, ... 15
    the Democratic party never admitted that a change of, was required in regard to paper circulation, 97
    of the Democratic party in regard to the tariff, . 99
Political Power, of the South augmented by the importation of slaves, ... 78
    slave owners, needed new States for, . . 8
    slavery would have been without, . . . 9
    the love of, an inducement for the extension and defense of slavery, ... 11, 12
    the establishment of an equilibrium of, and the tendency to overthrow, caused sectional struggles, ... 13
    an equilibrium of, established in 1820, . . 13
    the re-distribution of, required by the Constitution, 14
Polk, James K., represented the Democratic party in the canvass of 1844, ... 15
    an open advocate of the annexation of Texas, . 15
    his election treated as an endorsement of the scheme, 15, 16
Polygamy, and slavery, in the territories, condemned by the Republican party of 1856, . . 23
Population, dependent directly upon labor for means of subsistence, ... 81
    of the North, increase of, from 1790 to 1860, . 8
    the increase of, not controlled by statutes, . 14
    the larger part of, in California, north of the line 36° 30′, ... 16
    in California, sufficient for a State, . . 16
    excess of, in the North, due to its superior civilization, ... 21
    distribution of, in the United States, . . 108
    tendency of, to cities, ... 86
    increase of, ... 91
Power, at the close of every decennial period, a new distribution of, in the House of Representatives and in the Electoral Colleges, . . . 14, 16, 17
    the representative of, Slave to Free States, . 14
    to furnish a bank currency, lodged with general government, ... 98
    to decide the quantity and quality of currency an essential incident of sovereignty, . . 77
Powers, to borrow money and to levy taxes supreme, and essential to national existence, . . 70
Pre-emption laws, ... 85
President, and Vice-President, slave power in the election of, in 1819, ... 7
    negroes found on slave-traders, were to be delivered to, and returned to Africa by, . . . 12

President, asked for authority to borrow four hundred
    million dollars, at the extra session of Congress,
    which began July 4, 1861, ... 66
  the sinking fund system put in operation by, . 72
  the opinions of Buchanan, harmonized with the
    purposes of the Secessionists, . . . 30
  announced that the government had no power to
    interfere with Secession, ... 30
  every executive act would require the concurrence
    of both, ... 17
  Mr. Calhoun advocated having two, one from the
    North and one from the South, with equal
    powers, ... 17
Presidency, sold in the market, ... 15
  John Tyler succeeded to, upon the death of President Harrison, in April, 1841, . . . 15
  Mr. Clay lost, by making open surrender on the
    question of the annexation of Texas, . . 15
Presidential elections in 1876 and 1880 in peril, because of
    usurpation in the South, ... 104
Presidential election, it was always possible for the slaveholding class to decide, ... 15
Prodigal ways, owners of slaves indulged in, . . 8
Products of labor, the demand for diminishes, when the
    demand for labor itself is checked, . . 81
Profits of cotton culture and the value of slave labor
    increased by the invention of the cotton-gin and
    press, ... 11
Property, valuation of in 1880, ... 91, 92
  valuation of in 1860, ... 91
  Mr. Buchanan attempted to assert a right of, in the
    custom-houses and forts, ... 30
Protection of the Slave States from free negroes by the
    statute of 1807, ... 12
  and free-trade not referred to in the Republican
    platform of 1856, ... 23
  to domestic labor, the Republican party identified
    itself with the doctrine of, . . . 25
  to domestic labor and the new financial policy can
    never be secure until the equality of man is recognized, and enjoyed by the former slaves, . 25
  necessary to guard against over-production in foreign countries, ... 101
  a "revenue system with incidental" cannot be,
    practically, ... 101
  there may be a system of, that shall incidentally
    yield a revenue, ... 101
  the Republican party a unit, upon the question of, 102
  the organization of the Democratic party hostile to
    the system of, ... 102
  influence of our system upon Europe, . . 108
  position of the Democratic party in reference to, . 113

Protection, to domestic labor advocated by Washington and
      Jefferson, ... 76
    the advantages of, cannot be better stated than
      they were by Hamilton, ... 76
    under the system of, only one interest has lan-
      guished, the foreign carrying trade, . . 81
    and revenues upon a war basis, when secured, . 67, 68

Raids, by ruffians tolerated, if not encouraged, in Kansas, 25
Railway, to the Pacific Ocean, the projects for, was com-
      mended in the platform of the Republican party
      of 1856, ... 23
Railways, grants to, of lands, ... 83
Rebellion, organized, etc., ... 9
    the Southern half of the Democratic party en-
      gaged in, ... 96
    slavery, our chief peril in, ... 107
    war of, influence of, upon Europe, . . 109
    supported by slavery, ... 40
    war of, ... 59
    condition of the country, at the opening of, . 111
Receipts, from Internal Revenue, ... 69
Reconstruction, of Union, laws of, ... 63
    during the administration of President Johnson, 71
Remedy, no effectual, has yet been applied to the usurpa-
      tions in the South, ... 105
    is with the Republican party for the protection of
      citizens, against the systematized scheme to de-
      stroy the equality of men, and the equality of
      States, ... 106
Repeal of the Missouri compromise, Senator Douglas
      became the responsible author of, . . 20
    of the Missouri compromise precipitated the con-
      test of arms between the two forms of civiliza-
      tion, ... 21
    of the Missouri compromise, the words of, . 21
    of the Missouri compromise, the far-reaching
      results of, ... 21
    of the Missouri compromise divided the Demo-
      cratic party of the North, . . . 23
Representation, of slaves, under the Constitution, . . 78
    if basis of, had been limited to free persons, . 5
    the equilibrium of, in House of Representatives
      destroyed, ... 15
Representatives, of the minority party seized South Caro-
      lina and Louisiana, in 1877, . . . 103
    the South gains more than thirty in Congress, by
      emancipation, and an equal number in the elec-
      toral-colleges, ... 104
Republic, the harmony of, disturbed by the tendency to the
      overthrow of the equilibrium of political power, 13
    Mr. Lincoln the second personage in the history of, 28

Republic, in a, there can be no baser political crime than a usurpation by which millions of men are robbed of their rightful share in the government,	104
Republican ideas, dissemination of,	110
Republican Party, a necessity,	9
through it the people have destroyed slavery, reformed the Constitution and reconstructed the government, etc.,	9
its existence is still a necessity,	10
is alone authorized to speak for, or defend what has been accomplished,	10
the measures of which it may boast, and on which its claim for public confidence rests, have all been resisted and often denounced by the Democratic party,	10
accepted and continued the great struggle to abolish unjust features of the Constitution,	10
has made secure the equality of all men before the law,	10
upon it rests the obligation of securing practically certain conceded rights,	10
destined to destroy slavery, and preserve the Union,	13
the anti-slavery sentiment organized in,	13
the child of events,	22
the name of, an incident,	22
its principles and purposes the vital facts,	22
at first divided as to the abolition of slavery in the District of Columbia,	23
there was at first in, a general opposition to interference with slavery in the States where it existed,	23
in its declaration of 1856, no reference made to slavery in the States, in the District of Columbia, or to rendition of fugitives,	23
the platform of, in 1856, demanded the admission of Kansas as a free state, and denounced the proceedings there,	23
the platform of, in 1856, condemned slavery and polygamy in the territories,	23
commended the project of railway to the Pacific Ocean,	23
commended the improvement of rivers and harbors,	23
was silent upon the question of protection and free trade,	23
resisted secession, prosecuted the war, overthrew slavery, adopted the amendments to the Constitution, and reconstructed the government,	24
asserts the equality of men as the only sure basis of the equality of States,	25
created a new system of finance,	25
identified itself with the doctrine of protection to domestic labor,	25
strengthened by the disorders in Kansas,	25

Republican party, a minority of the Democratic party, not
    exceeding one-fourth of the entire organization,
    united with, during the Rebellion, . . 96
  pledged to the system of redemption of all paper
    money in coin, ... 99
  a unit, substantially, upon the question of pro-
    tection, ... 102
  a very general opinion, that there shall be a full
    and fair trial of the system of civil service reform, 102
  would command a large majority, etc., if the elec-
    tions in the old Slave States were free, and the
    returns were honest, ... 104, 105
  the remedy is with, for the protection of citizens
    against the systematized scheme to destroy the
    equality of man and the equality of States, . 106
  should stake everything upon the effort to redeem
    its supporters and allies in the South from the
    domination of a minority, . . . 106
  character of, ... 111
  its merits in preserving the union, . . . 111
  responsible for amendments to the constitution, . 50
  its position as an historical party, . . . 46
  final policy of, in regard to slavery, . . 40
  early declarations of, in regard to slavery, . . 38
  policy of, in reconstruction, . . . 63
  a party of principle, ... 58
  policy of, ... 92
  when it came into power, in March, 1861, condition
    of the country, ... 64
  the financial policy of, first dictated by the exi-
    gencies of war, but afterwards adapted to the
    conditions of peace, ... 67
  acquired the control of Congress, upon secession
    of States, ... 67
  under the administration of the government by,
    the Union has been restored, . . . 72
  under the administration of the government by,
    the debt has been paid so rapidly that the four
    per cent. bonds have been sold at twenty-five per
    cent. above their par value, . . . 72, 73
  the country is indebted to the, for financial suc-
    cesses of the government, ... 73
  Mr. Lincoln aided in the organization of, . . 27
  indebted to Mr. Lincoln, ... 27
  Mr. Lincoln the first personage of its history, . 27, 28
  Mr. Seward recognized as the leader of, in 1860, 28
  by September, 1860, was not merely united, but
    firmly compacted, and sustained by its principles, 28
  rendered enthusiastic by the certainty of success, 28
  the platform of, in 1860, in many particulars
    a contrast to that of 1856, . . . 28
  the Union re-established by, . . . 81
  met the enemy at the point of attack in 1856, . 23

Republicans, opposition of, to emancipation,	38
Resignation of Senators and Representatives,	67
Resistance to the admission of California based upon the ground that her people formed a Constitution without the authority of Congress,	18
Resolution of March 1, 1845, extended the Missouri compromise line across Texas,	16
Resources, natural, how made valuable,	110
Revenue from public lands,	83
there may be a system of protection that shall incidentally yield,	101
Revenues, upon a war basis, and protection were secured by the acts of March 2, 1861, August 5, 1861, July 14, 1862, and June 30, 1864,	67, 68
Revolution, events were the masters of the leaders of,	24
Revolutionary War, at the close of, England, France, and Holland, possessed all the skill in manufactures, etc.,	74
at the close of, the United States had neither capital nor skilled labor,	74
Rhode Island, population of,	108
Right to continue the foreign slave-trade insisted upon by Georgia and South Carolina, etc.,	12
Rights, if there were no remedy for the gross violation of, the re-establishment of the Union could be regarded only as a mistake,	105
Rio Grande, named by Texas as its Southern boundary,	16
Gen. Taylor ordered to the left bank of,	16
Rule of the Democratic party has been perpetuated in South Carolina, Mississippi, and Louisiana, sometimes by force and sometimes by fraud,	103, 104
of the minority must be destroyed or the Republican idea will disappear in the South, or the downtrodden will rise in arms, etc.,	106
Savings Banks, the aggregate accumulation of deposits in, greater in 1880 than 1860,	80
Scheme, Mr. Calhoun's, for two Presidents designed, manifestly, to effect a dissolution of the Union,	17
Schools, influence of free,	88
established by Freedman's Bureau,	90
in the city of Washington,	89
Scriptures, a class of theologians maintained that slavery was not forbidden in,	12
Secession threatened in Mr. Calhoun's dying speech, unless equality of political power should be given to the South,	17
resisted by the Republican party,	24
promoted by opinions of Mr. Buchanan,	32
to the position of the Democratic party in reference to the threats and doctrines of, was due the impairment of the public credit,	65

Secession of States and the resignation of Senators and Representatives, left Congress in the control of the Republican party, ... 67
    Mr. Buchanan denied the right of, as a constitutional right, ... 30
    Mr. Buchanan denied the right of the United States Government to prevent, by force, . 30
    the ordinance of, adopted by South Carolina the 17th of December, 1860, . . 30
Secessionists, the opinions of the President harmonized with the purposes of, . . . 30
Secretary of the Treasury was only able to borrow seven million dollars in September, 1860, . . 65
    of the Treasury, in December, 1869, recommended the passage of a law authorizing a new loan, etc., 71
Selfishness, the spirit of, subservient to the cause of justice, 25
Senate, the equality of States and of representation in, could not be changed, except, etc., . . . 14
    the attempt to preserve the equality of the Slave States in, intensified the struggle, 15
    the Democratic members of, and of the House of Representatives, opposed the adoption of the National Bank System with great unanimity, . 96
    of the United States controlled by the Democratic party for a time, because of usurpation in the South, ... 104
Sentiment of anti-slavery organized in the Republican party, 13
Sentiments, bred of slavery, must disappear before the contest will end, ... 10
Seward, William H., the recognized leader of the Republican party in 1860, ... 28
Seymour, Governor, error of, ... 58
    President of Democratic Convention at Chicago, 1864, ... 58
    speech of, at Chicago, 1864, ... 58
Sinking Fund, the act providing for, also for the issue of six per cent. bonds, and for the issue of United States notes, was approved February 25, 1862, . 68
    the system was not put in operation until after the inauguration of President Grant, . . 72
Slave-holders, alliance of, with Democratic party, . . 52
Slave-owners, needed new lands, ... 8
Slave power, subordination of, to Democratic party, . 39
    its rule in politics, ... 39
Slave States, productive power of, in 1860 and 1880, . 92
    the attempt to preserve the equality of, in the Senate, intensified the struggle, . . . 15
Slave-trade, Free and Slave States did not antagonize each other upon the suppression of the foreign, . 12
    if Constitution had abolished instantly, . . 9
    penalties imposed upon vessels, etc., engaged in the foreign, by statute of March 2, 1807, . 12

INDEX. xli

Slavery, three provisions of the Constitution relating to, conflicted with the principles of the founders of the Northern States, ... 7
    the advocates of, achieved a victory in the framing of the Constitution, ... 7
    extended to new territories, and the number of persons pecuniarily interested largely increased, . 7
    land exhausted by, ... 8
    tendency to consume, under a system of, . . 8
    hatred of, taught in schools and churches, . . 8
    would have continued for years and perhaps generations in the South if, etc., . . . 9
    would have been without political power, . . 9
    would have been abolished by the individual action of States, ... 9
    the guarantees derived from the Constitution were all temporary, etc., ... 9
    provisions in the Constitution concerning, made a conflict inevitable, ... 9
    when it demanded new guarantees, neither of the existing parties was prepared to resist, . . 9
    has been destroyed by the people through the Republican party, ... 9
    the Democratic party has profited by the injustice of, ... 10
    the overthrow of, was resisted by the Democratic party, ... 10
    unjust to assume that the framers of the Constitution foresaw the evils to come from, . . 11
    the gradual destruction of, expected by the delegates from both South and North, . . 11
    the extension and defense of, induced by lust for gain and love of political power, . . . 11, 12
    imbedded in the Constitution, . . . 12
    protected by moral, theological, and financial defenses, ... 12
    protected by law, wealth, and theology combined, 12
    prohibiting the foreign trade in, the only action by the government which could or did affect the institution, ... 13
    the Democratic party yielded itself to the defense of, and subordinated its love of the Union to, . 13
    neither opposed nor defended by the Whig party, 13
    the destruction of, destined to be accomplished by the Republican party, ... 13
    existed in the Territory of Louisiana, . . 14
    prohibited in that part of the original territory of Louisiana north of parallel 36° 30′, by the act of March 6, 1820, except in the State of Missouri, 14
    Mr. Polk and Mr. Clay were both in the interest of, 15
    States formed south of 36° 30′, might be admitted either with or without, ... 16

Slavery, prohibited in States formed north of 36° 30′,   16
    gained fresh concessions by the acquisition of the vast Territory of Texas,   16
    contributed to the overthrow of its own power,   17
    wherever it existed manual labor dishonored,   17
    the exclusion of, the real reason for the resistance offered to the admission of California,   18
    the bill for the admission of California silent upon the subject,   18
    the statutes organizing the territories of Utah and New Mexico permitted them to be admitted into the Union with or without, as their Constitutions might prescribe,   18
    the bill for the surrender of fugitives from, carried under the lead of Mr. Clay,   18
    the organization of Utah and New Mexico a concession to,   18
    except for, the admission of California would have been considered separately,   18
    the Democratic party declared, in 1852, that peace upon the subject of, had been secured by the compromise measures of 1850,   19
    the power of, compelled President Pierce to violate his pledge,   20
    the supporters of, and of freedom, invited to a contest of arms,   20
    and freedom, antagonism between,   22
    and freedom, a struggle for the mastery between, went on for seventy years,   22
    triumphed in the early contest, allied with the Democratic party,   22
    the Republican party at first divided as to the abolition of, in the District of Columbia,   23
    no reference to, in the States or in the District of Columbia, is made in the declaration of the Republican party in 1856,   23
    and polygamy in the Territories condemned by the platform of the Republican party in 1856,   23
    the South asserted its right to establish, in all the Territories of the Union,   23
    the exclusion of, from the Territories, was the leading issue in 1856,   24
    the controversy over the exclusion of, from the Territories, led to secession, war, the abolition of slavery, the constitutional amendments, and the reconstruction of the government,   24
    overthrown by the Republican party,   24
    the sole surviving issue born of, is that of the equality of men and of States,   25
    the annexation of Texas, the consequent war with Mexico, and the vast acquisitions of territory, formed a scheme designed for the advantage of,   95

INDEX.

Slavery, it is no credit to the Democratic party that a scheme designed to foster the institution of, has been controlled for the advantage of freedom, . . 95
    defense of, by the Democratic party, . . 96
    not exceeding one-fourth of the Democratic party contributed to the destruction of, . . 96
    abolition of, in West Indies, . . . 107
    United States humiliated by, . . . 107
    our peril from, in the Rebellion, . . . 107
    defenders of, ... 107
    questions growing out of, ... 34
    influence of, statute of July, 1862, on, . . 34
    effect of abolition of, on representation, . . 48
    the source of inequality of political power, . 46
    its influence on parties in the North, . . 46
    the effect upon parties of overthrow of, . . 39
    the cause of the war, ... 43
    aid to States for the abolition of, . . . 42
    final abolition of, ... 46
    Mr. Lincoln claimed that the ordinance of 1787 made the institution of, local, . . . 27
    after the passage of the act for the organization of Kansas, all territory in the United States was open to, ... 27
Slaves, the number of, augmented by the foreign slave-trade, ... 7
    of the South were set off against the freemen of the North, ... 8
    the importation of, stimulated by the invention of the cotton-gin, ... 11
    the value of, increased in the tobacco and grain sections by the invention of the cotton-gin, . 11
    Congress passed a penal statute in 1794 against the exportation of, ... 12
    and against their transportation between foreign countries, in American vessels, . . 12
    the importation of, insisted upon by Georgia and South Carolina to check monopoly, etc., . 12
    the importation of, prohibited by Congress March 2, 1807, ...
    emancipated, not citizens, ... 48
    agency of in supporting the Rebellion, . . 40
    the value of, had been increased by the cotton-gin, 17
Solid South, by whatever of peril the civil service, the financial system, or the industries of the country are menaced, is due to the fact of, . . 106
    means the rule of the minority, etc., . . 106
South, poor, ... 8
    government of the country by, . . . 8
    the pecuniary interests of, were promoted by the legislation prohibiting the exportation of slaves, 12

South, hoped that slave States could be formed from the territory south of 36° 30' in set-off to the Free States that might be formed north of that line, . 14
    achieved a victory in every presidential election from 1828 to 1856, inclusive, unless that of Harrison be an exception, ... 15
    usually dictated the candidates of each party, . 15
    ruled by the slave-holding class, - . . 15
    received a fresh opportunity by the admission of Texas, but fraught with peril, - . . 16
    the representative power of, broken down, . 17
    control of the House of Representatives, lost to, 17
    Mr. Calhoun, in his dying speech, threatened secession unless equality of political power should be given to, ... 17
    the demands of, always accompanied by threats of dissolution, ... 19
    subjected political organizations to its will, . 19
    asserted its right to establish slavery in all the territories, ... 23
    in large portions of, the right of the negro to vote is practically denied, . . . 24
    sent men and money into Kansas, . . 25
    the Democratic leaders of, dictated the annexation of Texas, ... 85
    the systematic suppression of votes in the States of, 103
    gains more than thirty representatives in Congress by the present basis of representation, and an equal number n the electoral colleges, . . 104
    by usurpations in, the negro race and many white persons are deprived of the privileges and immunities to which they are entitled, etc., . . 104
    never, until elections are free in the States of, can the voters of the North enjoy an equality of power in the government, . . . 105
    has enjoyed the fullest right of representation, but at the same time one-third of its inhabitants have been excluded from all part in the government, ... 105
    effects of a free vote and an honest count in the States of, ... 106
    the Republican party should take everything upon the effort to redeem its supporters and allies in, from the domination of a minority, . . 106
    effects of emancipation upon the, . . . 47, 48
    elections in, ... 52
    condition of, in 1864, ... 62
    Mr. Breckinridge the Democratic candidate of, in 1860, ... 29
    peace and justice alike demand the assertion of the doctrine of equality of rights in the States of, . 106

South, no effectual remedy has yet been applied to the usurpations in,	105
South Carolina insisted upon the right to continue the foreign slave trade,	12
seized by representatives of the minority in 1877,	103
the State of, adopted the ordinance of secession,	30
Sovereignty, the power to decide the quantity and quality of currency, is an essential incident of,	71
Speech, of Mr. Lincoln accepting the nomination for the Senate in 1858, inaugurated a discussion that has no equal in American politics,	26
State, once a State, always a State,	40
upon Mr. Buchanan's theory it was competent for the smallest, to declare the Union at an end,	80
State rights, to its notions of, was due the opposition of the Democratic party to the National Bank System,	97
the Democratic doctrine of, has become odious to the people,	95, 96
in obedience to the doctrine of, the Democratic party continued in the persistent defense of slavery,	96
States, slave-owners needed men, for political power,	8
citizens of, are citizens of the United States,	97
slavery would have been abolished by the individual action of,	9
free and slave, did not antagonize each other upon the suppression of the foreign slave trade,	12
compromise between, on the slave trade,	12, 13
of the original thirteen, seven had become free and six were slave in 1820,	13
eleven were free and eleven slave, in 1820,	13
representation in the Senate of, could not be changed except by the admission of new ones, etc.,	16
the representative power of slave to free, was, in 1820, as 88 to 100,	14
the representative power of slave to free was, in 1810, as 92 to 100,	14
the representative power of slave to free was, in 1800, as 85 to 100,	14
the representative power of slave to free was, in 1790, as 87 to 100,	14
the equilibrium between the free and slave,	14, 15
the greatness of the future of, was not foreseen, etc.,	15
apparent that the equality of, could not be maintained, etc.,	15
Congress guaranteed that not more than five might be formed out of the territory of Texas,	16
formed south of 36° 30′ might be admitted either slave or free, as their people might desire,	16
formed north of 30° 30′, slavery was prohibited in,	16
the annexation of Texas made an open way for new slave States,	16

States, to be formed from the territory of Texas were to be set-off against those to come from the north-west, ... 16
 at the close of the Mexican War the Union was composed of fifteen slave and fifteen free, . 16
 the census of 1850 showed the relative representative power of slave and free, as 63 to 100, . 16, 17
 the overthrow of equilibrium between the free and slave, admitted in Mr. Calhoun's dying speech, . 17
 Mr. Calhoun's plan for re-establishing the equilibrium, ... 17
 no reference to slavery in, in the declarations of the Republican party of 1856, . . . 23
 upon the basis of the equality of, and of the equality of men, the Government was reconstructed by the Republican party, . . 24
 the old Government recognized the equality of, and disregarded the equality of men, . . 24
 the new Government asserts that the equality of, can only be secured through the equality of men, 24, 25
 the question of the equality of, and of men, is the only surviving issue born of slavery, . . 25
 in the old slave, men are deprived of their right to vote, either by force or by fraud. . . 25
 the equality of, is destroyed by the denial of the right of men to vote, ... 22
 there is a class of duties that may be performed by, if the National Government does not assert its better right, ... 97
 until 1863, the furnishing of a circulation of paper was left to, ... 97
 within the limits prescribed by the Constitution, the question whether a particular power shall be left to, or exercised by the General Government, is for Congress, ... 97
 Congress composed of representatives of, and of the people, ... 97
 have been seized by usurpation, and held by a minority, through fear and force, . . 104
 never until elections are free in those of the South, can the voters of the North enjoy an equality of power in the Government, . . . 105
 seizure of governments of, ... 106
 the remedy against the systematized scheme to destroy the equality of, and the equality of men, . 106
 effects of a free vote in, ... 106
 the secession of, ... 67
 a direct tax upon, ... 69
 all the territory outside the thirteen original, was dedicated to freedom when the Constitution was adopted, ... 27

INDEX. xlvii

States, equality of,	63
eleven voted for Mr. Breckinridge in 1860,	29
Statesmen of the South had as a policy the annexation of Texas,	15
Stephens, A. H., views of in 1862,	112
Sumter, Fort, attacked,	34
Supplies consumed by the laborer and his family are largely obtained in the vicinity,	76
consumed by the laborer, are, in the main, furnished by the agricultural population,	76
Supremacy, the contest for began when the leading men discovered that the equilibrium between the sections could not be preserved,	16
in commerce, in manufactures, and in the inventive arts was due to the superior civilization of the North,	21
Supreme Court has sustained the authority of Congress to provide for the issue of United States notes, and to make them a legal tender.	70
Tariff, the policy of the Democratic party in regard to, either uncertain or dangerous,	89
bill, the purposes of the authors of are more important to understand than are the effects of the measure itself,	100
Tax, a direct, upon the State, was provided for by the statute of July 1, 1862,	69
Taxes, the power to levy, and to borrow money is supreme, and essential to national existence,	70
Taylor, Gen., ordered to the left bank of the Rio Grande,	16
opposed to the compromise measures of 1850,	19
the death of, in 1850, made it possible to secure Utah and New Mexico to the chances of slavery,	18, 19
Texas, the annexation of inured to the advantage of freedom,	9
the State of, declared its independence of Mexico,	15
called the "Lone Star State,"	15
the annexation of, the policy of President Tyler,	15
Mr. Polk an open advocate of the annexation of,	15
the annexation of, opposed by the Whig party of the North,	15
Congress provided for the annexation of, by joint resolution approved March 1, 1845,	16
the resolution of Congress guaranteed that not more than five States might be formed out of the territory of,	16
the annexation of, an open way for new Slave States,	16
the admission of gave the South a fresh opportunity, but one fraught with peril,	16
named the Rio Grande as its Southern boundary,	16

Texas, by the annexation of, the United States accepted the existing controversy and war, . . 16
    the resolution of March 1, 1845, extended the Missouri compromise line across, . . . 16
    the annexation of, and consequent war with Mexico, caused California to be presented for admission as a Free State, ... 17
    was paid ten million dollars for the portion of New Mexico North of 36° 30′, . . 18
    all advantage gained by the extension of the Missouri compromise line across, was abandoned, . 18
    the annexation of, in 1845, dictated by the Democratic leaders of the South, . . 95
    the annexation of, made possible during that presidential term, by the death of Harrison, . 18
    capacity of, to support inhabitants, . . . 108
Theologians, a class of, maintained that bringing negroes to this country transferred them into civilization, 12
    a class of, maintained that slavery was not forbidden in the Scriptures, ... 12
Thirteenth Amendment to Constitution, effect of, . . 108
Towns burned in Kansas, ... 25
Trade, no foreign in American cotton in 1790, . . 11
    in slaves inaugurated between the States of the Potomac, and of the Gulf of Mexico by the invention of the cotton gin, . . . 11
    Virginia and the other border States willing to prohibit the foreign in slaves at the earliest day, ... 13
Traditions, bred of slavery must disappear before the contest will end, ... 10
    of the Democratic party and its history, found expression in the platform of 1880, . . . 100
Treasury of the United States was empty when the Republican party came to power in March, 1861, . 64
    amount in, was inadequate for the safe management of a first-class bank, . . . 65
Treaty, France ceded Louisiana to the United States by, in 1803, ... 14
    of Guadalupe Hidalgo signed February 2, 1848, 16
    of Guadalupe Hidalgo, the result of the annexation of Texas, and consequent war with Mexico, caused California to be presented for admission as a Free State, ... 17
Trial by jury, denied to alleged fugitives, . . 8
Tyler, John, was allied to the slave-holding class, . . 15
    succeeded to the presidency upon the death of President Harrison in April, 1841, . . 15

Union, the more perfect, being a necessity, the friends of the Constitution could not adjust the differences between the South and North, . . . 7

INDEX. xlix

Union, of the nine States admitted into, previous to 1820,
  five were slave and four free, . . . 13
 the Democratic party subordinated its love of, to
  slavery, ... 13
 the preservation of, was destined to be accomplished
  by the Republican party, . . . 13
 Maine applied for admission to, in 1820, . . 14
 Arkansas was admitted into, in 1836, . . 14
 Michigan was admitted into, in 1837, . . 14, 15
 at the close of the Mexican War, composed of
  fifteen Slave and fifteen Free States, . . 16
 Mr. Calhoun, by his scheme for two Presidents,
  manifestly designed to effect a dissolution of, . 17
 resistance to the admission of California into, . 18
 the statutes organizing the Territories of Utah and
  New Mexico permitted them to be admitted into,
  with or without slavery, as their Constitutions
  might prescribe, ... 18
 threats of dissolution of, ... 19
 nullification of the laws of, successfully resisted
  in 1832, ... 19
 the South asserted its right to establish slavery in
  all the territories of, . . . 23
 vain appeals for the admission of Kansas into, . 25
 bank currency equally valuable in every part of, 98
 the reëstablishment of, could be regarded only as a
  mistake, if there were no remedy for the gross
  violation of personal and public rights, . . 105
 the reëstablishment of, a necessity, . . 105
 preserved by the Republican party, . . 111
 its restoration and preservation, . . . 105
 old, failure of, ... 40
 restoration of old, ... 40
 as it was, ... 40
 restoration of, on pro-slavery basis impossible, . 63
 restored by the Republican party, . . 31, 72
 ceased to exist on the 17th of December, 1860, by
  the admission of Mr. Buchanan, . . 30
 ceased to exist by the aggressive acts of one wing
  of the Democratic party, and by the non-action
  of the representatives of the whole party, . 31
United States, France ceded Louisiana to, by treaty, in 1803, 14
 annexation of Texas to, ... 16
 citizens of the States are citizens of, . . 97
 when the governments of States are seized by force
  and fraud, the nation can not remain indifferent, 106
 humiliation of, in days of slavery, . . 107
 influence of, in affairs of the world, . . 107
 capacity of, to support inhabitants, . . 108
 military power of, ... 109
 fortunate condition of, (London "Times,") . 111
 influence of example of, in China and Japan, . 110

INDEX.

United States, financial ability of, ... 110
    had neither capital nor skilled labor, at the close
        of the Revolution War, ... 74
    the farmers of, supply the laborers of Lowell and
        Pitsburgh, ... 76
    the political party in, most hostile to Great Britain,
        was also the one most hostile to protection, . 76
    the operatives in the manufactories of, enjoy more
        of the comforts of life than in 1860, . . 79
    the number of inhabitants in, in 1880, of the age
        of ten years and upwards, . . . 81
    of the inhabitants of, in 1880, number employed
        in agriculture, trade, transportation, mechanics,
        manufactures, and mining, . . . 81
    of the inhabitants of, in 1880, number employed
        in manufactures, ... 81
    policy in regard to expatriation, . . . 93
    valuation in, ... 92
    notes of, ... 68
    the public debt of, in March, 1869, . . 71
    the bonds of, in March, 1869, sold at eighty-three
        cents on the dollar, in gold, . . . 71
    the debt of, in August, 1865, . . . 72
    the debt of, June 30, 1883, ... 72
    the financial success of, the government of, is
        unexampled in the history of the world, . 73
    after the passage of the act for the organization of
        Kansas, all the territory in, was open to slavery, 27
    acquired a vast territory from Mexico by the treaty
        of Gaudalope Hidalgo, ... 16
United States Notes, the issue of, the only financial
    measure of the war that has been assailed, . 69, 70
    the Supreme Court has sustained the authority of
        Congress to provide for the issue of, and to make
        them a legal tender, ... 70
    the act of February 25, 1862, does not permit the
        issue of, except upon a pledge of redemption in
        coin, ... 70
    in 1862, constituted the only means by which the
        army was to be paid and kept in the field, . 70
Upper California, was ceded to the United States by the
    treaty of Gaudalope Hidalgo, . . . 16
Usurpation, anything in the nature of, is impossible with
    Congress, ... 97
    States have been seized by, and held by a minority,
        through fear and force, ... 104
    in the presence of, the votes of two Democrats in
        South Carolina have as much weight in the gov-
        ernment as do those of five citizens of New
        York, ... 105
Utah, the bill for the organization of the territory of,
    approved the same day as that for the admission
    of California, ... 18

INDEX. li

Utah, the whole of the territory of, north of the parallel
36° 30', ... 18
    the organization of the territory of, a concession
to slavery, ... 18
Utah and New Mexico, by the death of President Taylor,
in 1850, were opened to the chances of slavery, 18, 19
    it was claimed that the bills for the organization of
the territories of, were an abandonment of the
principles of the Missouri compromise, . . 20

Valuation of property in 1860, ... 91
Vessels, in the slave-trade, negroes found on after 1819
to be delivered to the President for return to
Africa, ... 12
Victory of the slave power in framing the Constitution was
temporary, ... 7
    was achieved by the South in every presidential
election from 1828 to 1856 inclusive, unless that
of Harrison be excepted, ... 15
    of slavery in every contest was due to its alliance
with one or both of the old political parties, . 22
Virginia, and other border States willing to prohibit the
foreign slave-trade, ... 13
    and the other border States willing that negroes
found on slave-trading vessels should be returned
to Africa, ... 13
Vote, the aggregate popular in 1860, exceeded four million
six hundred and eighty thousand, . . 29
    under the defense offered for the suppression of,
the minority may usurp the government, whenever the rule of the majority is disagreeable
or burdensome, ... 103
    the suppression of, is defended upon the ground
that it is impossible to live under negro government, ... 103
    the fact of the systematic suppression of, in the
South, is proved, and is often admitted by those
who profit thereby, ... 103
    all other issues are insignificant compared with that
springing from the systematic suppression of, in
the States of the South, . . . 103

Wages, the average for each person employed in manufacturing for 1860, was $288.00, and for 1880,
$346.00, ... 77
    the aggregate paid in 1880, and in 1860, . . 77
    rate of increase in Europe, . . . 109
    about two and three-quarter million operatives are
employed in manufactures, at an annual aggregate of, amounting to nearly one thousand million
dollars, ... 102
War, by the annexation of Texas, the United States accepted, &c., ... 16

INDEX.

War with Mexico opened in May, 1846, . . . 16
 with Mexico ended with the capture of the city, by Gen. Scott, ... 16
 to suppress the rebellion was prosecuted by the Republican party, ... 24
 not exceeding one-fourth of the entire Democratic party contributed their full share to the prosecution of, and the destruction of slavery, . . 96
 the exigencies of, compelled Congress to assume jurisdiction of the subject of paper circulation, 97
 commerce is the first and easiest victim of, . . 75
 the primary object of, ... 40
 would have been a failure if it had been conducted by the Democratic party, ... 41
 the issue of United States notes is the only financial measure of, that has been assailed, . . 69, 70
 Mr. Buchanan asserted a right of property in the custom-houses and forts, which could not be visited except as an act of, . . . 30
Washington and Jefferson were advocates of protection to domestic labor, ... 76
 schools in the city of, ... 89
Wealth, law, and theology had combined for the protection of slavery, ... 12
Westborough, Massachusetts, Eli Whitney of, invented the cotton-gin between 1788 and 1800, . . 11
West Indies, emancipation in, ... 107
Whig and Democratic parties were rival bidders for southern support, ... 15
Whig party, could not command efficient support, &c., . 13
 would neither oppose nor defend slavery, . . 13
 disappeared, ... 13
 was represented by Mr. Clay in the canvass of 1844, 15
 of the North was opposed to the annexation of Texas, ... 15
 ceased to exist as a national organization, after the repeal of the Missouri compromise, . . 23
 effect of destruction of, ... 39
White persons, surrender of as an incident of the system, 8
Whitney, Eli, of Westborough, Worcester county, Mass., invented the cotton-gin between 1788 and 1800, 11
Woodward, Geo. W., opinion in regard to Enrollment act, 55

www.ingramcontent.com/pod-product-compliance
Lightning Source LLC
Chambersburg PA
CBHW031728230426
43669CB00007B/284